LIBERAL NATIONALISM

STUDIES IN MORAL, POLITICAL,
AND LEGAL PHILOSOPHY

General Editor: Marshall Cohen

LIBERAL NATIONALISM

Yael Tamir

PRINCETON UNIVERSITY PRESS
PRINCETON, NEW JERSEY

Published by Princeton University Press, 41 William Street,
Princeton, New Jersey 08540
In the United Kingdom: Princeton University Press,
Chichester, West Sussex

Library of Congress Cataloging-in-Publication Data

Tamir, Yael.
Liberal nationalism / Yael Tamir.
p.   cm. — (Studies in moral, political, and legal philosophy)
Includes bibliographical references and index.
ISBN 0-691-07893-9 (cloth)
ISBN 0-691-00174-x (paperback)
1. Nationalism.   2. Liberalism.   I. Title.   II. Series.
JC311.T295   1993
320.5′4—dc20   92-40490

This book has been composed in Adobe Palatino

Princeton University Press books are printed on acid-free paper
and meet the guidelines for permanence and durability
of the Committee on Production Guidelines for Book Longevity of
the Council on Library Resources

Third printing, and first paperback printing, with new preface, 1995

Printed in the United States of America

3   5   7   9   10   8   6   4

To my parents
ADA AND YEHUDA TAMIR
who educated me to believe that
to be a Zionist means to respect individuals,
their rights, and their national aspirations,
and to my daughters
CARMEL AND TAL
who I hope will choose to respect
the same values.

Seminar Plan.
1. Kant + ind. self-det. > why modern ?
ii. Appropriation by German romantics ? >
        ind - cult - nation + state

iii - structural constraints + B. U. M.

_____

Tamir > reclaiming ind. choice for theory
    of self-determination.
    1. ind as self in society / contextual
intermediate position (q. p. 13 + 14). + p. 33.
    2. Criticisms of liberal theories - e.g. Mill
    + Irish nationalism.
    micro- — thin - ← thick (strong nationalist).
            moral (liberal) v. communal (nationalist)
3 Criticisms of thick - denies ind. rights.
    cultural choices, like religion, are
    constitutive choices (meaning ?)   p. 41
    _____ - as non-secessionist. p. 57
    Ch. 3. NSD.
            self rule v. self-determination e.g.
    p. 71.

CONTENTS

PREFACE

In the short time since *Liberal Nationalism* was published readers and reviewers have generously shared with me some of their thoughts as well as some of their objections regarding the theory presented in the book. Many of them raised difficult issues that cannot be answered in a short preface such as this. I would like, however, to take the opportunity that a second edition's publication presents to clarify three major issues: the nature of the justification of national rights, the educational implications of liberal nationalism, and the ramifications of the theory for the Israeli-Palestinian conflict.

National Rights: A Remedial or a Universal Justification?

While nationalism was generally overlooked until the mid-1980s, *bon ton* now dictates that it should be acknowledged but in derogatory terms, usually in reference to the atrocities in former Yugoslavia or Rwanda. According to this view nationalism is the main cause of bloodshed in our times; some—forgetting the past atrocities caused by religious wars or economic interests—are tempted to suggest that nationalism is the main cause of evil in human history. These claims imply that we should strive to curtail the power of nationalism as much as possible and forgo new national claims whenever they arise unless they serve as a means to rectify damages caused in the process of national conflicts. National rights are therefore seen as corrective means, as a way to right a wrong, to compensate those who were victimized by nationalism. This type of argumentation has both moral and political value and could lead to some desirable outcomes, but it cannot substitute, nor can it be a part of, a coherent theory of nationalism.

This claim could be clarified by the following analogy: Suppose one would defend freedom of speech by making reference to the fact that a certain group has suffered from a long history of defamation. Members of this group, one would argue, are entitled to defend themselves and should therefore enjoy freedom of speech. The problem with this type of reasoning is that it runs together a theoretical and a practical claim: a justification of a basic right and a policy recommendation to use a certain means—freedom of speech—to assure the accomplishment of a particular political goal. Mixing the two types of claims creates a false impression that the former depends on the latter. But the justification of freedom of speech is independent of the history of any particular group; it is derived from basic interests individuals are believed to have regardless of their own personal history.

By providing a remedial justification one might indeed pursue a worthy cause and bring about desirable results. Yet one cannot cast a theory of nationalism or of freedom of speech in these terms, as remedial justification must rest on the contingent features of particular cases rather than on universal justification.

Moreover, the claim that the demand for actual statehood can only be based on an experience of violence, sufficiently protracted and widespread to convince any observer that such people can only be secure if they have an effective means of self-defense, that is, a state of their own, is rather puzzling. Do nations, secure and content in their own states, lose their right to have such states? If so, a rather ironic vicious circle is created—suffering nations have a remedial right to a state of their own that will grant them security and protection. Yet, no longer threatened and intimidated, they seem to lose the main prop buttressing their right to statehood. Should it then be demanded that they forgo this right and allow other "suffering nations" to take their place until their national survival is again sufficiently endangered to regain their national rights? And who is to judge what is a sufficiently protracted and widespread experience of violence, or which are the nations that can only be secure if they have a state of their own?

Yet the most troubling consequence of this approach is that it leads to the sanctification of suffering. The Museum of Barbarism, established by the Turkish Cypriots to illustrate in the most graphic and harrowing way the atrocities done to them by the Greek Cypriots, is a good example of the way national tragedies are not merely remembered but fostered and used politically to support national claims. The mandatory visit, for every official visitor to Israel, to Yad Va-Shem—the museum commemorating the victims of the Holocaust—also demonstrates the way past atrocities are employed to achieve present political gains. If suffering is what qualifies a nation for national rights, then these rituals are inescapable. The sanctification of suffering fosters hatred and mistrust and—worse still—a backward-looking politics that perpetuates conflict. If suffering is what qualifies a nation for national rights, then backward-looking politics are inescapable; if national rights could be supported on different grounds, then nationalists might adopt forward-looking politics that foster hope for forgiveness and reconciliation. Hence my reluctance to adopt the remedial approach has both practical and theoretical reasons.

I also refrained from supporting national rights by making reference to arguments concerning the survival of the group. Members of certain nations may indeed seek to acquire national rights, especially the right to establish their own nation-state, because they believe that this entity *alone* will protect them from the violence and the intimidation of their neighbors. Such arguments may be politically very persuasive yet they are theoretically unsound, and quite often factually false. Worse still, they inevitably entail dangerously illiberal consequences.

The effectiveness of "survival arguments" has led nationalists to describe every national conflict in existential terms. If what is at stake is not the right to express one's national identity but rather the nation's survival, then no restrictions can be placed on what one might be justified in doing. All means, including conquest and occupation, terror, torture, and disregard for the rights of others, or even for those of fellow members, are justified. In discussing the case of Pueblo Indians, Svensson recognizes that members of this community persecute dissenters. He brings the testimony of one of them, Delfino Concha. "I was subject to the most cruel injustice done to anybody," Concha says, "that of imposing upon myself outright intimidation, and isolation from social affairs enjoyed by the community simply because I did not conform to the religious function."[1] Svensson's response to this testimony is sympathy not with the persecuted individual but with the persecutors. The tribe's reaction to religious dissent is more understandable, he argues, "when it is remembered that in tribal societies, and even more particularly in one which is a theocracy, religion is an integral part of the community life which cannot be detached from other aspects of community. Violation of religious norms is viewed as literally threatening the survival of the entire community."[2]

The term "survival" seems to be doing most of the justificatory work in the above argument; if the freedom of individuals is weighed against the survival of the community, the latter seems to have much more weight. This would not be the case, however, if the dissenter's interests were weighed against those of other individuals, especially if they were weighed against external preferences.[3]

Taylor also uses the language of survival to justify restrictions on individuals rights. It is axiomatic for the Quebec government that the survival and flourishing of French culture in Quebec is a good, he argues; "it is not just a matter of having the French language available for those who might chose it. . . . Policies aimed at survival actively seek to *create* members of the community, for instance, in their assuring that future generations continue to identify as French speakers."[4] Behind this delicate phrasing lurks firm support for language laws that force individuals to identify as French speakers. The common element of these measures "is that some of the recognized rights and liberty of liberal citizenship are limited and unequally distributed in order to preserve a minority culture."[5] The term "survival" is thus too often used to trump individual rights.

If the suffering and the survival approaches appear questionable on theoretical grounds, they are even less tenable factually. Will Uzbeks, Georgians, and Azeris be more secure when they have their own states than they were before? Were the United Nations capable of imposing a settlement in Yugoslavia dividing it into several nation-states, would this ensure that Serbs and Croats would no longer attempt to intimidate each other? States created as solutions to national conflicts may continue a struggle begun before the states were established, only with improved means of mutual destruction. It is indeed well known that more people have been killed in wars between nation-states than in intrastate ethnic conflicts. As the peoples of Czechoslovakia, Afghanistan, and Kuwait learned in 1939, 1989, and 1990, statehood is not necessarily a barrier to intimidation.

In their long and tormented history, Jews suffered major national catastrophes at times of the destruction of the First and Second Temples, when they did have a state, and during the Holocaust, when they were stateless. The establishment of the state of Israel, one ought to remember, did not save Jews from violence and intimidation at the hands of their neighbors, nor from threats of annihilation, as their plight during the Gulf War attests. Jews were determined to live in Israel and establish their homeland despite these dangers. They knew that Israel was not a safe haven but a place where survival entailed a struggle.

Jews are not an exception; for most nations the main concern is not survival but the development of a shared public sphere where the national culture, language, and traditions attain expression. Were biological survival the main consideration, it would appear that in an age facing atomic and chemical weapons as well as the danger of ecological disaster it would be prudent for nationalists to spread their risks by avoiding territorial concentration at all costs. Nationalists, however, measure their success not by the continued contribution of their nation to the gene pool but by the flourishing of their national life and culture. To achieve this goal, they are ready to assume risks.

This implies that merging measures necessary for the survival of particular nations with measures required to right past wrongs, and making both a precondition to the allocation of national rights, may lead to a confused theoretical argument as well as to misguided political actions. Only when these issues are kept apart can one draw a distinction between policies that are motivated by certain national needs and those that are motivated by national rights. For these reasons remedial arguments, effective as they may be, occupy no role in my theory.

The Realm of the Political

Placing a cultural claim rather than a political one at the heart of nationalism prompted some uneasiness; some readers took this distinction to imply the depoliticization of nationalism. This criticism fails to notice the delicate difference between two claims. The first argues that at the core of nationalism lies a cultural rather than a political claim, that national movements are motivated by a desire to assure the existence and flourishing of a particular community, to preserve its culture, tradition, and language, rather than merely to seize state power.

This claim does not amount to a second, rather different, claim that nationalism has no political goals. By placing a cultural rather than a political claim at the heart of nationalism, I suggest that nationalism should not be seen as a mere striving to control state power and institutions; political power is the means, while the end is cultural. Yet claiming that certain actions should be seen not as intrinsically important but as a means for some other goals is not to render them unimportant or redundant. Political action is an important part of nationalism, but it is not its essence.

My claim that nationalism does not necessarily embody a right to establish a nation-state should also not be read as an attempt to privatize nationalism. There is a whole range of political activities that are both public and political in the sense that they are acted in the public sphere with the intention of influencing political institutions, but which are not meant to control state power.

Nowhere in the book do I divorce nationalism from this kind of political activity. Nowadays the power of the state, especially if it is a welfare state, is so pervasive that no party can ignore it; if a state supports any kind of associations, sport associations for example, then any such association would struggle to acquire state funding to provide special classes in schools to raise the public awareness of that particular field of sport, subsidize the creation of a national team, allocate land or resources for sport facilities, and the like. Every association thus strives to influence the process of political decision making, but this does not make it a political association. National groups are no exception to this rule.

Activities motivated by national interests are political even in a deeper way as they attempt to influence the shape of the public sphere; this is the essence of what is now called the politics of recognition. National groups aspire not only to be accepted or tolerated but to reshape the public sphere in a way that will reflect their own particularity. This implies that they must become active participants in the political game.

If political expression is required for the sake of national self-determination, why stop short of national self-rule? The answer to this question depends on the contingencies of each particular situation. National interests are not the only interests individuals have; a proper balancing between the pros and cons of every particular solution must therefore determine the nature of the most desired political settlement. If, as I have anticipated, the move from the centralized nation-state, anxious to present itself as representing a homogenous nation, to regional or international organizations that are explicitly multinational will ease the pressure on minorities and help to ensure their rights and interests within the larger framework, then many may find that such frameworks provide them with a more feasible and desirable way to satisfy their national as well as their economic, ecological, and strategic interests. In light of these newly developing conditions, it seems as if the burden of proof lies with those who claim that national self-determination can be practiced only in the form of an independent state and not vice versa. I did not find a persuasive argument to support this claim, or to exclude the possibility that the right to national self-determination can be realized in a variety of different ways: cultural autonomies, regional autonomies, federations, and confederations. In the concluding chapters of their comprehensive survey, *Minorities at Risk*, Gurr et al. suggest that ethnic conflicts are by no means unmanageable, and that minorities' rights and needs can be secured by a combination of power-sharing and autonomy. The fear that such arrangements will inevitably lead to secession and civil war, they argue, is unfounded.[6]

Such a process of devolution is even more likely to succeed if it takes place under the umbrella of a regional organization. In regional organizations the traditional concepts of majority and minority no longer apply, as these organizations are genuinely multinational. Many of the arguments against the secession of national minorities from existing nation-states will lose their validity. As long as the various national units commit themselves to be part of regional political, economic, and strategic systems, their own independent viability is no more an issue. "If choices can cease to be between rival claims to soverign statehood over disputed territories and populations, but can become choices about the allocation of levels of political authority within a transnational community embracing many nationalities and cultural traditions or groupings, a choice guided by some version of the principle of subsidiary, some dilemmas are greatly eased. The recognition of one identity ceases to be necessarily at the price of denying another."[7] In the European case this would allow small stateless nations like the Scots, the Basques, the Corsicans, or the Welsh to develop their own cultural and political autonomy if they will remain part of the European community. The expansion of the Union, MacCormick writes, "first to the Nordic countries and Austria, and later perhaps further east into the democratizing and liberalizing states beyond the former iron curtain, is almost a *fait accompli*, and may be the best road to undercutting atavistic nationalism that may otherwise spread like wildfire across the continent."[8]

It is evident that unification did not restrain but encouraged the flourishing of national, ethnic, cultural, and lingual sentiments. These conclusions apply not only to members of the European Community; such a transformation of national identity, Greenfeld argues, "is a necessary condition for the democratization of post–Soviet societies."[9]

In Support of Common Sense

This brings me to a further point that has attracted quite a lot of criticism: some readers have felt that my reliance on common-sense solutions attests to a desire to avoid difficult issues. I still believe that reasonableness and untidy compromises are the main key to any workable political solution. This, however, does not imply that I either try to blunt the sharp edges of liberalism or nationalism or that I turn to "strategic imprecision." Any theory that endorses more than one value must turn to such reasonable—untidy—compromises or else it would lead to a political disaster. Theories purporting to justify both property rights and social equality, the right to free speech as well as the right to personal and communal respect, the right to privacy alongside the right of women and children not to be abused would be able to offer no more than guidelines for decent compromises. The need for such compromises is not evidence of the vagueness or imprecision of concepts used but of the incompatibility and incommensurability of values and the complexity of the social reality we are facing.

In fact, one way to avoid the necessity of untidy compromises is to obscure the difference between different schools of thought—democracy and nationalism, or racism and nationalism—and thus to render practical solutions either too simple and straightforward or utterly impossible. A careful analysis that reveals the true complexity of the concepts involved must leave the issue of particular settlements open.

Imagine a theory of freedom of speech that attempts to provide a final list of all the cases in which free speech should be protected; such a list could not be drawn up without making reference to cost-benefit analysis that will define when freedom of speech should be protected and when it should give way to other values. Such judgments, however, depend on the particular circumstances of each case and cannot be decided a priori. The only way to avoid such calculations and the compromises they lead to is to develop a unidimensional theory that takes one value to be dominant over all others; needless to say, liberal nationalism, by its nature, cannot be such a theory.

Education for Citizenship; Education for Nationhood

Some readers remarked that the theory of liberal nationalism calls for a corresponding theory of education. This claim is fully justified: every political theory must explain the ways in which it will foster the conditions necessary for its functioning and sustain itself over successive generations.

Moreover, as educational goals reflect the political vision of a society, following the changes and developments in the sphere of education may shed light on the nature of political transformations. By looking at the development of modern education, we might be able to understand better the changes the term "state" has undergone and their effect on the relations between this term and the term "nation," and portray in a more lucid and intelligible way the complex nature of liberal nationalism.

In the course of the twentieth century the ideal of the nation-state has reached its zenith and begun to decline, grabbing with it the ideal of nation-building through education. It is now widely accepted that most states are not, never have been, and are unlikely to become nationally homogeneous. This transformation in the self-image of the state, represented by a shift from the politics of national homogeneity to the politics of multiculturalism, calls for a redefinition of the role of most political institutions, and especially of schools. The goal of education can no longer be to consolidate all citizens into one homogeneous public, but to find ways of coordinating among individuals who openly profess their differences.

Note that in my account of nationalism the terms multiculturalism and multinationalism can be used interchangeably. This is not merely a semantic point; it emphasizes the similarities between issues confronting multiethnic states like the United States, multinational states like Israel, multinational federations or confederations like Belgium or Canada, and regional organizations like the European Community, all of which confront a similar issue: how to retain diversity on the one hand and unity on the other.

The politics of multiculturalism offers a new balance between two basic trends that have dominated the educational realm for the last two centuries: national and civic education. In their development, civic and national education shared a long and troubled path; in each stage along this path the success of the one type of education made the other imperative. The emergence of the nation-state at the end of the eighteenth century was marked by the emergence of public education, whose main goal was to galvanize all citizens into one homogenized nation. The spread of the notion of universal citizenship introduced a new conception of equality: individuals were equal not only before God, but also by law. This change prepared the ground for the emergence of the notion of state neutrality, which until recently was seen as the most fundamental characteristic of civic education. The state, it was argued, has to ensure an equal, inclusive, and unifying education to all. The inclusiveness of the educational system made all citizens, including members of disadvantaged groups and national minorities, aware of their powers and liberties. These newly empowered individuals demanded that their rights, especially their right to retain their unique culture, be respected. These changes in turn prepared the ground for the emergence of multiculturalism and the revival of separate national-ethnic education. The latter stage marks the complete disengagement of the notion of *state* and *nation* and the reestablishment of two distinct spheres of education—civic and national. Yet the multinational state

that wishes to bridge differences and foster cross-communal understanding must foster some shared values that will provide a basis for
social and political cooperation. Hence, the growing importance of
national and ethnic feelings increases, rather than lessens, the importance of liberal-democratic civic education, with its emphasis on
those features that are common to all members rather than those
features that are unique to each of them.

In what follows I will define civic and national education and establish the difference between the two. Then, by briefly following
the delicate interplay between these two forms of education, I will
reveal the inevitable interplay between liberal and national values.

The Essence of Civic and National Education

The creation of a state school system was a landmark in the development of the modern state. Schools were meant to promote literacy,
inculcate shared values and respect for the law, and reinforce citizens' loyalty to rulers as well as to fellow citizens. In 1763, Louis-
Rene Caradeau de la Chalotais, the attorney general of the parliament of Brittany, wrote his *Essay on National Education*, which was
the first major modern proposal for state education. The children of
the state, he argued, "should be educated by the state."[10] Chalotais
believed education to be a civic affair whose purpose is the development of efficient, content, and loyal citizens.

Following the revolution, the ideal of state education acquired
greater popularity. In 1792, the Marquis de Condorcet wrote a report to the Revolutionary Assembly calling for the establishment of
state-sponsored education. The failure of the government to establish schools for all citizens, he argued, means that individuals are
deprived of their basic right to develop their natural abilities and
acquire a modicum of knowledge necessary for performing their
civic duties. Consequently they are less qualified to discharge their
political responsibilities. Education is meant to coach each individual "to direct his own conduct, to enjoy the plenitude of his own
rights and to insure the perpetuation of liberty and equality."[11]
The development of state education was thus seen as a necessary
condition for fostering the rights, freedoms, and responsibilities of
citizens.

The newly emerging United States of America granted no less importance to civic education. Faith in education was part and parcel
of the American dream. State education, it was believed, would supply the best protection against civil or ecclesiastical tyranny, anarchy, factionalism, and the disruption of law and order. Knowledge,

Webster believed, "must be diffused among all classes of citizens; and when they understand public affairs, they will not do wrong." Make them intelligent, he argued, and "they will be vigilant—give them the means of detecting the wrong and they will apply the remedy."[12]

Civic education was thus meant to impart knowledge and foster active, reflective political participation grounded in respect for the law. Let reverence for the laws be taught in schools, Lincoln said, "let it be preached from the pulpit, proclaimed from the legislative halls and enforced in the courts of justice. . . . Let the old and the young, the rich and the poor of all sexes and tongues and colors and conditions, sacrifice unceasingly upon its altars."[13] In their capacity as citizens, all individuals were alike, and it was this sameness that civic education emphasized.

Defined in these terms, civic education can clearly be distinguished from national education, the direct object of which is the preservation and strengthening of the nation and its culture. The most true and desirable form of national education, argues the Zionist leader Achad Ha'am, is one that will "bring children to absorb the spirit of their nation inadvertently, by transmitting to them general human contents in national form."[14] The study of the national language and the national literature are the most powerful of all instruments. Through the best of national literature, "the child internalizes a world of sublime moral and aesthetic ideals which gradually become part of his spiritual self. A firm bond is thereby created between the child and his nationality, a bond he comes to see as the source of everything that is humanly noble and inspiring."[15]

In the *Treatise on the Government of Poland*, Rousseau advises the Poles to focus on the education of their young if they wish to redeem their nation:

At twenty a Pole should be nothing else; he should be a Pole. When he learns to read, he should read of his country; at ten he should know all its products, at twelve he should know its provinces, roads and towns, at fifteen all its history, at sixteen all its laws; there should not be in Poland a noble deed or a famous man that he does not know and love, or that he could not describe on the spot.[16]

Only by following this advice, Rousseau says, will the Polish nation emerge from the crisis through which it is passing.

Like Rousseau and Achad Ha'am, Fichte too believed that education could redeem a nation from its crisis and allow it to regain its glory. If the German people wished to reemerge and occupy its rightful place as a leader of the civilized world it must educate its young, suppress individualism (which Fichte considered to be the main reason for Germany's defeat), and foster among citizens common loyalty and service to the social organism. Hence,

> schools have to be established in which children could be separated from the reigning social habit of self-seeking and nurtured in the atmosphere of social service and cooperation. If Germany was to be saved, the nation must be taken as the unit of social organization. Germany must know its character and destiny, and through a conscious control of education it must liberate all the potentialities—moral, intellectual, physical, vocational—for national service, that existed within the children of all people.[17]

Fichte's organic and illiberal notion of national education profoundly differs from both the individualistic, humanistic notion of national education offered by Achad Ha'am and the collectivist though universal and polycentric notion of national education offered by Rousseau. This should not surprise us, for each form of nationalism introduces an analogous form of education. Common to all forms of national education are the veneration of the nation's language, traditions, and practices and the celebration of its freedom. A nation, Achad Ha'am argues, cannot exist unless it transmits its cultural assets from generation to generation through education. Without education it has no future and is destined to wither away.

In terms of the above definitions, the theoretical distinction between civic and national education seems quite clear (especially if compared with the distinction between state and nation offered in chapter 3). But the development of the nation-state fused the two types of education to the point where it became almost impossible to distinguish between them. In a period characterized by a deliberate attempt to obscure the difference between nation and state, national education came to be identified with civic education.

The Marriage

The purpose of education, according to the leaders of both the American and the French revolutions, was to foster a sense of brotherhood and dedication to the nation. In a democratic state, Washington argues, "in which the measures of government receive their impression so immediately from the sense of community, as in ours, knowledge is proportionally essential." Every man, Lincoln claimed, should receive "at least a moderate education, and thereby be enabled to read the histories of his own and the other countries, by which he may duly appreciate the value of free institutions." If a nation expects to be ignorant and free, Jefferson declared, "it expects what never was and never will be." Education for all was thus seen as a precondition for the development of a unified nation and a stable democracy, as well as for the preservation of the American way of life, its values, and its constitution.

The identification between national and civic education unfolded also in France; education, Rousseau argued, must shape the minds of children in a national mold, "direct their tastes and their opinions, till they are patriotic by inclination—by instinct—by necessity."[18] A child should see his fatherland when first opening his eyes, and till death should see nothing else. "The true republican sucks in with his mother's milk the love of his country, that is, of law and liberty. This love makes up his life; he only sees his fatherland, and only lives for his fatherland; alone, he is nothing; his country lost, he lives no more; if not dead, he is worse."[19]

An analysis of Jewish education in Israel before and after the establishment of the state offers an interesting illustration of the process whereby national education comes to be identified with civic education. In the prestate period, Jewish education falls mainly under the rubric of national education. But already in 1927, twenty years before independence, Arnon, an active member of the teachers' association, says: "The end of Jewish schools should not merely be to educate individuals to become national Jews, but also future citizens."[20] After 1948, the civic aspects of education began to overshadow the national ones. In 1953, a state law ensuring free, state-sponsored education for all was enacted. The aim of the law, Minister of Education Benzion Dinur stated, is to create citizens who are knowledgeable and respectful of the law, understand their rights, and assume civic responsibility. Jewish children should also receive Jewish education and be aware of the shared destiny of the Jewish people. For Jews, he argued, citizenship in the state of Israel "is only a partial citizenship; as we are also citizens of a great people, and it is this feeling of belonging to both state and nation that we should cultivate in the hearts of our children."[21]

Dinur's words expose the fragile nature of the equation between state and nation: as the Israeli case clearly shows, the nation and the state do not necessarily overlap.[22] Desperate attempts were thus made to foster this unity. The educational system was to serve as a "melting pot," dissolving the differences in an attempt to produce free and equal citizens. This educational ideology embodied two seemingly contradictory, yet in fact complementary, schools of thought, which could be labeled as "neutral" and "assimilationist" education.

Keeping the Parts Together

Attempts to foster homogeneity were reinforced by democratic commitments and supported by two powerful ideas: "First, that free government was only possible under conditions of cultural unity; second, that free individuals would choose to live with their own kind, that is, to join political sovereignty to national and ethnic community."[23] Even immigrant states like the United States adopted during the eighteenth and the beginning of the nineteenth century educational policies intended to transform all their members into fellow nationals. J. H. Smart, president of the National Education Association, described this policy in 1881:

> I believe that the American school-room is a place in which that wonderful change takes place, by which the children of every land and every tongue, of every religious creed and of every political faith, are transformed by the subtle assimilating process, from aliens and strangers into a sympathetic membership in the greatest and best political organization the world has ever seen.[24]

Americanization, Walzer argues, was aimed at people susceptible to cultural change, "for they were not only uprooted; they had uprooted themselves. . . . The fact is that the men and women who were to become Americanized were, already, many of them, patriotic Americans."[25] This description of the educational "melting pot" and the process of Americanization avoids a critical question: Who is a sympathetic member? Who is an American? It is now clear that the melting pot did not manage to form, nor was it intended to form, a new person that faithfully and equally reflected all of the different social groups. Instead it was used to mold all children into one specific version of Americanism—a white, some say male, English-speaking, Protestant one.

At the end of the nineteenth century, when Smart delivered his speech, the liberal-democratic political discourse was oblivious of this cultural bias. It fashioned itself as culture-free, based on universalistic principles that were independent of color, race, gender, or religion.

It is at this point that the melting-pot strategy meets the ideal of neutral education on the one hand and assimilation on the other. Both were supported on the grounds that they ensure members equal treatment, allowing individuals to shed their particularities and acquire the universal status of citizenship. Citizenship was presented as an embodiment of abstract humanity, of those human qualities that unite all human beings. In the same vein schools were assumed to be culturally, morally, and politically neutral, reflecting the strength of legalism and codification, motivated solely by the desire to foster respect for the law and principles of fair play and thereby equally accessible to all citizens.

Civic education was thus expected to rid itself of all divisive features. Family affiliations, religious allegiances, and ethnic ties all were viewed as private matters and hence unessential, even disturbing, to civic life. An advertisement for *McGuffey's Eclectic First Reader*, published in 1884, stresses its neutral nature as it greatest virtue:

> No sectarian matter has been admitted into this book. . . . It has been submitted to the inspection of highly intelligent clergymen and teachers of the various Protestant and Catholic denominations, and nothing has been inserted, except with their united approbation. . . . No sectorial matter reflecting upon the local institutions, customs, or habits of any portion of the United States, is to be found among their constants, and hence they [the readers] are extensively used at the South and at the North, in the East as well as the West.[26]

But the biased nature of the melting pot was exposed in times of crisis when some other version, not an Anglo-Saxon one, seemed to be gaining ground. This was the case in the early days of the American experience just as it is true nowadays. Motivated by a fear that the melting pot would not produce what was, for him, the desirable result, Benjamin Franklin said: "This [Pennsylvania] will in a few years become a German Colony; Instead of their learning our language, we must learn theirs or live as in a foreign country."[27] It is in light of these words that one should look again at the statement of another Pennsylvanian, Benjamin Rush, in 1798: "The education of our youth in the country to be particularly necessary in Pennsylvania, while our citizens are composed of natives of so many different kingdoms in Europe. Our schools of learning, by producing one general uniform system of education, will render the mass of the people more homogeneous, and therefore fit more easily for uniform and peaceful government."[28]

The new immigrants acquiesced to cultural naturalization, Walzer argues, this was especially true in the area of language: "there has been no long-term or successful effort to maintain the original language of the newcomers as anything more than a second language in the United States."[29]

Reading Franklin's and Rush's words one may wonder what would have happened if a serious attempt to preserve the German language, or any other language, was pursued. It is now clear that the educational melting pot was not meant to produce citizens who were abstract, universal beings, but Americans who were to adopt English as their language and espouse a set of norms, traditions, and moral principles that was considered American. That no attempt to resist this trend arose may be a sign of acquiescence, but it may also be a sign of self-denial motivated by a cruel choice between preserving one's identity and carving a place for oneself in the new society.

Despite claims to the contrary in the French case, the national nature of citizenship was no less evident. A belief in the importance of education and its ability to correct environmental differences, together with adherence to the Enlightenment view that reason is universal, led Helvetius, Condorcet, and Renan as well as other French social thinkers to assume that humanity should be educated in the noble, rationalist, French tradition. "The evolution of the French spirit has passed from the Romans to Christian universality, and from that to a purely human universality," wrote Fouille.[30] Hence, whatever was proper for the French was good for humanity at large.

From these assumptions, it was easy to derive the conclusion that France should promote the assimilation of all human beings into the great French tradition. We wish, said Renan, to "establish everywhere the government which is suitable to us and to which we have a right."[31] Yet when Gabriel Hanotaux described the French civilizing mission, he resorted to national rather than universal categories. The essence of the French mission, he wrote, is to extend overseas

> to regions only yesterday barbarian the principles of a civilization of which one of the oldest nations of the world has the right to be proud. It is a question of creating near us and far away from us so many new Frances; it is a question of protecting our language, our customs, our ideals, the French and Latin glory, in face of furious competition from other races, all marching along the same routes.[32]

Hanotaux's words highlight the belief, prevalent among French thinkers of his time, that there were strong affinities between their national and universal mission, between the desire to bring the principles of the Enlightenment to remote countries and the yearning to convert members of these countries to Frenchhood. This affinity between the cultural and universal aspects of French citizenship was evident to Isaac Beer, a Jewish merchant who, together with other Jews, was granted citizenship in 1791. In a letter to his fellow Jews he writes:

> We are now, thanks to the Supreme Being and to the sovereignty of the nation, not only Men and Citizens, but we are Frenchmen! . . . Our [the Jews'] fate, and the fate of our posterity, depends solely on the changes we shall effect in our mode of education. . . . French ought to be the Jew's mother tongue, since they are reared with and among Frenchmen. . . . [And] why should we continue to bear the names of German or Polish Jews, while we are happily French Jews?[33]

Beer's words demonstrate the tendency of members of minority cultures to endorse and support the image of the state as culturally and normatively neutral. This tendency was even more evident in the United States. It was first expressed by new immigrants wanting to assimilate into the American experience and then by women and black people, struggling to assure their place as equal citizens. In their attempt to gain equality, members of these groups tended to reject any deviation from universalist arguments, fearing it would legitimize discrimination. Disillusion, strangely enough, came hand in hand with success, with the fall of the colonial powers and the political empowerment of national minorities. The strange alliance among neutrality, universality, and assimilation came to an impasse; new forms of political discourse and educational theories were about to develop.

The Unavoidable Awakening

Members of disempowered national minorities soon discovered that a set of formal civic rights is insufficient to ensure them equal status, and they realized that they faced a choice between two evils: they could remain estranged and marginalized or integrate at the price of self-effacement. This is the dilemma Diaspora Jews are often forced to face and which the establishment of the state of Israel was meant to resolve:

Being a citizen in an independent state is a heavy responsibility which we have never experienced. We have been used to have a wall between us and general citizenship. . . . We have always been personally and nationally a mechanical combination of two mental spheres that are unable to be reconciled. . . . A Jew must always be also a person—i.e., a citizen, and this duality is still vivid for us Israelis. We are unable to shell off, at once, the burden we have accrued in our long years of the Diaspora.[34]

For Diaspora Jews, Palestinian citizens of Israel, or Basque citizens of France, being a citizen entailed an entirely different state of mind than being a member of the nation; for such individuals, general citizenship was no more than a codeword for a choice between assimilation and exclusion. Members of national minorities thus became increasingly aware that the ideal of a neutral public sphere embodied a dangerous and oppressive illusion.

Haunted by the shadows of "separate but equal" policies originally meant to preserve segregation and social inequality in education, members of minority groups were reluctant to demand special schools or classes aimed at fostering their own tradition, language, and history. They were facing a dilemma: demanding such measures would imply not only acknowledgment but also acceptance of the particularized nature of the state; ignoring their importance would considerably reduce the minorities' chances of retaining their identity. It was only when it became clear that no struggle for equal rights could turn the state into a culturally neutral institution that national minorities began to demand special treatment in the name of equality.

Yet even if such educational measures are provided, members of minority groups will still feel alienated from the public sphere, less able to understand its cultural origins, less capable of playing according to the "rules of the game." They can, of course, decide to become acquainted with the culture of the ruling nation, but this demands that they devote time and efforts that members of the majority culture can invest elsewhere. We thus cannot realistically assume that granting minority groups either formal rights or means to preserve their identity will solve the issue of marginalization. This is, however, true not only for national minorities but also for communists in a liberal capitalist state that is committed to the celebration of private property, for vegetarians in nonvegetarian eating clubs, for political philosophers in some philosophy departments, and so on.

It was the problem of minorities that evoked the realization that being granted equal rights is not enough, and that strict adherence to a principle of equal treatment tends to perpetuate oppression or disadvantage. The notion of universal citizenship therefore had to be replaced by a notion of "differential citizenship." The most evident implication of this development is the separation between civic and national education.

The Divorce

The reconceptualization of the notion of citizenship rejects the traditional liberal distinction between the public sphere as the realm of general reason "in which all particularities are left behind" and the private sphere as "the realm of affectivity, affiliation, need, and the body."[35]

> As long as that dichotomy is in place, the inclusion of the formerly excluded in the definition of citizenship—women, workers, Jews, blacks, Asians, Indians, Mexicans—imposes a homogeneity that suppresses group differences in the public and in practice forces the formally excluded groups to be measured according to norms derived from and defined by privileged groups.[36]

The public sphere in a multicultural, multiethnic state is supposed to be varied, to reflect the particularities of all its members. Citizens are no longer expected to transcend their particular self-interested lives in order to participate in public discussion and collective decision making. Yet if those aspects of the liberal philosophical tradition that set out to address a transcendental subject, to define an essential human nature, and to prescribe a global human destiny and collective human goals are rejected at the outset, on what grounds would it be possible to support the claim of all citizens, despite their differences, to equal concern and respect? Emphasizing diversity over and above a shared social vision leaves no basis for a rainbow coalition.

Rawls's overlapping consensus, or Dworkin's abstract egalitarian principle, seem to serve well the need for guiding principles. Suppose the parties in the original position, who have general knowledge of their society's basic features, are aware of the fact that their state encompasses various national and ethnic groups but are unaware of which particular group they belong to. Under such conditions they are likely to endorse Gutmann's view that "the dignity of free and equal beings requires liberal democratic institutions to be nonrepressive, nondiscriminatory, and deliberative."[37] They are also likely to accept Young's demand that institutionalized means be provided for the explicit recognition and representation of oppressed or disadvantaged groups. But members of these representative bodies still need to search for a common ground and a set of agreed upon principles, or else they will not be able to establish a common public sphere and a shared political system.

Barring this vision, granting representation to the different national and ethnic groups might lead to further oppression, as stronger groups might abuse and oppress the weaker ones, which in turn will use their power to exploit those weaker than themselves. In her critique of interest-group politics, Young argues that such politics forestalls the emergence of public discussion and decision making, since each group need not consider the interests of others "except strategically, as potential allies or adversaries in the pursuit of one's own. The rules of interest group pluralism do not require justifying one's interest as right or as compatible with social justice."[38] The opposite, she argues, is true for a heterogeneous public "where participants discuss together the issue before them, and are supposed to come to a decision that they determine as just or most just."[39] Young's criticism of interest-group politics, however, seems just as relevant to cases of ethnic and national heterogeneity. There is no reason to assume an inherent correlation between a particular type of politics, be it interest-group politics or the politics of difference, and a desire for justice.

It is puzzling to find that supporters of multiculturalism, who stress the importance of power relations, aim to revive the old liberal belief in social harmony inspired by an invisible hand. Yet this belief is the unavoidable, and unrealistic, outcome of the refusal to adopt liberal principles as the basis of political discussion and decision making; if no principles can be agreed upon, idealized, invisible-hand solutions seem the only available fallback position. Ideally, Young claims,

> a rainbow coalition affirms the presence and supports the claims of each of the oppressed groups or political movements constituting it, and arrives at a political program not by voicing some "principle of unity" that hides differences but rather by allowing each constituent to analyze economic and social issues from the perspective of its experience.[40]

But promoting an illusion of harmony within diversity is as dangerous and oppressive as the old liberal illusion of neutrality. It is only when this illusion is rejected that we are able to consider various models of conflict resolution and appreciate the advantage of the liberal-democratic model. The evident national, cultural, and religious diversity of our society makes a thin layer of civic education, introducing children to the liberal discourse of rights and rationality, necessary. Without such an introduction it will be impossible to generate cross-cultural discussions based on equal respect and concern for all participants.

In a nationally diversified political system, be it a town, a state, a federation, a regional organization, or a global society, it is especially important that all children learn to respect others who have different lifestyles, values, and traditions and view them—qua members of the political system—as equals. Beyond this thin layer, each national group should foster among its young knowledge that is relevant to its own particular community, its history, language, and traditions. Separating civic education from national education is thus the key for the continued peaceful existence of multinational societies.

The distinctions I make in the book between citizenship and nationhood allow us to understand the basis for such a division of labor; if educating individuals to become virtuous citizens and turning them into conscientious fellow nationals are not one and the same thing, then the state is justified in enforcing an education that will promote the former, but not the latter, type of virtues. National groups—minorities and majorities alike—should thus be given the freedom to have their own educational system (whether in the form of separate schools or, preferably, in the form of special hours or special days) alongside the civic one.

Civic education should attempt to create civic friendship among all, but it should attempt to do so not by assimilating all into one culture, but by respecting cultural diversity. All children should thus acquire some knowledge of the culture, history, and tradition of all national groups that share their political system, and be taught to respect them.

It is the strengthening of multinationalism and with it of national education that highlights the importance of civic education, and it is the belief in the importance of belonging to and respect for thick cultures that motivates the search for a thin layer of agreement. It was only recently that critics of liberalism took the thinness of the liberal discourse to be its major disadvantage. It now seems as if it is its major virtue.

This brief discussion suggests that the theory of liberal nationalism has implications for the restructuring not only of political institutions but also of educational ones. Moreover, by following the multifarious interplay between civic and national education, it is possible to clarify the intricate nature of the relations between nationalism and liberalism and expose the complicated way in which these theories serve both to criticize and to promote each other.

Grounds for Optimism

Two last remarks: Some critics wondered whether my theory contradicted my own commitment to support the establishment of a Palestinian state. The answer is straightforward: the Palestinians' right to national self-determination does not imply a right to an independent state of their own—no nation has such a right, including the Jews. Yet given the contingent features of the Israeli-Palestinian conflict, I believe that the establishment of such a state is the best possible solution. In light of recent developments, however, it is possible to hope that after a Palestinian state is established, Israelis, Palestinians, and Jordanians will join a confederation, renouncing aspects of their national sovereignty for the sake of regional prosperity. This move ought to be based on full-scale reciprocity requiring all parties to sacrifice the same degree of autonomy in order to attain equal benefits.

After long years of hostility, as Israelis and Palestinians embark on the troubled journey toward mutual reconciliation, we can dream that while this century staggers to its balkanized end, the next one will feature regional cooperation as its distinguishing characteristic.

Am I being too optimistic? Maybe. Indeed, some critics suggest that my theoretical conclusions that liberal nationalism is possible, and that there are ways of balancing different national claims, are unrealistically optimistic. This assertion, however, confuses two claims. The first is that a certain set of principles yields a valid inference; the second is that this conclusion can easily be implemented. My book makes only the former claim. Were it possible to define such theoretical claims as optimistic, then every theory offering valid justifications of virtue, justice, rights, freedom, or democracy would merit this label.

There is, however, also room for actual optimism. The political developments in South Africa, the gradual progress of the peace process between Israel and its neighbors and especially with the Palestinians, and the first signs of a compromise in Ireland suggest that liberal nationalism is more than an abstract theory; it could turn into a reality.

ACKNOWLEDGMENTS

My interest in liberal nationalism arose out of a process of self-reflection. Between 1977 and 1982 I was very active in the Israeli peace movement (Peace Now) and in the civil rights movement. In the course of these activities I was frequently required to justify the complex position held by supporters of the peace movement, and to vindicate its moderate version of national commitments as a legitimate Zionist approach. My attempts to explain these views made me aware of the vulnerability of the liberal nationalist position, forced to contend with the censure of both liberals and nationalists.

This book is the fruit of many years of personal political involvement, which eventually led me to a concern with the theoretical dimensions of liberal nationalism. I am grateful for the opportunity to spend three years doing graduate work on this subject at Balliol College, Oxford, and I am deeply indebted to the college for their support and for awarding me the Domus Scholarship.

When I embarked on this project, nationalism seemed almost an anachronistic topic. During my years in Oxford I exhausted a stockpile of phrases in answer to the comment, "How interesting!" (Oxfordese for "How weird!")—usually uttered after I reported I was writing a thesis on nationalism. In the years since, the situation has changed so radically that it is almost impossible to try and make sense of the political reality without giving thought to the pursuit of national ideals, and it now goes without saying that nationalism merits scholarly concern. The mostly aggressive character of the recent nationalist revival, however, placed me once again on the defensive, and I am now busy drawing up a new list of replies to "How interesting!"—apparently evoked by the term "*liberal* nationalism." In this book I try to show that, although it might be seen as an impossible match, liberal nationalism is a far more pervasive view than is usually assumed.

When writing the doctoral dissertation from which this book later developed, tutors and friends were generous with their guidance and advice. Sir Isaiah Berlin devoted a great deal of time to discuss with me the thesis developed in this book. His comments and criticism were invaluable, and I am grateful for the skillful and humorous way in which he led me to see my argument more clearly, and to accept that many questions would remain unanswered. After reading the final version of this book I have come to realise how deeply I have been influenced by his work and his temper as a philosopher. Alan Montefiore has closely followed my work over these years, and I have found his guidance and unlimited patience enormously helpful in confronting the philosophical complexities of the questions surrounding this work. His personal friendship and attention were very helpful in some of the hard periods I went through during these years. My tutorials with Steven Lukes introduced me to a whole range of questions in sociology and political science that I might otherwise have left unattended. I deeply appreciate his generous invitation to the European University in Florence and his willingness to read the final draft of my dissertation after he had left Oxford.

Charles Taylor and David Heyd kindly read parts of the work, and I am thankful for their very helpful comments. I would also like to thank Michael Freeden and Neil MacCormick for their stimulating suggestions. Michael Walzer and Amy Gutmann were very generous with their time and advice, read extensive versions of various drafts, and significantly contributed to my thinking on several thorny questions.

Being a graduate student at Balliol College meant that I was privileged to be part of a very stimulating and active group of political philosophy students. It is hard to overstate the contribution of this group to my work and to my intellectual development during those years. In particular, I would like to thank Valerie Monchi, Ragib Bhargaba, Seth Moglen, David Knott, and Mahesh Rangarjan, who read and commented on various drafts. I owe very special thanks to Michael Sarbanes, whose advice was always helpful, and who cheered me up at some of the most difficult moments. Following my return to Israel and in the course of working on this book, I benefited greatly from the remarks of Ruth Weintraub and Amnon Levav. This was a sceptical and critical audience, and although I tried to meet all their objections I am not at all sure I have managed to do so.

I wish to thank Ann Himmelberger Wald, philosophy and political theory editor at Princeton University Press, for her patience and her meticulous reading of the manuscript. Her comments were extremely helpful and are reflected in the final version.

I am very grateful to my editor Batya Stein for her comments, advice, and editorial skills. We have shared questions and doubts and the partnership between us has made this book what it is.

ACKNOWLEDGMENTS

It is customary to end acknowledgments by thanking one's family, and with good reason. Sharing one's life with someone engaged in writing a book is not, to put it mildly, a pleasant experience. Lonny, Carmel, and Tal patiently endured the closed door of my study and gave me the love and support without which this book could not have been written.

LIBERAL NATIONALISM

INTRODUCTION

There is no route back from reflectiveness. This phenomenon of self-consciousness, together with the institutions and processes that support it, constitute one reason why past forms of life are not a real option for the present, and why attempts to go back often produce results that are ludicrous on a small scale and hideous on a large one.
—*Bernard Williams*

As we entered the final quarter of the twentieth century, there was a widespread assumption that the age of nationalism was over, that we were on the threshold of a postnational era. It is now clear that this assumption was wrong. National movements are regaining popularity, and nations that had once assimilated and "vanished" have now reappeared. Estonians, Latvians, Corsicans, and Lombards awake from the long slumber that communist regimes or Western European nation-states had forced upon them, flex their muscles, and set out to march under the banner of national independence. These attempts to turn back the historical clock are often marked by bloodshed and by a violation of the rights of neighbouring nations. In their enthusiasm to regain their national identity and acquire recognition and self-respect, national activists often overlook the changes that have taken place in the surrounding political, economic, and strategic circumstances, and fail to realise that some national slogans have become obsolete. The era of homogeneous and viable nation-states is over (or rather, the era of the illusion that homogeneous and viable nation-states are possible is over, since such states never existed), and the national vision must be redefined.

The twenty-first century is unlikely to see nationalism fade away. Liberals, whom some had viewed as the great winners of the twentieth century, must come to terms with the need to "share this glory" with nationalism, and probably with religious fundamentalism too. Liberals then need to ask themselves whether national convictions matter to their way of thinking, to their values, norms, and modes of behaviour, to their notions of social justice, and to the range of prac-

3

tical policies they support. In other words, they must rethink their beliefs and policies and seek to adapt them to the world in which they live.

Some may argue that liberals should rather engage in a struggle against the national phenomenon, offer a universalist alternative, and rely on persuasion and education to eradicate national feelings. Although this attempt to manipulate individual preferences rather than meet them is obviously paternalistic, it could be viewed more favourably were we to agree that national aspirations are ultimately evil and there is nothing in them that merits our respect. But is this indeed the case? Even when viewed from a liberal perspective, nationalism advances an important claim, which can hardly be dismissed as manifestly and utterly irrelevant, false, or morally reprehensible. This is not to say that certain types of nationalism are not morally repugnant, but the same could be said of almost any political theory. The oppressive and at times murderous nature of people's democracies, the malicious neglect of the poor and the needy that follows from a rigid adherence to free-market libertarianism, clearly show the horrific results of pushing even the most virtuous of ideas to their logical end. National ideas have indeed fueled some of the most devastating regimes of this century, but they have also inspired some of its most glorious moments, when the struggle against colonialism and imperialism was waged in the name of national self-determination.

This work is an attempt to demonstrate that the liberal tendency to overlook the value inherent in nationalism is mistaken, and to explore ways in which nationalism might contribute to liberal thinking. This could prove to be a rewarding venture, particularly if it provides us with a better set of tools with which to confront some of the bitter conflicts tearing our world apart.

The treatment of nationalism and liberalism in this book is not symmetrical. Liberalism is taken as the starting point, and there is no attempt to justify the set of liberal values in light of which this work aims to reflect on, evaluate, and structure a theory of nationalism. In the pursuit of this task, it breaks away from the liberal tendency to describe nationalism as resting merely on irrational (some say primitive) fears of "the stranger," as motivated by a morally irrelevant attraction to what is familiar and similar, by an unscrupulous desire for power, or by a desire to grab advantages for one's nation at the expense of others. These elements obviously have a role in the understanding of nationalism, but they fail to exhaust the reasons for

4

its appeal. Underlying nationalism is a range of perceptive under-
standings of the human situation, of what makes human life meaningful and creative, as well as a set of praiseworthy values. Liberals
are challenged to accommodate those worthy elements, and lend
substance to national values within the boundaries of liberalism.

My attempt to introduce national values into the liberal discourse
is motivated by an ongoing personal commitment to pursue a national vision while remaining faithful to a set of liberal beliefs. I have
consequently refrained from taking a frequently offered piece of advice suggesting I renounce the concept of "nationalism" in favour of
a less emotionally loaded term, such as "people" or the much discussed "community." Although resorting to a less controversial and
less pejorative term might have made my position more acceptable,
I thought it would be wrong to bypass the concept of nationalism.
Liberals who give up this term and surrender it to the use of conservative political forces, or note the difference, to chauvinist and
racist ideologies, alienate themselves from a whole set of values
that are of immense importance to a great many people, including
liberals.

MacCormick excels in conveying the problems faced by liberals
who are also committed to a national cause:

> Whether 'nation' and 'nationalism' are antithetical to or com-
> patible with 'individual' and 'individualism' is a question of
> acute personal concern for me. I have been for a good many
> years a member of the Scottish National Party, and yet remain
> in some perplexity about the justiciability of any nationalistic
> case within the terms set for me by the other principles to which
> I adhere.[1]

Liberal nationalists confront a whole range of questions: Should I
prefer my liberal beliefs to my national commitments? Are both intrinsically valuable because they reflect different aspects of my personality? Is it really the case that my liberal values reflect rational
thinking and the exercise of choice, while my national attachments
are part of the emotional, inexplicable allure of the mysterious word
"my"—"my" people, "my" culture?

If the conflict between liberalism and nationalism is, as Gellner
describes it, "a tug of war between reason and passion,"[2] liberals
might feel obliged to give liberal values priority over national convictions. But if this description is simplistic and misleading, there
may be no easy way of ranking these two sets of values. Liberals

might then have to acknowledge that a wide range of incommensurable and incompatible values and norms are relevant to their life, and seek a reasonable compromise.

This book suggests that the liberal tradition, with its respect for personal autonomy, reflection, and choice, and the national tradition, with its emphasis on belonging, loyalty, and solidarity, although generally seen as mutually exclusive, can indeed accommodate one another. Liberals can acknowledge the importance of belonging, membership, and cultural affiliations, as well as the particular moral commitments that follow from them. Nationalists can appreciate the value of personal autonomy and individual rights and freedoms, and sustain a commitment for social justice both between and within nations.

Certain tensions between liberal and national values are, however, inherent. Some of these values lead to incompatible policies and many such conflicts, explored in the final chapter, are not the outcome of "a logical incomparability between duties abstractly defined, but between the actions they require in a given situation."[3] In other cases, liberal and national values are incommensurable, that is, there is no single scale on which they might be measured and compared. How can we determine which will be more valuable to the individual's well-being—a wide range of civil liberties or membership in a flourishing cultural group, full-scale autonomy, or a deep sense of belonging?

Arguing that national values should be acknowledged and respected, rather than dismissed as inherently groundless and irrational, entails a move toward greater moral complexity and more frequent collisions between rights and values. At best, these could be resolved by untidy compromises aimed at alleviating harm and suffering. Tidiness is not a proper end for heterogeneous societies, says Berlin; there are no perfect answers to social problems, and the pursuit of absolute solutions too often leads to oppression or bloodshed.[4] The search for a theory of liberal nationalism, which renounces the ultimate pursuit of one set of values at the expense of the other, is an attempt to avoid this peril.

The starting point of this work is a set of beliefs endorsing individual rights and liberties, affirming the right of individuals to equal respect and concern, and presuming that governments should be neutral and impartial vis-à-vis individual interests, preferences, and conceptions of the good, propositions endorsed by most contemporary liberal theorists. As far as the national dimension is concerned, this book does not embark on a descriptive account of the political, historical, sociological or economic circumstances that brought nationalism about, or allowed its development as a global force. It presents nationalism as a way of thinking about human nature and about a world order, from which prescriptive implications for moral and political thought might be derived.

My inquiry concerning the foundations of liberal nationalism, begins with the basic methodological postulate of every political ideology—a portrait of human nature. The idea that there are universal features that characterise human nature might seem more plausible to liberals than to nationalists. Yet, the nationalist emphasis on the importance of particular circumstances for the construction of personal identity does not contradict the universalist view of human nature. On the contrary, nationalists can endorse this notion and claim that, by nature, individuals are members of particular human communities. Outside such communities they cannot develop a language and a culture, or set themselves aims. Their lives become meaningless; there is no substance to their reflection, no set of norms and values in light of which they can make choices and become the free, autonomous persons that liberals assume them to be. Being situated, adhering to a particular tradition, and being intimate with a particular language, could therefore be seen as preconditions of personal autonomy, although they could also be perceived as restricting the possibility of choosing elements that are constitutive of personal identity, such as communal and cultural affiliations and a basic set of values. But would national, religious, and cultural movements be so fearful of conversion and assimilation were it not clear that individuals do indeed have a choice in these realms?

The first chapter discusses cultural choices in great detail, asking whether culture can be a precondition of reflective thinking and the exercise of choice, while in itself remaining an object of choice. It is argued in this work that although cultural choices are neither easy nor limitless, cultural memberships are not beyond choice. In this sense, the view of culture and communal membership developed here differs from the perfectionistic and collective approach generally adopted by communitarians, in that it cherishes openness, reflection, and individual choice.

Claiming that individuals can choose their communal affiliations does not imply that they approach their membership superficially, or that they consider it irrelevant to their self-definition. Several elements, although constitutive of our personal identity—religious beliefs, political affiliations, professions, and styles of life—are nevertheless subject to reflection and choice.

7

This emphasis on the elective aspect of personal identity has important implications for the theoretical understanding and the practical realisation of cultural and national rights, which are discussed in Chapters 2 and 3. Rights are viewed here as means to allow individuals to lead a life which, on reflection, they have come to value, rather than a life imposed on them by history and fate. It makes no sense to ensure individuals the ability to adopt a culture they despise, or to belong to a community they do not wish to be members of. The right to culture is meant to allow individuals to live within the culture of their choice, to decide on their social affiliations, to re-create the culture of the community they belong to, and to redefine its borders.

Notwithstanding the individualistic dimension of this argument, liberal nationalism recognises that culture and membership are communal features, whose worth can be fully enjoyed only together with others making similar choices. A right to culture thus entails the right to a public sphere in which individuals can share a language, memorise their past, cherish their heroes, live a fulfilling national life.

This approach presupposes a cultural definition of the term "nation," in which the nation is seen as an "imaginary community."[5] The concept "imaginary community" is used here, following Anderson, to describe a community too big to allow for direct personal relations among all its members. The boundaries of such a community and the notion of recognition that follows from it, are products of its members' ability to "think the nation" by the power of their imagination. Hence, rather than implying false beliefs or misrepresentations of reality, "imaginary" implies that, unlike the family, the tribe, or the people, the nation exists only when its members consciously conceive themselves as distinct from members of other groups. This "illusive" definition makes it hard to draw clear distinctions between a nation and other types of cultural communities. Less harm is likely to be caused, however, by accepting an ambiguous definition of the term "nation," which might lead to the inclusion of groups that would be left out by a stricter one, than by excluding borderline cases.

If culture, in its widest sense, is what holds a nation together and preserves it as separate from others, then the existence of a nation as a distinct social unit is contingent on the presence of a public sphere where the national culture is expressed, where an individual feels free to "develop without repression those aspects of his personality which are bound up with his sense of identity as a member of his community."[6] This demand for a public sphere in which the cultural aspects of national life come to the fore constitutes the essence of the right to national self-determination. This right is to be distinguished from the right to self-rule, which is the right to take part in the political institutions that govern one's life. Whereas the latter is derived from democratic theory, the former is grounded in a theory of nationalism. Chapter 3 develops this distinction and follows up its ℀ practical implications.

Historically, the nation-state has been the prevalent solution to nationalist demands for self-determination. National self-determination can indeed substantiate a claim for political institutions that members might see as "their own," and for a public sphere where the national culture might be expressed, but these ends can also be achieved through a variety of other political setups, including federative and confederative arrangements, local autonomies, or the establishment of national institutions. Were nation-states the only way of realising the right to national self-determination, its implementation would remain the privilege of only a fortunate few. The merits of a model suggesting that the political implications of this right be phrased in more modest terms, is that it allows all nations to enjoy it in some form.

Chapter 4 outlines in more detail the parameters of liberal nationalism, and demonstrates that it can be distinguished from some of its more notorious neighbours, such as fascism and nazism. Liberal nationalism is predicated on the idea that all nations should enjoy equal rights, and in fact derives its universal structure from the theory of individual rights found at its core. If national rights rest on the value that individuals attach to their membership in a nation, then all nations are entitled to equal respect. The justification of national rights is thus separated from the glorious or tormented past of each nation, from its antiquity, or from its success in attaining territorial gains.[7]

Chapter 5 turns to the question of justice. Theories of nationalism do not endorse a particular conception of social justice, although we can infer a certain moral approach from the basic set of beliefs underlying national thinking. Its most immediate consequences touch on the claim that membership influences the moral obligations of individuals. Members have certain special obligations and responsibilities toward each other, thereby sustaining a claim for partiality: Individuals thus have a reason, although not an ultimate one, to

9

prefer members over nonmembers. In the course of the discussion several distinctions regarding the subjects as well as the spheres in which this favouritism is justified are drawn.

Contrary to common wisdom, the conception of justice implied by liberal nationalism is no more egoistic and no less satisfying, but more consistent than that of traditional liberalism.

The inconsistencies found in liberal theories of justice reveal that many national elements, although unacknowledged, have been fused into liberal thought; some of them are explored in Chapter 6. For example, the liberal conception of distributive justice is particularistic and applies only within well-defined, relatively closed social frameworks, which favour members over nonmembers. The same applies to the liberal conceptions of membership and political obligations, which simultaneously embody two contradictory images of the political community: that of a voluntary association and that of a community of fate. This dualistic perception comes to the fore in the liberal stand on questions of naturalisation, as citizenship in a liberal state is more often a right acquired by birth than through voluntary consent. Indeed, this could almost be expected, since the modern conception of the state emerges from the amalgamation of liberal, democratic, and national ideas. Liberal nationalism is therefore a more common position than is generally assumed. Most liberals might disagree and tend to dissociate themselves from nationalism because they identify it only with its most extreme and intolerant versions. In so doing, however, they deprive themselves of the possibility of gaining a better understanding of the sources of their own thinking.

The national point of view grants prominence to several dimensions that liberal theory has tended to overlook: social attachments, cultural affiliations, the communal aspect of individual identity, and particular moral commitments that grow out of membership in associative communities. Once the importance of these dimensions is recognised, they could shed light on the liberal argument itself.

Were homogeneous nation-states possible, liberal nationalism would pose no problems. But most contemporary states are multinational, and under these circumstances, the demand that a state should reflect one national culture entails harsh implications for members of minority groups.

Drawing a line between the political and the cultural spheres could serve to alleviate some of the problems raised by multinationalism. The most important aspect of this distinction is that nationality, which is here used to describe membership in a nation and not

10

in its misleading yet widespread connotation of citizenship, should not be a criterion for participating in the political sphere or for the allocation of goods and services.

An open political culture, that compensates members of minority groups for cultural disadvantages, may lessen the problems faced by national and cultural minorities. Nevertheless, alienation from a system characterised by cultural features one does not share is a persistent cause of personal suffering and political unrest. These tensions are inherent in the national nature of the modern state, and cannot be dealt with unless we reconsider our understanding of its roles and functions.

The final chapter offers guidelines for such a reconsideration, keeping in mind that solutions are never simple, even under optimal conditions. The main merit of this discussion is not in its ability to unravel all possible entanglements, but in pointing to the irresolvable collision between worthwhile values. It addresses a plea to liberals to be attentive to the nature of national claims, and to seek ways of taking them into account alongside traditional liberal values.

Liberals often align themselves with national demands raised by "underdogs," be they indigenous peoples, discriminated minorities, or occupied nations, whose plight can easily evoke sympathy. But if national claims rest on theoretically sound and morally justified grounds, one cannot restrict their application: They apply equally to all nations, regardless of their power, their wealth, their history of suffering, or even the injustices they have inflicted on others in the past.

It is true that fanatic nationalism is a more dangerous tool in the hands of the mighty, and zealous nationalism can indeed lead to deplorable consequences. Even some of the moderate views suggested in this work could be used to justify evil policies if isolated from their overall context. At the risk of stating the obvious, it must be said that all decent solutions to the problems raised in this book require a fair degree of tolerance, open-mindedness, and common sense, and no theory, no matter how well-defined, could be of any help in their absence.

It could also be claimed that reflective nationalism is not nationalism at all and that, by nature, nationalism is holistic and ultimate, and could never be reflective, individualistic, and antiperfectionistic. Williams' words, which served as the epigraph of this introduction, seem appropriate in response: "There is no route back from reflectiveness." That is why past forms of life, as well as past forms of thought, are not suitable options. Some nationalists, as well as some

11

communitarians, might indeed hope to return to the intimate, close, authoritarian communities of the past that, in the haze of history, appear as a lost Eden. But the past has withered, and trying to force it back can, as we have recently witnessed, be "ludicrous on a small scale and hideous on a large one."[8]

The feeling that national thinking stakes an important claim if it could only free itself from the rhetoric of blood and soil and acknowledge that reflection and choice are as important as history and fate, is what motivated me to write this book. It is for the reader to judge whether I have succeeded in placing national thinking within the boundaries of liberalism without losing sight of either.

O N E

THE IDEA OF THE PERSON

> The ideas of every philosopher concerned with human
> affairs in the end rest on his conception of what man is
> and can be. To understand such thinkers, it is more impor-
> tant to grasp this central notion or image (which may be
> implicit, but determines their picture of the world) than
> even the most forceful arguments with which they defended
> their views and refute actual and possible objections.
> —*Isaiah Berlin*

What is the essence of human nature? This question is a central
methodological issue lying at the foundation of every political philosophy, as well as a very personal matter. To think about human
nature is to think about ourselves as individuals, as members of certain communities and associations, as political and moral agents.
When thinking of human nature we venture inwards and reflect on
what we are, what we ought to be, and what we could potentially
become. We expect a plausible description of human nature to
reflect, at least in some sense, the way in which we perceive ourselves. The view that neither the totally situated description of a "national self," nor the liberal description of a self antecedently free of
all attachments adequately portrays human nature is now shared by
many. This has motivated the search for a midway position able to
encompass the nationalist belief that individuals are the inevitable
product of their culture, as well as the liberal conviction that individuals can be the authors of their own lives.

"I have seen, in my times," says De-Maistre, "Frenchmen, Italians,
and Russians. I even know, thanks to Montesquieu, that one may be
a Persian; but as for Man, I declare I have never met him in my life;
if he exists, it is without my knowledge."[1] This description sheds
light on one source of human diversity, namely, national and cultural affiliations. Mill suggests other sources, personal rather than
communal. Such are the differences among human beings in their
sources of pleasure, their susceptibilities of pain, and the operation

13

on them of different physical and moral agencies, says Mill, "that unless there is a corresponding diversity in their modes of life, they neither obtain their fair share of happiness, nor grow up to the mental, moral and aesthetic stature of which their nature is capable."[2] These two very different, although not necessarily incompatible, descriptions of human nature are at the heart of this book's endeavour to outline a theory of liberal nationalism. Finding a common ground between the liberal and nationalist views of human nature will not ensure that all conflicts between these two schools of thought will fade away, but it could provide an adequate framework for discussion.

Several political philosophers have recently attempted, with considerable success, to bridge the gap between the liberal and the communitarian approaches to the question of human nature. Although not specifically concerned with the liberal nationalist debate, their writings have a bearing on the issues with which this book is concerned.[3] In an attempt to present a concept of human nature that both liberals and nationalists might find acceptable, this book takes as its starting point the central argument emerging from these writings, that is, that embeddedness and choice are not necessarily antithetical. I shall only refer to issues directly relevant to this attempt, as covering all aspects of this philosophical argument would far exceed the scope of this book.

Two main methodological difficulties hinder the search for a midway position. The first is that it is hard to infer a shared interpretation of the concept of human nature from the writings of different nationalist thinkers. Herder or Mazzini suggest a radically different notion from that offered by Schelling, Treitschke, or Fichte, who himself entertained different interpretations of this concept at various stages of his life. It therefore seems quite impossible to identify *the* nationalist point of view. The second stems from the fact that nationalists and liberals have adopted radically different modes of discourse regarding this issue. Since this book takes liberal theory as its starting point, it attempts to "translate" nationalist arguments into liberal language. In so doing it relies on the current terms of communitarian discourse, which is akin to the nationalist one in its content.

The idea of the person developed in this chapter is inspired by both liberalism and nationalism, and combines the notions of personal autonomy and communal belonging. These concepts are viewed here as complementary rather than conflicting, suggesting that no individual can be context-free, but that all can be free within a context.

What Is Natural about Human Nature?

It is no surprise that the question of human nature features so prominently in liberal literature, while it is hardly ever mentioned in nationalist writings. The notion of a universal human nature is clearly more plausible to liberals than to nationalists. This should not immediately lead to the conclusion, however, that a theory of nationalism cannot accommodate the notion that individuals share some universal human features, as liberal theory need not deny the importance of particularistic circumstances in the structuring of personal identity and individual traits, preferences, and modes of behaviour. The tensions among the different interpretations of the concept of human nature adopted by these schools of thought centre around altogether different issues: What constitutes the stable core of universal human nature? What human characteristics vary in line with specific cultural environments? What is the status of these two types of features? Is it justified to claim that only universal characteristics are constitutive of our humanity whereas culture-bound features are of secondary importance? Can elements constitutive of our identity be a matter of choice?

Some preliminary remarks are in order before we plunge into the substance of the discussion. It is worth noting that the descriptive, empirical language often used in discussions about human nature is misleading. The body of knowledge made available through the natural and social sciences underdetermines "true human nature." Consequently, every description unavoidably relies on normative assumptions, which are meant to fill the gap between what we know about human beings and what we think should be the essence of humanity. Thus, claims that human agents are, by nature, rational or nationally embedded, reflect moral and social convictions and are not merely descriptive. They interpret our knowledge in light of some ideal and suggest that we ought to treat human beings as if they have the *potential* to be rational, make free choices, or harbour strong national feelings, that these attributes are distinctively human, and that, if allowed to develop them, individuals will be better able to realise themselves. This does not mean that we can attribute to human beings any feature serving our theories, but rather that our interpretation of what we know is heavily biased by our theoretical perspective.

Social scientists can, nevertheless, be helpful in clarifying the terms of this debate. Geertz makes an important contribution when he ridicules the hope to uncover the "fundamental unchanged na-

15

ture of man." Unmodified human nature has never existed and "could not, in the very nature of the case, exist."[4] Geertz criticises the "stratigraphic" view of human nature as a composite of layers, and rejects the notion that, after stripping off culture and social organisation, we shall uncover a series of natural psychological factors or basic needs, and still below some biological foundations—anatomical, psychological, or neurological components that have developed independent of culture. There is no human nature independent of circumstances. Human beings have developed in close interaction with culture; they are "incomplete or unfinished animals who complete or finish themselves through culture—and not through culture in general but through highly particular forms of it."[5]

Geertz's criticism suggests that the term "human nature" is meaningless. It is therefore preferable to place at the focus of this discussion a different notion, namely, the idea of the person. This notion emphasises that the argument concerns those characteristics ascribed to human beings as part of a cetain picture of the world. Our idea of the person has developed alongside civilisation:

> From a simple masquerade to the mask, from a "role" (personage) to a "person" (personne), to a name, to an individual; from the latter to a being possessing metaphysical and moral value; from a moral consciousness to a sacred being; from the latter to a fundamental form of thought and action—the course is accomplished.[6]

Many have questioned the linear, evolutionary assumption latent in this description. Nevertheless, it is still the case that our idea of the person has developed hand in hand with "different societies, systems of laws, religion, customs, social structures and mentality,"[7] and is "both culturally specific and a historical product."[8]

Formulating this discussion in terms of the idea of the person rather than of human nature enhances the relevance of the nationalist approach. If the human qualities essential to our discussion are not context-free, then terms like "culture," "membership," and "embeddedness," which are central to the national discourse, become pivotal.

On Atomised and Situated Selves— ### Two Polarised Ideas of the Person

Nationalism and liberalism are modern movements. Both share the view that free, rational, and autonomous human beings are capable of exercising full responsibility for the conduct of their lives, and both share a belief in the human ability to attain self-rule, self-expression, and self-development. Despite this broad consensus, nationalism and liberalism have developed radically diverse interpretations of these human qualities.

Liberals emphasise and celebrate the plurality of desires, beliefs, and conceptions of the good adopted by different individuals, and assume that "where not the person's own character but the traditions or customs of other people are the rule of conduct, there is wanting one of the principal ingredients of human happiness, and quite the chief ingredient of individual and social progress," namely, the element of unimpeded individual development.[9]

Nationalists stress the inescapable social aspect of personal identity, and suggest that the only way in which individuals can realise themselves to the full is by identifying with the nation, serving it, obeying its customs, and unreflectively celebrating its greatness.

Nationalists approach societies as natural organs incapable of division into independently viable parts. The social whole is therefore seen as "prior to, more important, and greater than all its parts."[10] Individuals are reduced to being parts in a whole, means for safeguarding the latter's existence and well-being. According to this view, national ends have priority over individual ends, and personal freedom is attainable only through identification with, and subordination to the "national will."

Liberals do not altogether reject the organic description of society, but stress that social relations among individuals are based on mutual advantage. Society allows individuals to profit from the complementary nature of their inclinations by enabling them to enjoy, through the activities of others, those aspects of their own personality that they "have not been able to cultivate."[11] Hence, from a liberal perspective, self-expression and individual diversity are the crux of the organic view of society, and these elements should enjoy priority.

Nationalists view the liberal idea of the person as an empty abstraction, to which liberals reply with an analogous counterclaim: Community, they claim, is a "fictitious body," and the interest of the community is merely the sum of the individual interests of its members. A people, claims MacDonald, "doesn't exist except as an abstract conception; the only realities are the individuals who actually make up the people."[12] Thus, "no rational person could elevate the supposed interests of a fiction above the real interests of real individuals."[13]

As described by nationalists, liberals are committed to an idea of the person as antecedently free, and as a rational, reflective agent "for whom group membership is voluntary."[14] Liberals are accused of misunderstanding the power of social affiliations, and of promoting an atomistic, alienating notion of association based on competition, mistrust, and narrow egoism, inevitably leading to national decadence, defeat, and humiliation.[15] For their part, liberals have described nationalism as antithetical to rationality, and as rooted in primitive forces tending to overpower judgment and freedom. They have accused nationalists of endorsing the view that "human beings are totally constituted by the social relationships in which they are necessarily to be found,"[16] and have warned that such views can be used, and indeed have been used, to justify the brutal oppression of individuals.

But these descriptions, however widespread, rest on simplistic and radical interpretations of both liberalism and nationalism. They invite us

> to see the moral universe in dualistic terms; either our identities are independent of our ends, leaving us *totally free* to choose our life plans, or they are constituted by community, leaving us *totally encumbered* by socially given ends; either justice must be independent of all historical and social particularities or virtue must depend completely on the particular social practices of each society.[17]

These extreme portrayals reflect the fact that nationalism and liberalism tend to emphasise different features in the idea of the person, to the point where both become easily refutable "straw men." A closer look will reveal that liberals need not reject the importance of cultural contextualisation, whereas nationalists need not ignore the importance of personal freedom. A much more balanced idea of the person, revealing broad areas of agreement between these seemingly opposing views, thus emerges.

For example, both schools of thought can agree on a characterisation of individuals as agents who look to society to lend context to their personal thoughts, namely, as agents who acknowledge that their ends are meaningful only within a social context, but who do not necessarily accept socially dictated ends unreflectively. Their conception of the good is neither totally individualistic nor wholly communal, and they may at times place their personal good before the common one while overturning their priorities at others. Society is thus seen as essential for the fulfillment of some ends, and as an obstacle hindering the attainment of others.

In fact, this is a rather common view among liberals. Gaus claims that the modern liberal theory of man combines a view of the individual as a unique manifestation of humanity, an end in himself, with that of the individual as a member of a social group. He shows that six modern liberals—Mill, Green, Hobhouse, Bosanquant, Dewey, and Rawls—all attempt to "develop a theory of man that reconciles the pursuit of individuality with sociability and membership in a community."[18] Although Gaus's argument does not apply equally to all six, most liberals do see individuals as rooted in society, and as dependent on communal relations for their moral and personal development.

The sociability of human beings must not be understood in a trivial fashion, claims Rawls. It does not merely imply that living in a community is essential for fulfilling the needs and interests of individuals, nor is it exhausted by the truism that social life is a necessary condition for developing the ability to speak, think, and take part in the shared activities of culture. "We need one another as partners in ways of life that are engaged in for their own sake, and the successes and enjoyment of others are necessary for and complementary to our own good."[19] Society, according to this view, is necessary to enable individuals to reach self-development, self-expression, personal happiness, and satisfaction.

The definition of individuals as social beings does not seem to evoke strong controversy. The conflict between liberals and nationalists lies elsewhere, and concerns the process whereby individuals acquire membership in particular social groups, and the links between these memberships and personal identity.

Most contemporary liberals, such as Rawls, Dworkin, Raz, and Ackerman, do not ignore the fact that affections, loyalties, and social ties are constitutive factors of individual identity. Indeed, the situated nature of individuals, their attachment to particular communities, and the way in which such attachments influence their decision-making, motivated Rawls to seek a thin overlapping consensus rather than a thick moral and cultural understanding. The parties in the original position thus needed to be placed behind a veil of ignorance, allowing them to make judgments unencumbered by their constitutive affiliations. Citizens, suggests Rawls, "may regard it as simply unthinkable to view themselves apart from certain religious, philosophical and moral convictions, or from certain enduring attachments and loyalties."[20] They may therefore find it impossible to stand apart from, and objectively evaluate, these affiliations from the point of view of their purely rational good.

Rawls' claims presuppose that individuals are social beings and that social membership is a constitutive element of personal identity, but this view leaves open the question of how individuals define this identity: Is it, as nationalists claim, a matter of discovery, of disclos-

19

ing the ways in which communal relations mould identity, or is it a matter of choice? This is an essential point of contention between liberal and nationalist conceptions of the self.

Choice, Discovery, and the Formation of Identity

Liberals acknowledge the importance of social relations and communal affiliations, but they presume that individuals can distance themselves from their social roles and affiliations, "adopt, perform or abandon any at will (though not all, and probably not even many, at once)."[21] Will, choice, reflection, and evaluation are therefore central to the liberal idea of the person.

In this respect, the communitarian or nationalist idea is the reverse of the liberal one. It sees social roles and affiliations as inherent, as a matter of fate rather than choice: "Who I am is answered both for me and for others by the history I inherit, the social positions I occupy, and the 'moral career' on which I am embarked."[22]

There is therefore an apparent incompatibility between these two approaches. Once again, however, the gap seems greater than it really is. A distinction between two types of identity may sharpen the focus of this discussion: Moral identity, built around the question of what sort of person I would like to be, reflecting the conceptions of the good, the moral values and convictions, the life-plans and interests of individuals; and communal identity, reflecting their social affiliations.

Indeed, these two aspects of identity are closely related: The latter sets the terms of discussion for the former, while the former helps shape the critical evaluation of the latter. As far as the ability to define and reflect on personal identity is concerned, however, the two may be viewed separately. We can therefore define four models of identity formation as follows.

1. The strict discovery model. This model assumes that both our moral and communal identities are wholly prescribed for us by our history and our social affiliations. Therefore, they can only be discovered and cannot be a matter of choice.

2. The communal choice model. This model suggests that our communal identity is a matter of choice, but once defined, it dictates our values, permissible ends, and conceptions of the good, and thus prescribes our moral identity.

3. The moral choice model. According to this model, history and fate define our communal identity, which can therefore only be discovered, but our moral identity is left undefined. Our communal

membership may set the limits of our moral horizons, but it does not determine our conceptions of the good and our life-plans.

4. The strict choice model. This model claims that individuals can reflect on and choose both their communal and their moral identities. This model does not assume, however, that we are free to detach ourselves from all our communal and moral attachments at once, and reflect on them from some Archimedean point. Yet, it claims that we can, in the course of our lives, reflect on and choose our ends, our conception of the good, and our life-plans, as well as our communal affiliations. According to this model, individuals can distance themselves from both their moral and communal identities.[23]

It should be noted that, since we do not usually embark on a process of comprehensive change that questions our moral and communal identities all at once, discovery retains an important role in the latter model. Consequently, at every point in the course of reflecting on our identity, we engage in a process that combines discovery and choice. The ability to discover our social position is thus as essential to this model as the ability to reflect on it. Choice, reflection, and discovery are thus seen as mutually complementary rather than antithetical.

Liberals view the ability to choose as the most essential characteristic of the human agent, and in fact, the only one that is beyond the limits of human choice, as choosing not to choose entails a choice. But living a life in which choice plays an important role does not entail living an eclectic life, choosing one thing today and its opposite tomorrow. Choice is not to be identified with change. In the context of an argument against the notion of choice as intrinsically important, Kymlicka tries to refute the claim that life is more valuable the more we exercise our capacity for choice by means of the following example: We do not suppose, he argues, that someone "who has made twenty marriage choices is in any way leading a more valuable life than someone who has no reason to question or revise their original choice."[24] This is obviously true, yet this argument is based on the fallacy of identifying choice with change, and overlooks the fact that staying in a marriage also reflects a choice. How do we know that we have no reason to question and revise our original choices unless we reflect on them and decide on them anew? Our lives may be better if upon reflection, we choose to remain with our spouses or preserve our communal identity, but not if we do so out of convention and routine.

Introducing choice into the process of shaping a communal identity does not imply that this identity is unsubstantial or marginal,

21

but rather that even its constitutive elements are subject to choice. Not only are our communal affiliations—or, for that matter, our marriages—not weakened by the constant exercise of choice, they are in fact strengthened by it.

Granting choice such a central role requires an explanation of how individuals make choices bearing on their most fundamental attachments and values. This is the concern of the next section.

Choosing a Moral Identity

Individuals are unable to make choices *simultaneously* touching on all realms of their lives. It therefore seems more plausible to assume that they usually behave in line with one of the combined models of choice, namely, they hold constant one aspect of their identity, either their communal membership or their moral identity, and reflect on the other.

Reflecting on issues concerning moral identity is dependent on the presence of a cultural context. The importance of a cultural context is evident even in relation to the most casual everyday decisions. The answer to a question such as "What shall I have for breakfast?" often reflects national affiliations. An English breakfast is not the same as a French or an Israeli one, and all reflect shared social norms and beliefs about what is healthy, respectable, or fashionable.

Lest we end up selecting options at random, choice is contingent on having a socially acquired set of values that serve as criteria for evaluation. Taylor's concept of the strong evaluator clearly captures this interplay between choice and context.[25] Strong evaluators do not judge preferences on the basis of their contingent incompatibility with other alternatives, but on a qualitative evaluation of the alternatives "as higher and lower, noble and base, and so on."[26] The set of values they rely on in order to make these judgments is not an external instrument picked at random but a constitutive element of their identity; and as long as they adhere to it, some of their choices are inevitable.

Both liberals and nationalists could see strong evaluators as incarnating their own views. The ability of strong evaluators to reflect on and evaluate preferences and interests could be seen as a liberal attribute, whereas nationalists might view the evaluators' embeddedness in a cultural context and the precedence given to social membership as a precondition for choice, as an instance of national thinking. Liberals, however, face the question of whether the process of socialization, which enables individuals to become strong evaluators in the first place, might not prevent them from distancing themselves from their social context and from reflecting critically on its fundamental values.

Taylor assumes that certain fundamental features are "insepara‐ ble from ourselves as agents."[27] Our personal identity, as well as our basic values and norms, reflect our background, and to reject them would imply rejecting ourselves. But if we have no way of reflecting on the values prescribed by our background, the liberal self disap‐ pears and a well-situated agent takes its place. Having begun with a choosing agent and progressed through the need for context and socialization, we now find that the liberal self has not only lost the antecedent to social affiliations, but is confined to a restricted set of values drawn from this background. When taken to extremes, this position may only leave room for trivial choices.

If we are to restore the idea of a choosing agent, we must assume that one can at least distance oneself from some basic moral values provided by society and adopt a new or reformed set of values. Such a radical process of reflection may lead us to claim that a person is no longer the same person: "We know what this means: we refer to a profound and pervasive shift, or reversal in a person's final ends and character."[28] Although such extreme changes may shatter the most basic characteristics of the self, this does not necessarily mean that they are impossible.

How does this process take place? What is the nature of radical reflection? Some claim that individuals can distance themselves from constitutive elements of their identity through a gradual pro‐ cess of reflection. It seems, however, that this assumption cannot, in and of itself, explain our ability to embark on a radical reflective process. If a person's set of fundamental values is consistent, then keeping some of them constant while reflecting on the others cannot generate radical change. The assumption that reflection is a gradual process is therefore of little help in explaining radical change. What options are we then left with? On the face of it, it would appear that if we have a consistent set of values, to reevaluate some of them we must appeal to values that are outside our "horizon of evaluation." This would require us either to invent a totally new and detached set of values, or to appeal to some prevailing elsewhere, an approach Collini terms the "offshore" model.[29] This latter process entails moral mimicry, imitation, and adaptation. It is a modern phenome‐ non, contingent on the ability of individuals to be exposed to ways of life, belief systems, and sets of norms other than their own. The discovery that others hold a different set of norms and beliefs might tempt us to reconsider our own.

Suppose that an ultra-Orthodox Jewess comes across secular women and becomes aware of the fact that they act in ways different than hers. She finds herself both repelled and attracted by their behaviour. As she becomes more familiar with alternative ways of life, she is tempted to imitate them, despite the fact that, according to her values secular behaviour is sinful. She may then be tempted to reflect on her own set of values in the light of the secular values she has encountered, and decide that ultra-Orthodox tradition discriminates against women. At this point, the status of women might become the overriding variable in light of which she evaluates different forms of life. She may then seek a compromise enabling her to continue to adhere to some of her religious values while accommodating her newly found beliefs, or may gradually reach the conclusion that the inability of her old set of values to incorporate the new ones implies she should reject it altogether. At the end of this process, she may possess a totally new set of values.

Anthropologists speak of an analogous process known as "going native." This is what happened to Father Jack in Brian Friel's play *Dancing at Lughansa*. Father Jack, a missionary priest, is sent to Uganda and gradually embraces the native culture, to the point of including himself in the "we" that he uses to describe native rituals. With deep longing he tells his sisters about the Mass he used to hold in Uganda. When he had a church, he recalls,

> Okawa—my house boy—summons our people by striking a huge iron gong. . . to offer sacrifice to Obi, our Great Goddess of the Earth, so that the crops will flourish. Or maybe to get in touch with our departed fathers for their advice and wisdom. Or maybe to thank the spirits of our tribe if they have been good to us; or to appease them if they're angry.[30]

But does this a process entail choice, or is it a slow and unconscious drift, whereby one first yields to curiosity and temptation and only later seeks to rationalise it? In most cases, we do not begin with choice, just as the ultra-Orthodox Jewess probably did not set out to meet secular women with the deliberate intention of changing her life. Similarly Father Jack was sent to Uganda to bring the natives under the wings of the church, and had no intention of becoming a Ryangan.

Once this process is set in motion through the encounter with other forms of life, individuals become aware of the presence of dif-

THE IDEA OF THE PERSON

ferent options. Although aware of certain disadvantages inherent in their original set of values, they may nevertheless decide to uphold it, or may decide to adopt a new set of values. In this sense, this process does indeed involve choice.

Do we not imply that a radical process of reflection and choice has taken place when we praise someone for becoming a certain type of person "despite his background"? Might not this be the reason for our greater disappointment with certain individuals of privileged background who choose to follow a different, and in our judgment, less worthy set of values? Why otherwise the need to explain how someone who grew up in a communist home became a broker on Wall Street? Or what happened to a nineteenth-century aristocrat who opted to become a member of the working class? Or to Patricia Hearst when she joined her kidnappers and became part of a criminal gang?

It could indeed be claimed that when moral changes are radical enough, they imply joining a radically different social framework. Instances such as those of the broker, the aristocrat, or Patricia Hearst, show that radical moral changes are possible without necessarily changing one's national affiliations.

Individuals could, however, follow a less radical process and challenge the conventional understanding of the basic set of social norms and values prevalent in their society in terms advocated by these same values. In such instances, the motivation for reflection and change is rooted in tensions and inconsistencies internal to the system. These reflections might lead to a reinterpretation of socially held norms and values, or to the broadening of their scope. Collini refers to this process as "the voice of the underdog." The social changes advocated by feminism and the civil rights movement illustrate well the workings of this type of reflective process.

Rejecting the assumption that individuals have the potential to reflect on and refuse the values and norms offered to them in the course of their socialisation sets us on a slippery slope leading to social and cultural determinism. Every conception of the person acceptable to liberals must therefore include the notion of this potential.

Adopting a National Identity

We now turn to the second combined model of choice, namely, one where individuals hold constant their moral values and norms and make choices concerning their communal affiliations. In this section,

25

the discussion will focus on national choices. In line with my definition of "nation" as a form of cultural community, cultural and national choices are used interchangeably.

Can one choose a nation to belong to? Can individuals, from a situated position, distance themselves from their national culture, reflect on it, and make choices? Nationalists would like to deny this possibility, since they view cultural and national affiliations as a matter of fate rather than choice. Why, then, do nationalists contemplate assimilation as a nightmare and celebrate the renewal of national identity? This suggests that, at least in practice, nationalists admit that individuals are indeed capable of changing their national affiliations. From a national point of view, the question then is not whether assimilation is possible, but whether it is desirable or permissible. Nationalists think it is undesirable because it leads to the disintegration of the nation, and it is morally wrong since it reflects a betrayal of one's cultural loyalties.

Before entering the discussion of these normative aspects, a preliminary question seems in order: What is implied by the assumption that individuals can make national choices? First, it means that a statement such as "I would like to be French" is meaningful. This statement differs from the statement "I am French" or "I feel French." It is a statement of preference about communal affiliations. I can express a preference for being French, whether I am French or not; I may be French and happy with my lot, or I may not be French and wish I were. Both these claims share the assumption that I can have preferences regarding my national identity. But can I act on them?

Concepts such as "assimilation" and the "renewal of national identity" imply that one can do more than reflect on these matters, namely, one can indeed decide to adopt a new national identity. This statement needs to be qualified to some extent:

1. Individuals who decide to adopt a new national identity can act in ways that will bring them closer to this goal, but cannot be assured that they will in fact succeed in attaining this end. Similarly, individuals may sincerely desire to become good persons and decide to behave in ways that they believe are required to accomplish this goal, but may nevertheless fail in their endeavour.

2. "Full-scale" assimilation is rarely possible and relies on a variety of factors, of which individual will is only one. It remains a fact, however, that irrespective of the hardships involved in any process of conversion, and despite the almost insurmountable hurdles faced

by those attempting to become "real members," individuals do choose to change their national affiliations.

3. Membership is based on acceptance and mutual identification. Convincing others that one has become a member is the most difficult aspect of assimilation. It involves a readiness to adopt the national culture as well as to exhibit a sense of identification with, and responsibility toward, other members of the same national group.[31] Incidentally, this could encourage those wishing to assimilate to adopt rather conservative interpretations of the new national culture, hoping to gain acceptance and recognition in the eyes of veteran members.

These qualifications notwithstanding, individuals can assimilate or embrace the national identity of their forefathers, even though they might be completely estranged from it, and they make these choices in much the same way in which they reflect on their moral identity. In both instances, mimicry, temptation, and curiosity, largely facilitated by modern communication, are essential elements of the choice process. Very few isolated communities remain in the modern world, and most individuals are acquainted with more than one way of life and more than one national community. It is precisely for this reason that national communities strive for closure—if choice were not an option, closure would be unnecessary.

But how can members of one nation opt for membership in another that they only know superficially? It seems preposterous to suggest that one can choose a national identity merely on the basis of partial and fragmentary information. Yet if such choices were only possible following intimate acquaintance with alternative cultures, they would be extremely rare. One would have to closely study and live in a variety of cultures before making a choice, a relatively exceptional occurrence.

"Members of one culture can, by the force of imaginative insight, understand (what Vico called *entrare*) the values, ideals, the form of life of another culture or society, even those remote in time and space."[32] They may, of course, misinterpret the other culture, modify or distort a language to create their own dialect, detach symbols and rituals from their original use. Nonetheless, their contact with a new culture, or with their own image of it, however distorted and spurious, may assist them in reflecting on their own culture and bring about change.

Admitting that individuals can choose their communal identity still leaves open the question of whether they can choose to adopt

27

any national culture or whether their choices are restricted. It is patently evident that individuals can make far-reaching choices and succeed in implementing them. Even a cursory look at the way in which the House of Windsor became English, or the House of Bernadotte Swedish, will show that complete assimilation is indeed possible. The most recent and interesting example may be the attempt to suggest that Sonia Ghandi, an Italian-born woman, should become the leader of the Indian nation.

Had the young Sonia Ghandi been asked to which national group she would prefer to belong and had she answered, "The Indian people," the most likely reaction would have been to express surprise, and misgivings about her chances of ever accomplishing this wish. But had this young Italian girl had Indian ancestors, even if she had never met them and herself knew very little about Indian culture, her choice would have seemed more plausible. Why do we think that it is more "natural" and less strange for individuals to adopt an identity embraced by their parents or grandparents? Why do we tend to think that individuals of Jewish origin who decide to define themselves as Jews, although they know very little about Judaism, are "renewing" their identity? What does "renewal" mean in this context? Why is it that, although we no longer believe it is "natural" for a shoemaker's son to be a shoemaker and for the daughter of a working-class family to remain in her parents' social stratum, we still think it is "natural" for the son or the grandson of a Jew to be one too?

We welcome social mobility. The age of guilds is over, and watchmakers want their sons to be lawyers and not necessarily watchmakers. Individuals want their children to move out of the old neighbourhood, to have more successful lives, to belong to another class, and to make new friends—but they still want them to retain their national identity.

Why is this so? First, in the professional sphere, as is the case with neighbourhoods and classes, there is an accepted hierarchy. It is possible that the shoemaker will think it is better to be a lawyer than a shoemaker, and will welcome such a change for his children. No such agreed scale exists in the national sphere, and individuals tend to see their children's assimilation as the rejection of something that is dear to them, in favour of an alternative that is not demonstratively better. It is only when individuals view another culture as superior to their own, as was and is the case for certain groups of immigrants, that they welcome assimilation.

Second, continuity and respect for the past are inherent in national-cultural identity. Nationhood and culture are conceived as a progression through time, based on the transmission of language, traditions, and norms from one generation to the other. According to this conception, it is the duty of each generation to pay their debts to their ancestors by remaining within the fold. In this metaphysical sense, individuals are born with a set of communal duties they are meant to fulfill. By assuming the identity they have inherited from their forefathers, individuals take it upon themselves to comply with this duty. The term "identity renewal" thus reflects a belief about a certain continuity of identity across time. It assumes that when an individual of Jewish parentage chooses to define himself as a Jew he is thereby returning to his roots, renewing his ties with his past and embracing an identity that could have been his. George Perec, a French author of Jewish descent, once said in a television interview about a script he wrote for a film on Ellis Island: "This place is, for me, part of a potential memory, of a possible autobiography."[33] It is this sense of potentiality that is captured by the term "renewal." Individuals renew an option, a potential identity offered by their past. Although it may seem philosophically awkward, this concept is an essential aspect of our thinking about national identity.

Identity renewal and assimilation teach us that individuals can reflect not only about the kind of human beings they would like to be, but also about the kind of communal identity they would like to develop. The notion of identity renewal may indicate why individuals are more likely to choose to be what they are, or what their forefathers were, while assimilation reminds us that they can also choose to adopt a foreign culture to which they seem in no way connected.

No doubt, individuals are motivated to make specific choices by a variety of religious, social, political, and economic reasons, as well as by their own psychological makeup, all of which are beyond the scope of this work. It is also true that not all choices are similar, that some cultures are more difficult to leave or enter than others, that a particular colour of skin or certain physical features can make assimilation more difficult, and at times impossible. But this is also true regarding other choices. Take, for instance, career choices. Some careers are harder to embark on than others, and some demand qualifications that most individuals might never obtain. If my mother is a lawyer and has her own law firm, my chances of becoming a successful lawyer are greater than if she is a factory worker. Nevertheess, we still assume that individuals can make career choices. The claim that it is possible to make choices merely requires showing that a person has some options, not that all options are open to him. The same is true about choices concerning national identity: It is enough to show that an individual has some plausible options to claim that he has a choice.

The concept of communal choices is important for our discussion because it singles out two of the most important aspects of modern identity—the need to live one's life from the inside and the need to be rooted—and thus captures the duality inherent in the image of the modern individual. It is important to note that individuals will be unable to exercise their right to make cultural choices unless they live in a culturally plural environment. Since we have assumed that human beings must be embedded in a culture, reflecting critically on their culture can only be productive if there are others to which they can compare their own, from which they might learn or borrow, and into which they might assimilate. The plurality of cultures thus acquires an intrinsic value, as Raz rightly suggests: "If having an autonomous life is an ultimate value, then having a sufficient range of acceptable options is an intrinsic value."[34] Hence, the right to make cultural choices is only meaningful in a world where the plurality of cultures is protected.

Individuals can benefit from cultural plurality in two distinct ways. In the "strong sense," cultural plurality ensures that reflections about one's own culture take place within a genuine context, one offering models for imitation and even options for assimilation. In its "weak sense," cultural plurality is aesthetically valuable. Just as we prefer a stimulating cultural enviroment where we might enjoy the precision and elegance of Japanese painting, the naturalistic perfection of ancient Greek sculpture, and the power and irony of modern American art, we prefer cultural plurality because it broadens the range of possibilities for pleasure and enrichment. Cultural plurality is to be valued not only because it offers alternative life-options but also because it is a way of improving our lives within our own culture and preserving "different types of Men as variant species of the same genus." The loss of valuable forms of life can therefore be seen as a "failure of mankind to protect and value its own capacity to be different."[35]

In the modern world, cultures are forced to compete for the attention of their followers, give an account of themselves and defend themselves against their opponents. Mill holds unreasonably naive

30

and optimistic expectations about the inevitably positive outcome of competition as leading to the disappearance of the "least morally worthy" cultures and the proliferation of better and richer ones. It is not even safe to claim that the most liberal cultures, which encourage cultural pluralism, are those best equipped to "win" in an open cultural contest. In fact, many individuals find the feelings of closeness, solidarity, and assurance offered by authoritarian cultures very attractive. Hence, support for the plurality of cultures is not synonymous with an attempt to eradicate all nonliberal cultural options. It simply means that individuals are the best judges of what cultural enviroment is most suited to their needs: If in their exercise of cultural choices individuals do not try to hinder others from exercising theirs, there are no grounds for preventing them from pursuing their life-plans as they see fit.

Mill assumed that absorbing a developed people into a less advanced one is an evil and a loss to humanity, whereas when an improved, cultured nation overpowers a small, "backward" one, we experience a net "gain in civilisation." For example, he thought it would be best for the Irish to unite with their nearest neighbours, who were not only wealthier but "one of the freest, as well as the most civilised and powerful nations of the earth."[36] Needless to say, most Irishmen disagreed with him. Raz offers a modern version of Mill's argument and suggests that, when a liberal culture encounters an illiberal one, whose members do not endorse "the condition of autonomy," it would be justified to take action "to assimilate the minority group, at the cost of letting its culture die or at least be considerably changed by absorption" since illiberal cultures are "inferior to the dominant liberal culture."[37] Raz does acknowledge that wrenching individuals out of their communities may destroy their ability to live the autonomous life he would like them to have, and recommends toleration, although he is motivated by prudential reasons rather than by respect for illiberal ways of life. Raz thus seems to give priority to the preservation and proliferation of the conditions of autonomy, over the preservation and proliferation of forms of life that individuals may autonomously decide to pursue. This is equivalent to saying, however, that a life lived from the inside is a worthy life only if it is a liberal one, and that personal autonomy is to be respected as long as the range of choices includes only liberal alternatives. Therefore, if we have chosen to lead an illiberal life, it is justified, although costs must be taken into account, to oppose our choice, either actively or passively. It then seems that what is being respected is not actual individual choices but the abstract ability to exercise choice and that the latter is more valuable than the former.

Yet, if we wish to respect individuals as the authors of their own lives, we must accept that some of their choices will seem to us less valuable than others. Although they may choose to lead illiberal lives, follow authoritarian traditions, join Opus Dei or Hare Krishna, or dedicate themselves to what one might think of as a meaningless project, their choices merit respect as otherwise, autonomy and pluralism become devoid of all content.

Three different arguments can thus be offered in favour of cultural pluralism, relying on the interests of three distinct groups:

1. The participants—members of the particular cultural group

2. The potential users—those who may choose to assimilate in a particular culture, or may learn from it, borrow its norms and values, imitate its rituals, and use it as a trigger for reflecting on their own

3. All others—nonmembers who do not view the culture as an option for assimilation, for whom the existence of any culture enriches their own experience of what it means to be human

Preserving the plurality of cultures is thus a valuable resource to all human beings. Individuals, says Walzer, are like "artists and writers who pick up elements of one another's style, or even borrow plots, not for the sake of imitation but in order to strengthen their own work. So we make ourselves better without being the same."[38]

The Contextual Individual

The views presented in this chapter may appear to be diametrically opposed to conventional nationalist wisdom. The "thick" national approach indeed rejects the notion that we can make cultural choices, and assumes that individuals are imprisoned within the culture they were born into. This leads not only to a reprehensible moral position, but also overlooks the fact that, in reality, individuals do assimilate, break cultural ties, and move from one national community to another.

Yet, the approach presented here does not imply that individuals have "a view from nowhere," that they can make choices as entities

Taylor

lacking all background, attachments, or commitments. Reflection always begins from a defined social position, but contextuality need not preclude choice.

The claim that, if given to choice, identity features cannot be constitutive, seems unreasonable. We readily accept that life-plans, religious beliefs, and social roles are objects of reflection and choice, yet constitutive of our identity. Cultural and national affiliations fall under the same category, of being both chosen and constitutive.

Our discussion so far suggests a concept of the person that embodies both the liberal virtue of self-authorship and the national virtue of embeddedness. It portrays an autonomous person who can reflect on, evaluate, and choose his conception of the good, his ends, and his cultural and national affiliations, but is capable of such choices because he is situated in a particular social and cultural environment that offers him evaluative criteria. Self-determination, autonomy, and faculties of critical reflection and choice are essential features of this concept of the person, but so are cultural affiliations, religious beliefs, and conceptions of the good, namely, the products of these choices. The discussion so far has thus led to the claim that individuals can behave in line with both the communal choice model and the moral choice model, thereby indirectly implying the plausibility of the strict model of choice, which assumes that individuals can reflect on both their national and moral identity, without requiring that they do so simultaneously or radically.

The idea of the person developed in this work, the "contextual individual," combines individuality and sociability as two equally genuine and important features. It allows for an interpretation of liberalism that is aware of the binding, constitutive character of cultural and social memberships, together with an interpretation of nationalism that conceives of individuals as free and autonomous participants in a communal framework, who conceive of national membership in Renan's terms, as a daily plebiscite. The concept of the contextual individual thus brings liberal and national theories one step closer.

Acknowledging that cultural affiliation, history, and language are constitutive for the contextual individual leaves a range of unresolved issues between liberals and nationalists, since this concept might be interpreted in two different ways. Whereas liberals would tend to see cultural and national rootedness as descriptive and stop short of deriving normative consequences, nationalists rely on them

to justify a broad range of moral commitments. The following chapters elaborate some of these tensions, beginning with a discussion of
the right to culture—namely, the right to preserve the national culture one chooses to adopt. This right lies at the core of both personal
and national self-determination, and is thus the cornerstone of
liberal nationalism.

NATIONAL CHOICES AND
THE RIGHT TO CULTURE

Sometimes a college student who has been talked out of his
stereotypes in a psychology course is amazed to discover, on
his first trip abroad, that the Germans really are different
from the Italians. —*Roger Brown*

This chapter goes a step farther in the attempt to delineate the parameters of liberal nationalism. Liberal nationalism attempts to capture what is essential to both schools of thought, drawing from liberalism a commitment to personal autonomy and individual rights,
and from nationalism an appreciation of the importance of membership in human communities in general, and in national communities
in particular. These are the two main concerns of the discussion on
national choices and the right to culture, which is the focus of this
chapter.

Why should the wishes of individuals to preserve their national
identity and adhere to their national culture be respected? There are
five different, although closely related ways of approaching this
question. All are meant to demonstrate that individuals view the
protection of the distinct national identity they have chosen as an
important aspect of their well-being, and as an interest that justifies
holding others under duty, substantiating the claim that individuals
have a right to preserve the culture of their choice.[1]

The first approach suggests that national membership is an important and constitutive element of personal identity. It could be
claimed that "there is no essence of 'being Greek' or 'being English'"—that is, of belonging to a particular nation. It is merely
accidental whether one is born in England, in France, or in the
United States, or whether one is born a red Indian, a black, or a Jew,"
but a person "is not accidentally human. Humanity is his essence or

35

nature."[2] Obviously, "being English" or "being Greek" is not an essential feature of our concept of the person—most individuals are neither English nor Greek and are nevertheless human. There is, however, something misleading in this presentation: Although X could be replaced by any number of variants—in our case, different national groups—this does not imply that one could be none of these, meaning that one could be totally dissociated from any cultural national reference and remain human. Membership in a national culture is part of the essence of being human. The fact that individuals can define themselves as "Greek," "American," or "Greek-American" does not mean that these memberships are of incidental importance to them.

The second approach emerges from the description of the contextual individual. This description portrays individuals as reflective and autonomous, but as pointed out in the previous chapter, these features are contingent on the presence of a context that allows them to become strong evaluators. Were autonomy an intrinsically desirable good, national and cultural memberships could be viewed as possessing instrumental value, as means for individuals to exercise their capacity for choice and self-reflection.

The third approach ties the instrumental value of culture to its voluntary acceptance. If culture is valued only on instrumental grounds, that is, in terms of its contribution to personal autonomy, then the claim that the choice of culture merits respect might seem irrelevant. One might suggest that we should agree on the culture or cultures most conducive to this aim, and that individuals should be discouraged or even prevented from adhering to their own culture if it seems less rich or less suitable to modern times, and be forced to adopt more suitable alternatives.

But this is a self-defeating proposition since the instrumental value of a culture is contingent on its being accepted. It is only when we choose to accept our cultural affiliations as well as the values suggested by them, that culture can indeed assume its instrumental value. If after a process of reflection we were to reject the culture we were born into, then this culture would lose its authoritative stand and its ability to provide us with an evaluative horizon that could serve to guide our choices.[3] It would be absurd to argue that individuals who decide to emigrate or to assimilate because they reject the cultural codes of their own national group should turn to the latter in search of an evaluative horizon. Similarly, it seems quite irrelevant to suggest that we should rely for this purpose on a set of values drawn from an unfamiliar culture that we neither know nor respect. The complex relations among acceptance, practice, and the instrumental use of culture go far beyond the scope of this book. Nevertheless, they have a direct bearing on our discussion because they imply that no argument for granting the right to culture can be detached from questions of acceptance and choice.

The fourth approach argues that unless we allow individuals to practice the national culture they willingly identify with we fall into a "paternalistic trap" that is best avoided. Respect is due to cultural preferences not by virtue of their intrinsic contents, but because they reflect autonomous choices. National cultures should therefore be protected if, and only if, their members express a reflective interest in adhering to them. Like religious and political loyalties, or the choice of a spouse, cultural affiliations should be respected because they express one's choices regarding the kind of individual one would like to be and the kind of life one would like to live. It is not thereby implied, however, that any culture individuals might be interested in should be protected. The right to culture is by no means ultimate, and other rights may override it in situations of conflict, an argument similarly used to justify restriction of other freedoms. For example, although freedom of speech is independent of the content of what is being said, if its exercise leads to the violation of the rights of others, the latter are given priority and freedom of speech is restricted.

The fifth approach is a prudential one, implying that classifying individuals as members of a national culture they do not choose to belong to or assuming that they ought to have an interest in their native culture even though they deny it, seems preposterous. It undermines their right to autonomy and self-determination, and leads to unwarranted oppression.

Just as our belief in freedom of religion is not oblivious to the fact that most of us are born within a particular religion, arguing for the view of national culture as a matter of choice merely suggests that, having discovered the cultural and national frameworks we were born into, we can reflect on them critically and exercise choices regarding our future commitments and affiliations. In other words, a national culture is not a prison and cultural ties are not shackles. Furthermore, not only should individuals have a right to choose the national group they wish to belong to, but they should also have the right to define the meanings attached to this membership, that is, they should be the ones to decide on the cultural practices they wish to adopt, and on the ways of expressing them. It is for this reason that specific cultural demands are entitled to favourable consider-

37

ation only when raised by members of a culture. For example, it is morally plausible to accept a demand for geographic distinctiveness when it is raised by members, while it is morally offensive to accept a demand by nonmembers that people belonging to a particular group ought to be isolated in a closed ghetto.

It is on these grounds that the choice of a national identity and its cultural implications are entitled to respect. The emphasis of this argument on the elective dimension of national membership, however, might place it on an equal footing with any other preference, thus lessening its value. Kymlicka illustrates this claim through the following example: Aboriginal peoples occupy vast areas that are necessary for the preservation of their special way of life, but other Canadians want to use these areas for different purposes. If the aboriginal way of life reflects individual choices rather than fate, then granting special rights to the aboriginal peoples "would be an unfair use of political power" as it would "insulate aboriginal choices from the market."[4] The right to culture, Kymlicka argues, is to be respected precisely because cultural membership is an innate and inevitable feature of one's identity rather than a product of choice.

Kymlicka's objection raises an interesting point, but could be contested on two counts: (1) It creates a tie between the right to culture and the innate nature of membership, thus unjustifiably depriving, for instance, converts. (2) His position fails to acknowledge that, although we have reasons to protect cultural choices, these should not be entirely isolated from "the market of preferences."

Sandel's discussion of religious freedom could be helpful in furthering this discussion. The struggle for freedom of conscience, he argues, was not a struggle for the right of people to choose their beliefs, but rather for their right to exercise their religious duties without suffering civil penalties or incapacities: "It is precisely because belief is not governed by the will that freedom of conscience is inalienable." Religious liberty therefore "adresses the problem of encumbered selves, claimed by duties they cannot renounce, even in the face of civil obligations that may conflict."[5] Sandel then cites two cases that he takes as showing that, when religious obligations are approached as merely a matter of choice, the state sees no reason to give them preference. Were religious rights perceived as "a right to exercise a duty" rather than as a right to make a choice, argues Sandel, the attitude of the courts would be different.

His first example is the Supreme Court's ruling against granting Sabbath observers the right not to work on the Sabbath, on the grounds that the same degree of respect is due to the preference of other workers for not working on weekends, even though the latter's decision was not made on religious grounds. The second comments on the Court's ruling upholding the decision of the United States Air Force not to allow Captain Simha Goldman, an Orthodox Jew, the right to wear a skull-cap while serving in a health clinic, on the grounds that "the essence of military service is the subordination of the desires and interests of the individual to the needs of the_ service."[6]

Sandel is right in claiming that these two decisions show a misunderstanding of the nature of religious obligations. He is wrong in suggesting that what is needed to correct the Court's mistaken attitude is to adopt the view that religious freedom implies the exercise of duties by encumbered selves unable to renounce the obligations religion imposes on them.

Captain Goldman could have converted or he could have decided to become a nonobservant Jew; Sabbath observers could choose not to keep the Sabbath or to leave Judaism altogether. There are many precedents to such decisions. Until their hypothetical conversion, Captain Goldman and the Sabbath observers were encumbered by Judaism, but after renouncing this membership, it would obviously be morally wrong for the Court to force Captain Goldman to wear a skull-cap because he was born Jewish, or to forbid Jews to work on the Sabbath even had they wanted to, on the assumption that Jews cannot but wish to observe Jewish law.

Let us look at the same problem from the opposite angle and assume that Captain Goldman has converted to Judaism only recently. Would his demand to wear a skull-cap have carried less weight then? If it cannot be proven that this ought to have made a difference, then the issue is not that Captain Goldman's Jewish feelings are so deeply embedded that he cannot but act in a particular way, but that he has chosen a certain course of action.

Neither Sandel nor Kymlicka would support a policy ensuring a right to culture to individuals only after looking at their family tree seven generations back. As claimed earlier, individuals should not be seen as encumbered by duties imposed on them by their history and their fate, but as free to adhere to cultures and religions of their choice. Indeed, after they have chosen, their memberships might impose on them certain duties, inherent in their understanding of a particular religion or culture. It should be recognised that, by making a religious choice, people have expressed a readiness to follow the practices and traditions constitutive of a particular religion. Hence, proof that a certain practice plays a constitutive role in the history of a certain religion should count as an argument in favour of allowing individuals to adhere to it.

This view makes the question regarding odd or idiosyncratic demands easier to handle. Some individuals could claim that their commitment to a certain particularistic worldview compels them to act in ways that most people would consider bizarre. If our commitment to religious or cultural practices is only a matter of choice and interpretation, why should such demands not be heeded? How can we distinguish between these claims and those staked by Captain Goldman or by the Sabbath observers?

The first question is whether it would be justified to view these demands as constitutive of these individuals' identity. This is a test of plausibility that most personal instances of eccentricity would fail to pass. (Even assuming that eccentricity itself is constitutive of a person's identity, not every specific eccentric act need be seen as such.) Were we persuaded that these behaviour patterns are indeed constitutive of these individuals' identity, however, we would now have to consider to what extent these preferences can be accommodated. It seems that the best guide for what would constitute an appropriate measure of accommodation is common sense.

Note that the intuition that eccentric preferences need not, as a rule, be accommodated, is not grounded on the fact that they were chosen but rather on their extravagant and easily noticeable nature. Captain Goldman made a modest request, and had his demand to wear a skull-cap been accepted, his appearance would differ only slightly from that of other officers. But let us assume that Captain Goldman had demanded permission to serve in the American army without wearing a uniform and donning the standard black garb of his Hasidic group. Would not Sandel have expressed different feelings about the appropriate course of action? We may infer from this example that our readiness to accommodate personal preferences is influenced by the measure of their eccentricity rather than by the question of whether they are more or less authentic. A reasonable compromise should be sought in each case between the right of the individual to act "his own way" and factors such as the needs of the institution concerned, the degree of allowed divergence, the extent to which a precedent, perhaps a damaging one, is created for others, and the like. Claims formulated in terms of "this is our tradition" can only tilt the balance in certain cases.

The second reason Kymlicka's position is to be contested is that it lends itself to an interpretation whereby the right to culture is granted an overly predominant role. Suppose the aboriginal people do not live in Canada but in a densely populated area, and they still demand vast areas as essential for the preservation of their culture. Conceding to this demand would imply depriving others of a chance to build their own homes. Presumably it would be justified, under these circumstances, to take away part of their lands and give it to others, even if we thereby force changes in the aboriginal way of life. In other words, the claim that "this is how we do things in our community" is a reason for special consideration, but not a conclusive justification.

Cultural choices, like religious ones, belong in the category of constitutive choices, which due to their importance to individuals, should be granted special weight. Religious allegiances take priority over a choice of restaurant, and political ideologies are more important than a preference for a specific make of car. We are therefore likely to agree to give people a day off to vote, but not to visit a car exhibition. Similarly, if Moslems or Jews work for our company, we shall feel obliged to ensure that pork is not the only option at the company's restaurant, but we shall not feel obliged to satisfy the needs of a worker who loves Japanese food. Aboriginal people should have priority when competing for land with others wishing to build a golf club, but their case would be much weaker if they were competing with members of a persecuted religious group who have no other place to build a church.

But cultural preferences might be at a loss even when competing with other, ostensibly nonconstitutive preferences, as the following example illustrates. Jews are forbidden to eat pork and are required to follow certain procedures in the slaughter of animals. Let us assume that a small Jewish community lives in a particular area where it is only profitable to raise pigs, and all other meat imported into the area is not ritually fit. Jews are forced to import their own meat, but this becomes prohibitively expensive and they are therefore unable to eat meat at all. Does respect for their religious rituals imply that others must subsidise the import of kosher meat in order to allow Jews the same level of nutrition enjoyed by the rest of the population? While the answer will have to take into account the costs of such a subsidy and the burden it places on other members of the community, the mere readiness to consider these demands already demonstrates that we recognise the importance of cultural and religious rights.

A special reason for making special concessions meant to help members of a minority group preserve their national culture is worth noting. Membership in a cultural community is a matter of personal choice, but this does not imply that members have chosen to be a minority. This status is imposed on them by the choices of nonmembers, and could be seen as supplying a reason to support their chances of leading a meaningful and worthwhile life without having to renounce their cultural commitments. This claim implies that the process whereby individuals find themselves belonging to a minority should be a factor in deciding the extent of support they are entitled to. For instance, individuals at times emigrate, although aware that they will thereby lose their majority status and will become members of a minority. Their cultural demands are weakened under these circumstances, as it could well be argued that they have deliberately placed themselves in this position and should therefore bear the consequences. The parents' motivations and decisions are not relevant, however, when considering demands raised by second- or third-generation children of immigrants, who were born into a given situation. The final chapter elaborates this issue more fully, and argues that the reasons motivating individuals to emigrate should also be taken into account.

It should be noted in this context that the demands of indigenous peoples or of groups that were forced to migrate—such as the blacks taken to America against their will, or the Russians forcefully evacuated to republics in the periphery of the former Soviet Union—carry the strongest weight, since these individuals were practically forced to become minorities.

Is the Right to Culture a Communal Right?

Our argument so far shows that, in point of fact, we are discussing two different rights: the right of individuals to choose their national identity and their right to adhere to the national culture of their choice. While it is quite clear that the first is an individual right, can the right to follow a culture also be considered an individual right? The right to culture is generally regarded as a communal right, on the following grounds:

1. Individuals demand this right only by virtue of their membership in a collective, which in this case is the national community.

2. Individuals can realise this right only within a community of people sharing certain characteristics.

3. The interests of one individual in satisfying this right cannot justify burdening others with the costs of its satisfaction.

4. If the justification of a right is contingent on the good it promotes, then the right to practice a culture cannot be considered an individual right since it protects the pursuit of a collective good and can accordingly be judged only in reference to its collective benefit.

Let us examine these claims one by one.

The first claim is that the right to culture should be seen as a collective right on the grounds that the interest of individuals in preserving their cultural identity derives from their membership in a collective. Although this statement is obviously true, it is equally valid regarding civil rights or religious rights, in which we have an interest only by virtue of our membership in a particular political or religious community. But the fact that we acquire an interest due to our membership in a particular group does not alter its essential nature as an individual interest. Accordingly, the right protecting it should be approached as an individual right.

The second claim argues that the right to follow a national culture is a collective right since it can only be implemented by a collective. This argument can be contested in two ways. The first hinges on what is considered to be the implementation of this right, while the second refers to the fact that a right should be defined by its justification rather than by the ways in which it could be fully realised. These two points require further clarification.

What is entailed by the implementation of the right to follow a national culture? It is quite clear that one can declare oneself Israeli, Palestinian, Basque, or French even when alone, and that some features of national culture can be retained even in complete solitude, or within the boundaries of one's home (reading to oneself in one's own language, reciting poems, or practicing some traditional ceremonies).

Isolated individuals are undoubtedly more restricted in their ability to enjoy the full benefits of a culture, since a wide range of national cultural expressions requires the presence of a community. It is probably the case that the ability to express one's national identity grows in line with the size of the group, although there is a critical mass beyond which size does not necessarily influence the ability of members to lead a full national life.

But does this imply that individuals are not to be allowed to follow their national culture by themselves, to the best of their abilities? A musician can play solo, in a trio, in a quartet, in a chamber group, or in a philharmonic orchestra. Although the richness of the musical experience might vary with the size of the group, no one will claim that musicians, who for some reason cannot play in a philharmonic orchestra, would be better off not playing at all. Similarly, it makes no sense to suggest to those who cannot express their nationality and culture in optimal ways, that they should refrain from expressing them in more modest and restrained ones.

The second way of contesting this objection is to draw a distinction between the individual interest protected by the right to practice a national culture and the fact that these practices have a strong collective dimension. This distinction is by no means unique to the right to culture. Many individual rights have communal aspects. This implies that the practice of these aspects is contingent on the presence of a sufficient number of interested individuals, which justifies imposing a duty to allow, or even to support, their implementation. For example, individuals have religious rights, but the state's decision to allocate public space and public resources to establish houses of prayer or communal and educational institutions is contingent on there being sufficient numbers of interested citizens. It is quite obvious that the interests of a single individual cannot justify the establishment of a church, a Sunday school, or a community centre, and that an isolated individual could not put such institutions to use.

Similarly, individuals have a right of association but the practice of this right requires the presence of a group. If the association is to enjoy government assistance, society might even set a threshold and decide that only groups numbering more than one hundred individuals are to have free access to certain facilities necessary to the functioning of voluntary associations—tax-free status, meetings in the town hall, and the like. Such a decision could not be seen as violating the freedom of association of members in smaller groups, unless it could be proven that the threshold was set so as to exclude a particular group. As long as the threshold is determined in light of practical considerations—for instance, the need to limit the use of the town hall, or the expense entailed in sponsoring the activities of voluntary associations—it cannot be claimed that the members of smaller groups have been wronged simply because others, belonging to larger ones, are more successful in satisfying their preferences.[7]

Does this imply that the obligation to support the building of a church, the establishment of a Sunday school, or the granting of a tax exemption derives from a communal right? The nature of a right derives from its justification, not from the ways in which some of its aspects are best implemented. Since the justification of all these

rights, be they religious or political, is grounded in the interest that
individuals have in pursuing them, they should be considered individual rights. There is no reason why the right to follow a culture
should be an exception to this rule.

The third claim argues that the right to follow a national culture
should be seen as a collective right because its realisation might impose far-reaching demands on others. In and of itself, a person's interest cannot justify imposing such extensive obligations on so many
individuals. This conclusion obviously hinges on the assumption
that realising the right to culture will necessarily impose heavy burdens on others. The practice of a national culture, however, can be
realised at different points along a continuum, from the right of individuals to do whatever they can on their own, all the way to the
establishment of national autonomy. It would then be enough to
claim that the balance between costs and benefits should determine
when, and to what extent, one should seek to realise this right, but
this holds true for every right. Hence, there are no grounds for excluding in advance the possibility that some aspects of the right to
follow a culture may entail minor burdens, and it will therefore be
justified to grant it even to isolated individuals.

A distinction must be drawn between matters of principle and
matters of policy. As a matter of principle, the right to practice a
culture, like all other rights intended to protect the interests of individuals, is an individual right. As a matter of policy, it might be
justified to obligate others to carry the burdens that follow from the
realisation of this right only if there is a minimal number of individuals who will benefit from it. Hence, the size of the group deriving
benefits from a particular policy may influence the prospects of its
implementation: the larger the number of individuals who will
benefit from the implementation of a right, the stronger the justification to burden others with the costs entailed by this implementation.

The final claim relates to the fact that culture is a collective good:
If the justification of a right is contingent on the good it promotes,
then rights concerned with protecting the pursuit of collective goods
cannot be considered individual rights, and this for two reasons.
First, the value of collective goods can only be appreciated in reference to their collective benefit, namely, their benefit to the group as
a whole. Second, collective goods are nonexclusive, and even when
granted to isolated individuals, other members of the collective can
enjoy them. Communal goods, argues Waldron, cannot consequently be regarded as the subject of individual rights:

45

[A] claim of right does two things: it specifies a good, and it specifies a person—a beneficiary, a right-bearer—for whom, or for whose sake, the good is to be brought about. What is distinctive about a right is that the benefit to the individual is seen as the ground of the duty, as a "sufficient reason" for it, in Raz's phrase.[8]

Waldron defines communal goods as goods jointly produced and nonexcludable. Moreover, no account of their worth to anyone can be given except by concentrating on what they are worth to all. The duty to realise such goods, he argues, must be grounded in an adequate characterisation of their desirability. Since no adequate account of this desirability can be pinned on either X or Y or Z, there can be no point in saying it ought to be pursued as X's or Y's or Z's right.[9]

It is true that the desirability of communal goods cannot be fully captured by calculating their worth to particular individuals. The benefit of living within a prosperous culture, experiencing solidarity, sharing a language, or suffering from the destruction of such communal goods might be larger than the cumulative benefit or damage to specific individuals. But the fact that the value of a communal good exceeds the value it has for the individuals who enjoy it only suggests that such a reductive process will not capture the full worth of this good, yet it does not prove that we cannot estimate its value to individual members. It might then be the case that we desire to preserve a communal good—a national culture in our case—because of its comprehensive general value, but this would be different from granting individuals the right to preserve *their* national identity and participate in the social, cultural, and political life of *their* group. The latter must be based on the interests individual members have in following their culture, while the former might take into account the interest of nonmembers as well.

Note that if we base a claim for the right to preserve a particular culture on the interests of nonmembers we might find ourselves in the paradoxical situation of granting the right to culture to individuals who, in fact, wish to waive it. We may think, for instance, that Indian culture should be preserved because of its artistic and poetic achievements, but this cannot justify granting the right to culture to Indians if they do not care for it. The opposite is also true: Members of groups whose culture is not appreciated by others, or is even seen by them as decadent, have the same right to culture as members of groups held in high esteem.

If we accept that granting an individual the right to preserve and express a national culture in which he has no interest is not only absurd but could even lead to severe oppression, we must conclude that, in determining when a person should be granted a right, external preferences should not count.[10] The right to culture ought to be justified only in reference to its value to members, even if this value fails to capture the full worth of preserving a culture.

But what is the practical difference of granting a nonexclusive communal good to individuals rather than to a group? The difference lies in the status of individuals vis-à-vis the group, as according a right to a collective embodies a possible threat to individuals. The fact that a right is granted to a collective implies that it is incumbent on the group to decide whether to claim this right and how to implement it. This puts pressure on the group to define a unanimous, or seemingly unanimous, set of demands. Under these conditions, those wishing to withdraw from membership are pressed not to do so, and those who would like to realise this right in ways unacceptable to the majority are denied this possibility. The final outcome of granting rights to groups may therefore be that certain rights, to which all are entitled, are enjoyed only by some members of the group. For instance, Israeli law grants religious rights to the various religious communities in the country. This right is given to the community as a collective rather than to individuals, with the result that one group, Jewish Orthodoxy, dominates both the interpretation and the practice of this right while all other Jewish religious movements are excluded.

There is, however, another reason why the right to culture should be seen as an individual right, and it concerns the difficulty of defining the group. National groups, as demonstrated in Chapter 3, are informal, quite amorphous, constantly changing, imagined communities. Unlike commercial companies or other formal organizations, national groups lack clear criteria of membership, and the idea of granting them rights is fraught with theoretical and moral difficulties.

An interesting phenomenon deserves mention in this context. Policies reflecting an attempt to treat all individuals with equal respect could at times be mistakenly interpreted as directed toward groups. For example, a policy of affirmative action, or a policy that grants every group, irrespective of size, the same number of representatives in a governing body, could be interpreted as an attempt to ensure equal treatment to groups. The justifications of these policies, however, will reveal that they were devised in order to ensure equal

47

opportunities to the individual members of these groups. For example, granting equal voting powers to representatives of small and large groups, as is the case in the General Assembly of the United Nations or in the American Senate, is intended to safeguard the interests of *individual members* of these states and to protect them from being automatically outvoted. These policies are also meant to allow members of small groups the possibility of enjoying the benefits that derive from the public recognition of a group's uniqueness, and from the acknowledgment of its right to be an autonomous source of interests and preferences.

Similarly affirmative action can be described as a way of redressing wrongs inflicted on individuals whose self-image has suffered because they were not judged on their own merits, but rather in terms of their membership in humiliated and persecuted groups. This presupposes that the image of a group is a collective good to be either enjoyed or borne by all its individual members. It is individuals who profit or suffer from the group's image, and it is their personal suffering and the prospects of improving their individual well-being that motivate policies of affirmative action. Hence, policies granting representation to groups, or arguing that various groups should be proportionally represented in all public positions, are not motivated by concern for the welfare of the group, but by concern for its individual members.

The Problem of Authenticity

The tendency to view the right to culture as a collective right is spurred by an undesirable tendency to refrain from applying criteria of justice to intracommunal affairs. This tendency relies on two fallacies. First, it assumes that, in primordial communities, there is no need for rights and principles because matters are settled on grounds of affection and mutual interest. This approach comes through clearly in Sandel's description of ideal communities or in Rawls' decision to grant rights to heads of families rather than to their individual members, of which feminists have been highly critical. The second fallacy is that the right to culture is interpreted as the right to preserve the culture in its "authentic" form. This interpretation obviously serves the interests of those holding power within the community, but does it represent fairly the interests of all members? Interpreting the right to culture as the right of a community to preserve its authentic culture leads Kymlicka to endorse communal rights even at the expense of violating certain individual rights. For instance, Kymlicka accepts that Canadian Indian women should be denied the right to continue living on the reservation when they marry non-Indian men, although Indian men who marry non-Indian wives are allowed to remain in the community.[11] This is a clear example of how males, who presently rule the community, link the right to culture with the preservation of their dominant status, by depriving women who have chosen to marry outsiders of their right to make a cultural choice. Had the right to culture been granted to individuals rather than to the community, Indian women could have demanded that the community respect their right to marry non-Indians while allowing them to retain membership in the community. They could have required changes in the traditional patterns of decision-making, perhaps through an arrangement whereby the Indian spouse in a mixed marriage, whether male or female, would be the one to represent the family within tribal institutions, or else threaten to exercise their right to culture by establishing an alternative Indian community.

One might question the very notion of an "alternative community." But the right to culture is not only meant to grant individuals the right to follow their culture as given, but also to re-create it. The ultimate result of a series of moral and communal choices is a proliferation of ways of life, interpretations of culture, and the emergence of new national groups. In the process of choosing, individuals may draw from different national traditions and give rise to new, as yet undefined cultural versions. There will be cases in which it may be hard to indicate whether individuals have assimilated into another culture or changed their own. Many third world countries, which gained access to Western culture through their contact with imperialist powers, provide a good illustration of a variety of possible outcomes. In many cases, a new cluster of features emerged, a melange distorting both the native cultures and the colonial patterns and creating a new cultural reality. Describing the Kenyan elite, an English officer remarked: "The settlers played golf and polo, went to horse-races or on royal hunts in red coats and riding breeches. . . . The Black pupils now do the same, only with greater zeal: golf and horses have become 'national' institutions."[12] This might appear as a merely superficial adoption of cultural patterns, but for many Africans "cricket was not just a game. Rather, it was a uniquely British institution that embodied so many of the values and ideals which . . . they aspired to."[13]

The African example illustrates an important aspect of choice. Choice does not necessarily mean selecting between two well-structured alternatives, but can also involve creating a series of variations combining the old and the new, which may result in a proliferation of cultural alternatives.

Nationalists reject the proliferation of cultural options for two reasons. First, it challenges the aspect of continuity discussed above, opens the way for the disintegration of national identities based on cultural similarities, and brings about a proliferation of "private" cultures. Second, it is feared that new, modified traditions might be so thin as to lack all meaning.

The first concern would appear to be justified, at least to some extent. Individuals aware of the presence of options may indeed find it easier to leave their group of origin, or attempt to challenge the existing interpretation of their culture and aspire to change it. Such processes could challenge the integrity of existing frameworks and lead to the creation of new ones.

As for the fear that national cultures and consequently membership in national communities might become meaningless because of the "thinness" of newly emerged cultural options, this concern seems slightly exaggerated. Steinberg claims that the identity of American ethnic groups is threatened because the core elements of the traditional culture have been modified, diluted, compromised, and finally relinquished. For members of these groups, those elements of the traditional culture that have been preserved are "removed from the social and cultural matrix in which they once belonged."[14] Ethnic communities thus face a crisis of authenticity. Their cultural patterns, once rooted in the exigencies of life, appear to be increasingly irrelevant or even dysfunctional; ethnicity becomes symbolic, and thus culturally thin.

There is a dangerous dimension in claims about authenticity. These claims are commonly used to imply that there is one genuine interpretation of a national culture, whereas all the others are factitious and invalid. Agents of revision are therefore likely to be called disloyal and their products inauthentic. "And though authenticity is, one would think, always relative to a particular national history (and dubious even in its relativity, given the actual variousness and the internal contradictions of all such histories), nationalist intellectuals often reach for a stronger argument: that their culture, morality, and politics is authentic *tout court*—real, historical, orthodox, organic, faithful, uncorrupted, pure, and enduring—and so superior to all the synthetic, unnatural, and hybrid creations of other peoples."[15]

The term "authentic" could thus serve as an instrument of conservatism and social oppression. To claim that individuals should be authentic is to suggest that they should accept the identity or the roles ascribed to them by some "Council of Elders" and that, were they to deviate from these roles, they would be guilty of developing a false conscience or hiding their "true" selves.

In nineteenth-century England, for example, it was widely agreed that "a person who accepts his class situation, whatever it may be, as a given and necessary condition of his life, will be sincere beyond question. He will be sincere and authentic, sincere because authentic."[16] The idea that individuals were meant to be what they were born to be contradicts the view of individuals as free, choosing agents, as authors of their own lives. For those who embrace the discourse of authenticity, a converted Jew, a liberated woman, or a commoner marrying gentry are always guilty of fraud, since they will constantly be hiding what they were meant to be. There is, however, an alternative understanding of authenticity: The authentic person is someone who creates himself.[17] This position is expressed in its most extreme form by existentialists, who believe in the ability of every person to choose for himself his attitudes, purposes, values, and ways of life. According to this view, "the only 'authentic' and genuine way of life is that freely chosen by each individual for himself."

The debate about the nature of authenticity is closely related to the debate about the "thinness" or "thickness" of modern nations. The idea that a nation that has undergone a slow and organic process of development is more authentic than one that has developed in a less stable and continuous way, or that a society that exhibits a more congruous set of values and beliefs is more authentic than one that is new, pluralistic, and therefore heterogeneous, should then be viewed with some suspicion.

The assumption that individuals can exercise choice regarding both their communal affiliations and their moral identity entails respect for dynamic and pluralistic views of culture. It views with favour the fact that, at any given point in time, different cultural interpretations compete for recognition within each nation. Membership in the cultural community would then be expressed by participating in this debate, rather than by following one specific interpretation.

Interpretations of culture may spring from ancient sources, be recently invented, or bring together the old and the new. Modern cultures need not necessarily be the linear continuation of long historical traditions beginning in the rural practices of small, closed communities entrenched in an ethos of the soil. They can be urban, open, and democratic, even populistic. They can mirror such distinct spheres as rock music, soccer games, TV advertisements, talk shows, and newspaper columns. Such cultures are valued not because they revive old traditions or preserve a ruling culture, but because they allow individuals to participate in a cultural process they regard as their own.

If the only alternatives were closure and cultural coherence or openness and the destruction of culture, then all modern national cultures would be seriously threatened. Modern cultures are open to influence and change. They may not be preserved in their old structural form, and may include mutually inconsistent norms, values, and social habits, as well as largely symbolic acts, but they nevertheless play a significant role in their members' lives.

The revival of ethnic languages, the renewal of national identities, the search for roots, all suggest that, in the modern world, individuals attach great importance to the expression of their national affiliations. This is true irrespective of whether the national culture is self-professedly new, grounds a claim to authenticity on its ancient roots, or claims to be old wine in new vessels. Israelis do not care less than the members of long-established European nations about their national culture because it is newly invented, and are in fact more likely to be aware of it and more involved in its re-creation. Similarly, Palestinians, presently involved in the process of developing an independent Palestinian culture, show deep allegiance to the symbols of their newly emerging national identity.

It could be claimed that our ability to choose among national cultures is parasitic on previous generations, and on the closure and the thickness of past forms of life. Will such options be open to future generations? Will the newly emerging modern cultures provide future generations with a sufficient range of alternatives to choose from, or will we leave a wasteland behind us?

Such fears reflect the assumption that cultures are in the process of moving from the age of authenticity to the symbolic (used as synonymous with superficial) age. This assumption attempts to use "original" culture as a yardstick in light of which new variations are evaluated. But there is no Archimedean point from which we can evaluate the authenticity of cultures. Why are the Jewish practices of a New York Reform community less authentic than those of an eighteenth-century Orthodox community in Eastern Europe? Why is American-Italian culture less authentic than Italian culture in Milan? Is it because it is heavily influenced by American culture? But was not Italian culture itself influenced by neighbouring cultures? The view that in the past there were genuine and coherent cultures, while now we have thin and superficial ones seems questionable. It probably reflects our stronger awareness of change and innovation in modern cultures. Past cultures thus seem to us more comprehensive and rigid, less threatened by change and external influences, and therefore more valuable. But why identify the value of a culture with closure and rigidity? A common culture in our days, says Raymond Williams, cannot be "the simple all-in-all society of the old dream. It will be a very complex organization, requiring continual adjustment and redrawing."[18] The idea of a common culture brings together "at once the idea of natural growth and that of its tending. The former alone is a type of romantic individualism; the latter alone a type of authoritarian training. Yet each, within a whole view, marks a necessary emphasis."[19] Williams' words summarise well the importance of openness, creativity, and diversity within cultures.

The Individual Practice of the Right to Culture

What are the implications of the claim that the right to practice a culture is an individual right? What rights are due to a culturally isolated individual? This question is meaningful only if we admit that culture, although by definition a communal creation, has dimensions that can also be expressed individually.

Ms. X lives in Yland, a society that defines itself as liberal and fair. She is the only person practicing X culture in Yland. It is obvious that Ms. X's right to identify herself with the X community and to preserve its culture in her private domain should be recognised— her right to sing in her own language in the shower, to purchase and read books on her own culture, to wear special clothes, and so forth. This interpretation of the right to culture, however, is covered by the right to privacy.

Problems arise when individuals wish to carry their culture into the public sphere: when Jews wish to wear skull-caps, Algerian schoolgirls in France to don veils, Palestinians to tie kaffias around their shoulders, Scots to wear kilts, Sikhs turbans, and Indian women saris when other clothes are *de rigueur* for everyone else. As the case of Captain Goldman showed, even these minimal expressions of cultural distinctiveness could evoke conflict. Should a Sikh be allowed to wear a turban while working at a construction site where everybody is forced to wear a helmet? Should Moslems be free to leave work an hour earlier during the month of Ramadan so that they can get home in time for the evening meal? Should Hispanics be permitted to present their case in an American court in

Spanish? Should a Palestinian living in Israel be allowed to write matriculation exams in Arabic? Those who deny individuals the right to the public practice of their national culture often hide behind the claim that public life should be culturally neutral. But culture cannot be restricted to the private sphere, and only those living in a society expressive of their own culture could be oblivious to this fact. The separation of state and religion in French schools reflects their civic national culture. Compelling Jewish or Moslem children from religious homes to come to school bareheaded or without a veil is not merely to demand that they confine the practice of their national culture to the private sphere, but requires them to betray fundamental aspects of their culture. In these cases, refusing individuals the right to express their culture in the public sphere in compliance with the ruling culture compels them to forgo their identity. Note, however, that Jewish boys have a right to wear skull-caps and Algerian girls to don veils only if they have chosen to do so. Children may quite clearly be placed under pressure to conform with their parents' wishes, but it is of educational value to stress the relation between their choice and their right, teaching them not only to respect their culture but also their own individuality.

When no culture enjoys state support, the right to follow a culture merely amounts to the right to follow one's culture to the best of one's ability without state interference. If the state supports specific cultures, however, there are further implications to be considered. Suppose that Ms. X can prove that, in Y society, a certain amount of funds is spent in support of Y culture. She then claims that, as a taxpayer, she is entitled to receive her fair share of cultural funding and use it to practice those aspects of her culture she can practice on her own, or within a small circle of followers. This is a justified demand, and, as a matter of principle, Ms. X is entitled to her fair share of cultural expenditure. This approach calls for distributing an equal number of cultural vouchers to each citizen, and allowing individuals to consume culture according to their own preferences. (Note that individuals might decide to donate their vouchers to support the practice of a culture not their own.)

This does not imply that isolated individuals will have enough vouchers to materialise their cultural preferences, but it does suggest that state investment in cultural services should be based on a per capita calculation. In other words, if the state decides to distribute cultural goods, it should distribute them equally among all its members. State-sponsored language teaching, book publishing, social and historical research, the formulation of national curricula—

all should be equally assured to all citizens. The right to culture thus justifies the introduction of a relevant yardstick by which state spending in the cultural domain might be measured.

Satisfying these demands may require the creation of a pluralistic system providing differential services. The system of "separate but equal services," despite its notorious reputation, may thereby attain rehabilitation, demonstrating once more that it is crucially important to inquire who desires separate frameworks and why.

Even if Ms. X were to obtain a fair share of cultural vouchers, however, this would not solve her problems. Since Ms. X is culturally isolated, she may not be able to give expression to any of her culture's collective aspects, and her ability to practice her culture could thus be restricted to those activities she is able to perform on her own. Hence, at some point, Ms. X may decide to move to Xland, or to a community where there are more Xs, or to accept compromises in the expression of her culture, and there will be nothing unjust about that.

Let us now assume that several families that practice X culture move to Yland at some point. Adherents of X culture are now able to improve, although still modestly, the public practice of their culture. They soon realise, however, that since they are a relatively small group, their per capita expenses in organizing a festival, for instance, are higher than those of the rest of the population: Producing 10,000 flags, or bags, or hats, will make the production cost per item cheaper than producing only fifty. Therefore, members of the X community get the same number of cultural vouchers per capita, but can do much less with them than members of the Y community. If we wish to ensure that all cultural choices enjoy an equal chance, we may wish to supplement the funds granted to members of the X community. This may allow them to follow their culture in a more satisfying manner, but it will obviously not compensate them fully for the fact that they are a minority.

In the realisation of their right to culture, members of minority communities are affected by both an "internal" and an "external" restriction. Certain rituals or practices require a minimal number of participants, and this creates an internal restriction. Yet, when a cultural practice cannot be followed due to a lack of participants, it cannot be claimed that the right to culture of a particular individual interested in practicing it has been violated, unless it can be proven that deliberate obstacles were placed in the way of publicising an event, or in the attempts to convince individuals to participate, or that individuals were intimidated or prevented from participating.

opportunities
v.
outcomes.

In order to receive state support on a par with other citizens, members of minority groups must prove that there, in fact, is a sufficient number of individuals to make the practice feasible. For example, Jewish tradition requires a minimum of ten adult males in order to conduct public prayers; in a community where there are only five adult Jewish males, there is no basis for demanding that space be allocated to build a synagogue, even when other religious groups do receive state help to set up houses of prayer. (The definition of "a sufficient number" may differ among cultures, and among different practices within the same culture.)

The external restriction does not depend on the nature of a specific cultural practice and derives from the fact that, due to their size, minority groups may have to incur higher cultural costs to attain ends similar to those achieved by the majority. In most cases, irrespective of the state's fairness and generosity, unless sizable groups of individuals are interested in following a particular culture, vouchers given to isolated individuals will not suffice to ensure the provision of cultural services. Hence, even if social resources are fairly distributed, minority groups will be more limited in their ability to practice their national culture. Therefore, due to no fault of society, members of national minorities may feel culturally deprived and continue to wish that they lived in a community in which they constitute the majority.

These conclusions serve as the starting point of the next chapter, where I discuss a particular development of the right to follow the national culture, namely, the right to national self-determination.

T H R E E

THE RIGHT TO
NATIONAL SELF-DETERMINATION

A stable feature of human nature, over and above a normal
physical constitution, is the need to possess a distinct history,
which is one's own and not that of all mankind, and also to
cultivate that which is particular and that is believed to be
the best of this time and of that place, alongside and within
the universal and moral claims that are common to all people
as such. —*Stuart Hampshire*

Although the right to national self-determination has often been at
the heart of modern political discourse, theoretical analyses of this
right are rather rare. Mainly the work of international lawyers, these
analyses are heavily influenced by legal and political precedent. Political philosophers have also tended to infer the contents of this
right from past and present political arrangements, and have thus
suggested that the core of national self-determination is the right to
determine whether "a certain territory shall become, or remain, a
separate state."[1] The thrust of this right, in the interpretation that has
become prevalent in the postcolonial era, is that "a people—if it so
wills—is entitled to independence from foreign domination, i.e., it
may establish a sovereign state in the territory in which it lives and
where it constitutes a majority."[2] The right to national self-determination, however, stakes a cultural rather than a political claim,
namely, it is the right to preserve the existence of a nation as a distinct cultural entity. This right differs from the right of individuals to
govern their lives and to participate in a free and democratic political process. The present discussion of the right to national self-determination should therefore be seen as continuing and expanding the
argument developed earlier. This chapter takes the argument one
step forward and advances a claim that is central to the theory of
liberal nationalism, namely, that national claims are not synonymous with demands for political sovereignty.

There are two main advantages to a cultural interpretation of the right to national self-determination. First, it places this right in the general context of rights granted to different cultural groups, such as ethnic minorities and indigenous peoples. Second, it seems better suited to the present world, which is experiencing a tension between the clear advantages of transnational economic, strategic, and ecological cooperation on the one hand, and the increasing concern with the preservation of national and cultural uniqueness, leading to demands for partition and the establishment of autonomous national entities, on the other.

The second issue is more extensively discussed in the final chapter, but it is important to indicate at this point that this book suggests a significant modification in the traditional argument for national self-determination. Given the present state of affairs, it shall argue that it is the cultural rather than the political version of nationalism that best accords with a liberal viewpoint.

The view that the right to national self-determination is first and foremost a cultural claim is heavily dependent on the perception of nations as particular types of cultural communities. The first step will therefore be to substantiate this perception.

Nations, States, and Cultural Communities

The concept of "nation" is rather elusive, and it may therefore be advisable to begin by establishing what a nation is not. A nation is *not* a state. It may seem obvious that a state and a nation are not one and the same, but the fact is that these terms are often used interchangeably. A report on nationalism written by a study group at the Royal Institute of International Affairs defines "nation" as "used synonymously with 'state' or 'country' to mean a society united under one government." This sense of the term does not merely reflect a prevalent speech usage, but is found in such official expressions as "the laws of nations" or "League of Nations."[3]

This identification between state and nation is endorsed by Weil, who claims that "there is no other way of defining the word nation than as a territorial aggregate whose various parts recognise the authority of the same State."[4] Complementary claims are made by Deutsch, who defines a nation as "a people who have hold of a state,"[5] as well as by Hertz, who asserts that the identification of a nation with a people constituted as a state is very widespread and that, accordingly, "every state forms a nation and every citizen is a member of the nation."[6] The term "national" is usually employed for designating "anything run or controlled by the state, such as the national debt or national health insurance."[7]

These definitions might lead to the conclusion that "state" and "nation" are identical concepts, or at least two aspects of the same concept—one relating to the institutional sphere, the other to the individuals who participate in the formation and the activities of these institutions. It could thus be expected that, reciprocally, the definition of "state" would include parameters found in the definition of nation. Yet this is not the case: The concept "nation," if at all mentioned when defining a state, appears only in the combination "nation-state" as one of its various possible forms. The *Encyclopedia Britannica* defines "state" as the political organisation of society. There are two accepted meanings of the word "state,"—one more general, referring to a body of people that has organised politically, and the other more specific, implying the institutions of government. The state is distinguished from other associations by its goals, by the methods it employs in accomplishing these goals, by the marking of territorial limits, and by its sovereignty. Sovereignty distinguishes the state from other kinds of human associations: It entails the monopoly of power as well as the creation and control of law.

According to Dyson, the main characteristics of the state are the specific quality of its authority (its sovereignty), its extraordinary and growing resources of physical power, and its well-defined territory.[8] None of these features is considered an essential characteristic of the concept "nation."[9]

In his concluding remarks on the development of the concept "state" in *The Dictionary of the History of Ideas*, D'Entreves predicts that the nation-state will be replaced by "a new supra-national state." He follows this hypothesis with an interesting question:

But will this [the disappearance of the nation-state] mean the disappearance of the state, its 'withering away'—to use the familiar Marxist phrase? So long as there will be an organization capable of controlling force, regulating power and securing allegiances, one thing seems certain . . . that organization will still be a state.[10]

For D'Entreves, then, the link between states and nations is a historical coincidence, but this should not blur the conceptual distinction between them. As Seton-Watson rightly emphasises, a state is "a legal and political organization with the power to require obedience and loyalty from its citizens," while the nation is "a community of people, whose members are bound together by a sense of solidarity, a common culture, a national consciousness."[11]

What is the origin of this conceptual confusion between nation and state? It could be claimed that it is part of a deliberate attempt to obscure the difference between the claim that every nation *ought* to have a state—or rather, that every state *ought* to derive its legitimacy from a nation—and the claim that a nation *is* a state. The attempt to present the nationalist slogan "one people, one country, one language" as descriptive rather than normative, illustrates this tendency to suggest a complete identification between state and nation.[12] It seems, however, that the wide prevalence of this false identification cannot simply be attributed to a deliberate nationalist effort, but rather reflects the historical processes that accompanied the emergence of the modern nation-state.

Let us look back at this formative period, at the end of the eighteenth century. In line with Rousseau's philosophy, and revealing its influence on contemporary political developments, the state was identified with its subjects rather than with its rulers. The belief that the state should be the "institutional representation of the people's will"[13] formed the basis of the American and French revolutions, marking a substantial shift in the type of legitimacy sought by political institutions, from justifications based on divine or dynastic right to justifications grounded in popular voluntary consent. The underlying assumption of this view is that citizens have a right to rule themselves, and that the authority of the government is grounded in the people's will. This shift has placed the political democratic interpretation of the right to self-rule at the center of modern political thought. Self-determination came to be seen as "a democratic ideal valid for all mankind."[14]

This fit between democratic universalist ideals and the emerging national ideology reflected the sociopolitical realities of the time. The American Revolution created a new nation, comprising those politically empowered before the Declaration of Independence, and excluding non-property holders, women, blacks, and native Indians.[15] The right to self-determination was understood as equivalent to the taxpayers' right to political representation. A complete overlap was thereby created between the citizens of the state and the members of the nation. So strong was this identification between state and nation that it still holds today, and in the United States the term "nation" refers to the federal state.

A different process, although with similar results, unfolded in France. Whereas in America the new state had created a nation, the French Third Estate, in its search for an autonomous source of political legitimation independent from that of the old royalist regime, "invented" a nation, presented itself as its true representative, and demanded the right to self-rule. The state then became the official embodiment of the nation, the one true fatherland. As Abbe Volfius put it in 1790, "The true fatherland is the political community where all citizens protected by the same laws, united by the same interests, enjoy the natural rights of man and participate in the common cause."[16]

Consequently, at this particular historical stage, the question of who constitutes the people—the members of the state or the members of the nation—seemed irrelevant. The nation, now equated with the body of citizens, came to be understood as the "body of persons who could claim to represent, or to elect representatives for, a particular territory at councils, diets or estates." It became widely accepted that "the principle of sovereignty resides essentially in the nation; no body of men, no individual, can exercise authority that does not emanate from it."[17] The nation became the unique symbol of fellowship among *all* members of the political framework, as well as the tie between the rulers and the ruled. A new political norm ensued, fostering the belief that "the legitimating principle of politics and state-making is nationalism; no other principle commands mankind's allegiance."[18] The shift from a justification relying on democratic principles to one based on national ones, from a belief in the right of citizens to self-rule to one claiming support for the right of nations to self-determination, was thereby completed. New terms of discourse had been established, masking the possible internal contradictions between the democratic and the national approach.

In modern political discourse, the right of individuals to determine their government remains a basic tenet of both liberal and nationalist doctrines. But the course of history since the end of the eighteenth century has been marked by a series of social, economic, and political upheavals—migrations, the establishment of new states inhabited by more than one nation, and the inclusion of groups that had previously been excluded from the political process. All these undermine the identification between the citizens of the state and the members of the nation, and it is no longer plausible to equate the right of citizens to self-rule with the right of members of the nation to self-determination. But although there are hardly any nationally homogeneous states left, the political discourse has not adapted itself to these developments. As late as 1960, when the Covenant on Human Rights was drafted, it was clear that the terms "people" and "nation" had never been adequately defined, and a disturbing confusion reigned between these two and the concept of majorities.

Since the nation had become the only valid source of state legitimacy, every group of individuals who saw themselves as a nation yearned to establish an independent state, and members of every state hoped to transform themselves from a population into a nation. Governments were pressured to prove that they represented a nation rather than a mere gathering of individuals. As a result, they developed an interest in homogenizing their populations—they began to intervene in the language, the interpretation of history, the myths and symbols or, to put it more broadly, in the culture of their citizens. The modern nation-state thus became the agent for cultural, linguistic, and sometimes religious unification—it attempted to build a nation.

The holistic character of the nation-state found support in Rousseau's concept of the general will, in Burke's organic view of the state, and in Hegel's perception of the state as "the ethical whole, the actualization of freedom."[19] Burke ends his *Reflections on the Revolution in France* by suggesting an idealistic, holistic description of the state, emphasising the metaphysical link between state and nation, in contrast with the civic link discussed earlier. The state, says Burke, is not

> a partnership in things subservient only to the gross animal existence of a temporary and perishable nature. It is a partnership in all science; a partnership in every virtue, and in all perfection. As the ends of such a partnership cannot be obtained in many generations, it becomes a partnership not only between those who are living, but between those who are living, those who are dead, and those who are to be born.[20]

The state is thus seen as the sphere in which individuals are moulded socially, culturally, and ethically. It is the arena where morality and spirituality are created, transmitted, and perfected.

Two very distinct lines of thought emerge from the political interpretation of the right to national self-determination: the idealist one, best represented by Hegel, and the individualist-civic one, exemplified by Mill. As Burke insightfully suggests, the identification between individual and national liberties typical of the civic version was natural for a nation like England, which had developed a "pedigree of liberties" based on the Magna Carta. But in Germany and Russia, which had none of these traditions, identifying with the history and the "spirit" of the nation was likely to lead to a relinquishment of liberal-democratic values, and to the emergence of romantic, organic perceptions. These fears were actualised in Hegel's philosophy of the nation-state. The nation-state, argues Hegel, "is mind in its substantive rationality and immediate actuality and is therefore the absolute power on earth." At every moment in the history of the world, there is a nation "to which is ascribed a moment of the Idea in the form of a natural principle entrusted with giving complete effect to it in the advance of the self-development self-conciousness of the world mind. This nation is dominant in world history during this one epoch, and it is only once that it can make its hour strike."[21] In this spirit, Hegel strongly opposed the individualism embodied in the civic version, which he viewed as a glorification of egoism and individual capriciousness, as leading to a plutocracy. He criticised the German nation of his times for its internal schisms, its particularism and provincialism, and was moved to think that it could only be saved by subordinating the parts—be they individuals or local political units—to the whole. His views gave metaphysical justification to the union between the nation and the state, promoting the view that political independence was a precondition for a nation's ability to fulfill its historical mission and be "a vehicle" of a certain stage "in the world's mind."[22]

These two traditions dominated the modern understanding of the nation-state, and supported the identification between "state" and "nation." This identification has not stood the test of history, however, and there are almost no nationally homogeneous states today. Irrespective of the fact that nations may attempt to establish states, and states may prefer to present themselves as representing nations, the two no longer overlap.

So what is a nation? The discussion so far has been concerned with what a nation is not. We now approach the much more difficult task of clarifying what it is.

What Is a Nation?

In order to answer this question, we could begin with the modern concept of nation-building. The concern with the deliberate creation of a nation is guided by a certain idea of what a nation is supposed to be.

The inherent contradiction between the claim that nations are natural communities shaped by history and fate and the concept of nation-building is immediately apparent. In order to mask this tension, nation-builders compulsively search for "ancestral origins" to which the new nation might "return," cling to even the faintest testimony of historical continuity, and advance patently false claims locating the nation's roots in a distant past. By emphasising the "link to the past," nation-builders try to play down the fact that their nation is the outcome of a bureaucratic decision or an international agreement and its national consciousness is only beginning to take shape. They focus their attempts on projecting an image of "a real nation," a group sharing a common denominator based on history, culture, language, tradition, and rituals. "Nationalism itself teaches that all nations have a past by definition."[23] Hence,

> those movements which could not fall back upon a community with long and rich cultural heritage sought to imitate those which could do so by, if necessary, "inventing" or rather "rediscovering" and "annexing" histories and cultures for their communities, in order to provide that cultural base without which no nationalism can attain widespread legitimation.[24]

The history of all nations is therefore saturated with invented traditions.[25] Invented tradition is defined by Hobsbawm as "a set of practices, normally governed by overtly or tacitly accepted rules and of a ritual or symbolic nature, which seek to inculcate certain values and norms of behaviour by repetition, which automatically implies continuity with the past."[26] The national emphasis on a shared culture plays a similar role. By definition, culture has a past, a history; "the essential core of culture consists of traditional (i.e., historically derived and selected) ideas and especially their attached values."[27] Through this alleged connection with the past, culture supports the nation's pretension to be natural, genuine, and unique. The importance that nation-builders ascribe to the invention of tradition and to the notion of a shared history and culture hints at the role these ideas are meant to play in national life. They respond to the urge for continuity, the desire to see at least some parts of social life as unchanging and invariant, and to the need for a locus of identification.

Osterud's definition of nation-building as the sum of policies designed to promote national integration illuminates another aspect of the nationalist concept of the nation. Nation-building, Osterud argues, "is an architectural metaphor for the process induced within a state to integrate the country and tie the inhabitants together in a national fellowship."[28] The ideal of national fellowship symbolises a belief in the existence of special ties and obligations binding the members of a nation. Nationalists view this ideal as the natural outcome of a collective destiny, a shared culture, and a faith in a common future, emphasising the perception of the nation as "a caring community," where individuals are able to overcome their egoistic inclinations and cooperate for the sake of mutual prosperity.

The concept of nation-building also illuminates the tension between the subjective and the objective definitions of a nation. Although largely human creations, nations seek to validate their existence by reference to ostensibly objective features. Nevertheless, all attempts to single out a particular set of objective features—be it a common history, collective destiny, language, religion, territory, climate, race, ethnicity—as necessary and sufficient for the definition of a nation have ended in failure. Although all these features have been mentioned as characteristic of some nations, no nation will have all of them. A nation could thus be understood as a cluster concept, that is, in order to count as a nation a group has to have a "sufficient number" of certain characteristics. Although they do not necessarily share the same set of identifying features, all members within the category "nation" will, therefore, show some family resemblance. Only one factor is necessary, although not sufficient, for a group to be defined as a nation—the existence of national consciousness. The best we can say, according to Cobban, is that "any territorial community, the members of which are conscious of themselves as members of a community, and wish to maintain the identity of their community, is a nation."[29] Seton-Watson makes a similar claim when he argues that it is impossible to arrive at a scientifically precise definition of a nation. At best, a nation can be said to exist when "a significant number of people in a community consider themselves to form a nation, or behave as if they formed one."[30]

At this point, it is important to distinguish between two closely related terms: nation and people. Although in the literature they often appear interchangeably, a nation is a community conscious of its particularistic existence, whereas the concept of "people" belongs to the same social category as "family" or "tribe," that is, a people is one of those social units whose existence is independent of their members' consciousness. It follows then that there must be some objective fact, such as relations of blood, race, a defined territory, or the like, which will allow an outsider to define a people without reference to the awareness of its members. The endurance of peoples, unlike that of nations, does not depend on the presence of a national consciousness or on the will of individuals to determine themselves as members.

In the present work, a group is defined as a nation if it exhibits both a sufficient number of shared, objective characteristics—such as language, history, or territory—and self-awareness of its distinctiveness. An occasional group of individuals lacking any shared characteristics cannot, merely by the power of its will, turn into a nation, and hence the importance of the first part of the definition. An answer to the question of what constitutes a sufficient number of *distinct* characteristics whereby a group becomes a nation, however, cannot rely on objective features only. Drawing the boundaries of a nation involves a conscious and deliberate effort to lessen the importance of objective differences within the group while reinforcing the group's uniqueness vis-à-vis outsiders.

The Jewish nation provides an interesting example. Jews from Israel, Russia, Ethiopia, and the United States share few objective characteristics, including race or skin colour, although they claim to share a religion and a history. My Judaism is very different from that of an Ethiopian Jew, or that of the Lubavitcher Rebbe, or that of a newcomer from Latvia who never practiced her Judaism and was not even conscious of it until recently. It is in fact doubtful whether an outsider could ever define the Jews as one nation on the basis of objective features. The Palestinian nation offers a diametrically opposed example. Palestinians share many objective features with other Arabs, and it might well be the case that from a historical, cultural, linguistic, and religious point of view, Palestinians have more in common with Jordanians or Syrians than a native Israeli has with an Ethiopian Jew. Yet, Palestinians *feel* that they belong to a distinct nation, while Ethiopian Jews and native Israelis feel that they belong to the same national group. These feelings can of course change and bring about the destruction of nations or result in the emergence of new ones. Nations exist only as long as their members share a feeling of communal membership, and in this sense, Renan's metaphor of a nationhood as "an everyday plebiscite"[31] accurately captures the important role of "the will to belong" in the definition of a nation.

Hampshire points to the importance of a willed emphasis on similarities as well as of a conscious downplay of divergence in the construction of a nation:

> The self-conscious and willed reinforcement of differences in behaviour and in interests between groups of human beings is

the effect of a shared habit of thinking of these differences historically and under descriptions that identify the differences. This source of continual reinforcement of differences is, as far as we know, unique to human beings. . . . There are many thousands of languages in the different regions of the world, and they are used to preserve the distinct history and habits of a particular population; and this remembered history will in turn reinforce the consciousness of difference.[32]

Hence, as Renan claims, the emergence of a nation is dependent on both the "possession in common of a rich legacy of remembrances" and "a shared amnesia, a collective forgetfulness."[33] The French nation tends to emphasise its oneness rather than the specific history and traditions of Bretons, Provencaux, Burgundians, Germans, Basques, and Catalans, just as the English nation tends to disregard the differences among Britons, Anglos, Saxons, Jutes, and Danes in order to promote a feeling of unity.

Nations, old or new, tend to reshape their past, reinterpret their culture, forget differentiating features, and embrace common characteristics in order to create the illusion of a "natural" unit with a long, mostly glorious history and a promising future. This process takes place within a context and does not imply that "anything goes." Invention depends on the existence of some shared features that may be highlighted to reinforce feelings of unity and allow members to recognise each other, a major element in the building of a nation. The belief that "nation marketh man," the illusion that we can rely on the notion of a national character in order to set the borders of national groups, is essential to the understanding of modern nationality:

A mere category of persons (say, occupants of a given territory, or speakers of a given language, for example) becomes a nation if and when the members of the category firmly recognize certain mutual rights and duties to each other in virtue of their shared membership of it. It is their recognition of each other as fellows of this kind which turns them into a nation, and not the other shared attributes, whatever they might be, which separate that category from non-members.[34]

The set of specific features that enable members of a nation to distinguish between themselves and others is culture. Culture, says Williams, is the ordinary:

Every human society has its own shape, its own purpose, its own meanings. Every human society expresses these in institu-

tions and in arts and leanings. The making of society is the finding of common meanings and directions, and its growth is an
active debate and amendment, under the pressures of experience, contact, and discovery, writing themselves into the land.
The growing society is there, yet it is also made and remade in
every individual mind.[35]

Culture is seen here as embodying patterns of behaviour, language,
norms, myths, and symbols that enable mutual recognition. Consequently, two people are of the same nation if, and only if, they share
the same culture.[36]

Communities, Anderson argues, are to be distinguished not by
their falsity or genuineness, but by the style in which they are imagined. Nations are communities imagined through culture, and are
therefore "cultural artifacts of a particular kind."[37] Modern nations
are too large to allow all their members to encounter each other personally. Recognition of fellow members, the drawing of boundaries
between members and nonmembers, thus becomes a product of
human imagination, contingent on the belief that there are similarities among members.

This definition of nations as cultural communities demarcated by
the imaginative power of their members raises many difficulties.
There are many kinds of cultural groups, some as large as Western
civilisation and others as small as the Amish community. Intuitively,
we would not tend to classify such groups as nations, although they
might be seen as falling within the parameters of our definition.
How, then, can we distinguish between nations and other cultural
groups? There is no satisfactory answer to this question, nor can we
draw more rigorous boundaries. Greater precision, if at all possible,
would force us to overlook the immense variety of social phenomena laying claim to the title "nation." Established nations often set
criteria concerning numbers, territory, or language, aimed at preventing others from attaining recognition as nations, a status they
themselves already enjoy. There is no objective way to determine
when two cultures are too close to be separated, and when the differences between them are significant enough to justify the emergence
of a new group. Hence, when members of a particular group sharing
some identifying national characteristics define themselves as a nation, they ought to be seen as one, lest they become victims of a
needless injustice.

This definition is valid even if it creates problems regarding a
small number of borderline cases. It is a fact that most claims for
national self-determination are advanced by groups to whom the

term "nation" applies without great difficulty. The analysis of the right to national self-determination, developed in the next section demonstrates that fears about the possible fragmentation of the political system resulting from the adoption of too loose a definition of the term "nation" have been highly overrated. These fears have been nurtured by the suspicion that behind every demand for national recognition lurks a separatist claim for the establishment of an independent nation-state. This, however, need not be the case.

Justifying the Right to National Self-Determination

The right to national self-determination was contested at three turning points in the twentieth century: after World War I, during the days of Wilson's Fourteen Points; after World War II, throughout the process of decolonization; and at the end of the 1980s, following the social and political revolution in Eastern and Central Europe. At each of these points, the justification of this right was couched in different terms.

Historically, the interpretation of the right to national self-determination followed two distinct courses, each relying on a different definition of the term "nation," and deriving its justification from the protection of a different individual interest.

According to the *cultural* version, "nation" is defined as a community sharing a set of objective characteristics grouped under the rubric of culture and national consciousness. Consequently, the right to national self-determination is understood as the right of a nation or, more precisely, the members of a nation, to preserve their distinct existence, and to manage communal life in accordance with their particular way of life. The *democratic* version defines "nation" as synonymous with "the governed," that is, the group of individuals living under the same rule. Hence, self-determination is understood as the right of individuals to participate in the governing of their lives. This right relies on the principle explicitly affirmed in the 1947 Universal Declaration of Human Rights: "Everyone has the right to take part in the government of his country directly or through freely chosen representatives."

These interpretations offer two independent approaches to fundamental principles concerning the formation and development of states. Whereas the first version suitably reflects the national essence of the right to self-determination, the second does not derive its justification from national thinking but rather from liberal, democratic ideals.

69

Although most discussions of the right to national self-determination reflect a confusion between these two versions, self-rule and national self-determination are two distinct concepts. They differ in their individualistic and communal aspects, represent two distinct human goods, and derive their value from two separate human interests.

The individualistic aspect of both these rights celebrates personal autonomy and the right of individuals to make constitutive choices. Whereas in the right to self-rule this aspect points to the right of individuals to govern their lives without being subject to external dictates, in the case of self-determination, it concerns the way in which individuals define their personal and national identity.

In its communal aspect, national self-determination entails a process whereby individuals seek to give public expression to their national identity. Hence, it is often described as the right of individuals to a public sphere, thus implying that individuals are entitled to establish institutions and manage their communal life in ways that reflect their communal values, traditions, and history—in short, their culture. The communal aspect of self-rule refers to the right of individuals to participate in the determination of the aims and the policies adopted by the political group they belong to, that is, their right to have a say in the fundamental decisions affecting the political process. It thus places at its center the right of individuals to participate in their country's government.

Accordingly, if individuals have an opportunity to participate in a fair political process—where all members are given an equal chance to take part as well as to present their views and persuade others to join them—they can be said to enjoy self-rule. But enjoying self-rule does not mean having one's views accepted. In pluralistic and heterogeneous communities, as most modern states indeed are, one will inevitably be outvoted on a variety of issues. At the conclusion of a fair process, individuals may find themselves in a minority position, unable to influence, let alone imprint the political sphere with their culture, preferences, and norms of behaviour, yet they could hardly claim that their right to self-rule has been violated. Hence, when given a fair opportunity to participate in the political process that structures their lives, individuals can be said to enjoy self-rule, irrespective of the results of this process.

By contrast, the right to national self-determination is not only measured by the ability to participate in determining the cultural nature of the social and political system one belongs to, but also by the results of this process. National self-determination is said to be attained only when certain features, unique to the nation, find expression in the political sphere.

Some examples might shed light on the distinction between self-rule and national self-determination. The process of European unification may eventually lead to the creation of one European state in which all European citizens will probably enjoy a full range of civil rights. A European state would thus allow all Europeans to fulfill their right to self-rule, but would not necessarily provide opportunities for members of different nations to realise their right to national self-determination.[38] Conversely, an undemocratic nation-state would deprive members of the nation of their right to self-rule, but not of their right to national self-determination. The yearning for national self-determination is different from, and may even contradict, the liberal democratic struggle for civil rights and political participation. Indeed, history shows that individuals often desire to secure status and recognition for their nation, even at the cost of relinquishing their civil rights and liberties. The Human Rights Committee was therefore wrong to view the realisation of the right to national self-determination as an essential condition for the effective guarantee and observance of individual human rights."[39] Members of nations granted national self-determination can, and indeed have, set up regimes that restrict the human rights of their fellow nationals, while individuals can enjoy a full range of civil rights even when not governed by their fellow nationals. As is evident from the above examples, national self-determination has little to do with civil rights and political participation. It is a search, as Berlin defines it, not for Millian freedoms and civil liberties, but for status. This is neither a struggle for the "equality of legal rights" nor for the "liberty to do as one wishes," although one may want these too, but for recognition. It expresses the desire to live in a meaningful environment, where one can feel a sense of familiarity or even identification with the rulers, irrespective of whether this is indeed true or merely a comfortable illusion:

> It is this desire for reciprocal recognition that leads the most authoritarian democracies to be, at times, consciously preferred by its members to the most enlightened oligarchies, or sometimes causes a member of some newly liberated Asian or African state to complain less today, when he is rudely treated by members of his own race or nation, than when he was governed by some cautious, just, gentle, well-meaning administrator from outside. I may feel unfree in the sense of not being recognized as

n.s.d. as search for
* Berlin - status + recognition.

a self-governing individual human being; but I may feel it also as a member of an unrecognized or insufficiently respected group: I wish for the emancipation of my entire class, or community, or nation, or race, or profession. So much can I desire this, that I may, in my bitter longing for status, prefer to be bullied and misgoverned by some member of my own race or social class, by whom I am nevertheless, recognized as a man and a rival—that is as an equal—to being well and tolerantly treated by someone from some higher and remoter group, who does not recognize me for what I wish myself to be. This is the heart of the great cry for recognition on the part of both individuals and groups, and in our own day, of professions and classes, nations and races.[40]

Individuals wish to be ruled by institutions informed by a culture they find understandable and meaningful, and which allows a certain degree of transparency that facilitates their participation in public affairs. When they are able to identify their own culture in the political framework, when the political institutions reflect familiar traditions, historical interpretations, and norms of behaviour, individuals come to perceive themselves as the creators, or at least the carriers, of a valuable set of beliefs.

The right to national self-determination cannot be reduced to other human rights, and more particularly, is not synonymous with rights to political participation or with freedoms of speech, press, assembly, and association. It is thus mistaken to claim that when civic rights are fully respected, "it is difficult to see how the right to self-determination could be denied."[41] Members of national minorities who live in liberal democracies, like the Quebecois and the Indians in Canada, the Aborigines in Australia, or the Basques in France, are not deprived of their freedoms and civil liberties, yet feel marginalised and dispossessed because they are governed by a political culture and political institutions imprinted by a culture not their own.

If the right to national self-determination cannot be reduced to the right to self-rule or to a range of civil rights and liberties, what is its essence?

The Essence of Cultural Self-Determination

The cultural interpretation of the right to national self-determination developed so far views it as the right of individuals to express their national identity, to protect, preserve, and cultivate the existence of their nation as a distinct entity. The emphasis on the cultural aspect links this discussion to issues concerning the right to culture raised in the previous chapter. It now seems obvious that the right to national self-determination is merely a particular case of the right to culture. In this light, the right to national self-determination should be seen as an individual right, contingent on a willed decision of individuals to affiliate themselves with a particular national group and to give public expression to this affiliation. The discussion in the previous chapter suggested that isolated individuals can enjoy the right to national self-determination but are restricted in their ability to give it full expression in the absence of a shared public space. But does the claim that individuals have the right to a national public sphere entail a right to establish their own nation-state?

The full scope of the argument must be unfolded in order to answer this question. The justification of the right to national self-determination rests on six counts:

1. Membership in a nation is a constitutive factor of personal identity. The self-image of individuals is highly affected by the status of their national community. The ability of individuals to lead a satisfying life and to attain the respect of others is contingent on, although not assured by, their ability to view themselves as active members of a worthy community. A safe, dignified, and flourishing national existence thus significantly contributes to their well-being.

2. Given the essential interest of individuals in preserving their national identity, it is justified to grant them a set of rights aimed at the protection of this interest. Since rights are to be judged by their justification, as claimed in the previous chapter, the right to national self-determination should be seen as an individual right.

3. In order to preserve their *national* identity, *individuals* must be given the opportunity to express this identity, both privately and publicly. Indeed, the ability of individuals to publicly realise their right to national self-determination in the fullest and most satisfying way depends on the existence of others who share their interests. Nevertheless, as it is an individual right, individual expressions of its implementation, however restricted, merit respect and support.

4. The existence of a shared public space is a necessary condition for ensuring the preservation of a nation as a vital and active community. The ability to enjoy the liveliness of public life is one of the major benefits that accrue from living among one's own people. Only then can the "individual feel that he lives in a community which enables him to express in public and develop without repres-

sion those aspects of his personality which are bound up with his sense of identity as a member of his community."[42]

5. National self-determination is therefore tied to the aspiration to have a communal domain that is construed not only as an arena of cooperation for the purpose of securing one's individual interests, but also as a space where one's communal identity finds expression. The ability to conceive of certain social and political institutions as representing a particular culture and as carriers of the national identity is at the heart of the yearning for national self-determination. Political arrangements based on this right should allow for the establishment of public institutions that reflect the history, the culture, the language, and at times the religion of the national group, thereby enabling their members to regard them as their own.

6. The right to national self-determination can be fully realised only if the national group is recognised by both members and non-members as an autonomous source of human action and creativity, and if this recognition is followed by political arrangements enabling members of the nation to develop their national life with as little external interference as possible. It has commonly been assumed that this requires granting members the widest possible degree of autonomy, namely, the right to establish their own sovereign nation-state. The issue of the desirable degree of autonomy entailed by this right, however, should take into account that all nations are equally entitled to it.

Unquestionably, a nation-state can ensure the widest possible degree of national autonomy and the maximum range of possibilities for the enjoyment of national life. Yet, it is commonly assumed that the implementation of rights is to be restricted so as to assure all individuals an equal sphere of freedom. Rawls' first principle of justice illustrates this constraint well. Each person "is to have an equal right to the most extensive basic liberty compatible with a similar liberty for all."[43] On this basis, it could be argued that the freedom of members of each nation to enjoy the right to national self-determination is to be restricted in order to allow members of other nations to enjoy this right. This is the rationale that motivates Walzer to argue that "the goal is a world of states within relatively secure borders, from which no sizable group of people is excluded."[44] The gains some people have made by acquiring states of their own, he argues, "must become gains for every one."[45] Since not all nations can attain this degree of national autonomy, and since restricting the implementation of this right only to nations able to establish one would lead to grave inequalities, other solutions must be sought.

74

The right to national-self determination can be satisfied through a variety of political arrangements—the establishment of national institutions, the formation of autonomous communities, or the establishment of federal or confederal states—able to ensure individuals the opportunity to participate in the national life of their community. It is pointless to search for an overall guiding principle to determine when the right to national self-determination justifies a certain political solution. The particular conditions of each case will determine the best solution under the specific circumstances.

The costs of each solution should, in each case, be weighed against its benefits. This implies that luck plays an important role in the ability of nations to enjoy the right to self-determination in its most comprehensive sense. Nations living in large, isolated territories are more likely to gain autonomy than nations living in densely populated areas, and factors such as natural resources, arable lands, access to the sea, a temperate climate, or topographical advantages, are also influential. Another important consideration in this context is the size of the communities involved: the larger the group that would benefit from a certain policy, the heavier the burdens it would be justified to impose on others. As Raz suggests, although national self-determination is justified on the basis of the interests of individual members of the community, "the interest of any one of them is an inadequate ground for holding others to be duty-bound to satisfy that interest. The right [of self-determination] rests on the cumulative interests of many individuals."[46] Although it is hard to say how many is many, the argument does imply that the larger the community, the more extensive the range of rights its members will enjoy. The claim that size matters, however, is meaningful only if the right to national self-determination is perceived as a cumulative individual right. If approached as a collective right, it is hard to see on what grounds larger groups are entitled to a more extensive enjoyment of it. In this sense, the ability to enjoy the right to national self-determination is subject to the external and internal limitations discussed in the previous chapter.

It is therefore assumed that different nations will be able to implement their right to self-determination in varying degrees. As long as this variance only reflects the unequal distribution of the chance factors mentioned above, it is hard to claim that a wrong was done. We can then conclude that all nations are equally entitled to enjoy the widest possible degree of national self-determination allowed by their specific circumstances.

Adopting a cultural, individualistic view of the right to national self-determination enables us to place along one continuum the justification of the rights of nations—whether they are minorities or constitute the majority within a particular state—and the justification of rights granted to ethnic groups and indigenous peoples. Members of these groups share a vital interest in the preservation of their distinct cultural identity.

Members of national minorities are entitled to national rights because they have an interest in preserving their unique cultural essence. In this sense, the term "minorities" should not be understood as merely pointing to the group's proportional size but rather to the extent to which its culture is reflected in the public space. Dinstein indeed argues that "minority" should not be understood in numerical terms, and defines a minority as a group playing a "minor role in the affairs of the country."[47] But this definition might be misleading, as it could very well apply to the American Communist party, to stamp collectors, or to many other groups that, although likely to play a minor political role, are not entitled to the same rights as national minorities.

The cultural interpretation of the right to national self-determination highlights the importance of provisions aimed at protecting the cultural, religious, and linguistic identity of minorities and assuring them an opportunity to live alongside the majority, "co-operating amicably with it, while at the same time preserving the characteristics which distinguish them from the majority, and satisfying the ensuing special needs."[48] The following premise in the United Nations' charter, which uses a civil rights rather than a cultural rights terminology to formulate the rights of minorities to national self-determination, is thus particularly alarming: "In a world where individual rights are fully protected, minority groups will disappear with time and the 'nationality problem' would cease to pose a threat to world stability." In the guise of protecting the right of a minority to national self-determination, this statement could be used to justify assimilationalist policies.[49]

The demand for special rights put forward by indigenous peoples lends further support to the cultural interpretation of the right to national self-determination. Their claim is not merely a call for justice and for redressing past wrongs, but reflects their wish to ensure full expression of their distinct cultural identity. It is clear that translating the struggle of indigenous peoples into civic rather than cultural terms obscures the issue.

Moreover, a cultural, individualistic interpretation of the right, based on the distinction between the right to self-rule and the right to national self-determination, seems better suited to meet the challenges of the next century. The final chapter of this book elaborates on these ideas, casting doubts on the viability of independent nation-states and suggesting that state powers should devolve both to smaller, autonomous national entities on the one hand, and to larger, regional frameworks on the other.

FOUR

PARTICULAR NARRATIVES AND

GENERAL CLAIMS

> Some may think this too weak a version of nationalism to
> merit the name, others that any version of nationalism is
> merely a stalking horse for chauvinism and xenophobia. To
> both I would say that in this and in other matters there is
> much to be said for a golden mean. —*Neil MacCormick*

The present national awakening began in Europe, for a long time the
hearth of all nationalist fires. The nations of Eastern Europe have
taken to the streets waving their flags, singing their hymns, and un-
earthing national heroes buried in the shadows during the long
years of communism. In Great Britain, claims raised by the Irish, the
Welsh, and the Scots threaten the 400-year alliance among the nations of the British isles. At the same time, the Basques and the Corsicans stake claims for national autonomy, tensions escalate between
Flemish and Walloons, and signs of xenophobia appear wherever
immigrants concentrate. It is therefore hard to remember that, only
a few years ago, it was commonly suggested that the world had
reached a postnational era. Amos Elon, an Israeli journalist, wrote in
1987: "In one important sense, modern democracies already live in
a postnationalist era. Even in the relatively young nation of Israel,
few people seem nowadays to be in the mood for unreflective national celebration."[1] When making this claim, Elon was quite clearly
interpreting nationalism in the most extreme, ultimate and unreflective terms.

When approached as a set of definitive values nationalism may
indeed lead to social and political catastrophe. Although this is
probably the fate of any social or political ideal radically and
thoughtlessly pursued, a hidden assumption seems to be at work as
far as nationalism is concerned, which grants validity only to its ex-

treme interpretations and identifies it with fanaticism, violent struggle, and disaster.

So firm is this belief that MacCormick's interesting attempt to offer a moderate view of nationalism is met with great suspicion.[2] If MacCormick's view can be defined as "nationalism," argues Graham, then "a good many people are nationalists unawares." This conclusion, which will be defended in Chapter 6, seems too threatening, and Graham thus hastens to reassure us that "such a moderate nationalism is not really nationalism at all."[3] But why should nationalism be the only social ideal that must either be pursued in an ultimate manner or not at all? Moderate nationalism offers a coherent theoretical position, indeed, a more coherent one than its more extreme "relatives." Why should liberal nationalism, which places reflection, choice, and internal criticism at its center, and rejects the notion that nationalism must necessarily "exalt the idea of the nation above all other ideas,"[4] be defined as postnationalist?

The main characteristic of liberal nationalism is that it fosters national ideals without losing sight of other human values against which national ideals ought to be weighed. The outcome of this process is a redefinition of legitimate national goals and the means used to pursue them. Liberal nationalism thus celebrates the particularity of culture together with the universality of human rights, the social and cultural embeddedness of individuals together with their personal autonomy. In this sense it differs radically from organic interpretations of nationalism, which assume that the identity of individuals is totally constituted by their national membership, and that their personal will is "truly free" only when fully submerged in the general one. It is a direct descendant of the cultural pluralism of Herder and the liberal nationalism of Mazzini.

Liberal nationalism relies on the assumption that as liberalism is a theory about the eminence of individual liberties and personal autonomy, nationalism is a theory about the eminence of national-cultural membership and historical continuity, and the importance of perceiving one's present life and one's future development as an experience shared with others.

The parallel suggested by this comparison between liberalism and nationalism is frequently rejected. It is often suggested that nationalism is not a theory at all, that it lacks structure and consistency, and that it should therefore be regarded as merely a capricious mood, mirroring human desires and fears, "an irrational relic of, or retrogressive return to, a barbarous past."[5] Seton-Watson claims that the essence of nationalism is that popular sovereignty should be applied to the nation—"the rest of nationalist ideology is rhetoric."[6] Others agree that nationalism might be enormously important for historians and sociologists but claim that it would be absurd to treat it as if inviting serious rational criticism. And Popper, in what is probably the best known attack on nationalism, claims that nationalism is akin to a revolt against reason and the open society, which appeals "to our tribal instincts, to passion and to prejudice, and to our nostalgic desire to be relieved from the strain of individual responsibility which it attempts to replace by a collective or group responsibility."[7]

This attack on nationalism notwithstanding, this book attempts to describe an interpretation of nationalism that cherishes reason and the open society, rests on a systematic view of human nature and the world order, and on a coherent set of universally applicable values.

Arguing that one could approach nationalism as a theory entails an attempt to uncover the presence of some unifying characteristics able to cut across the myriad of claims raised by different national groups. The existence of these characteristics is often masked by the character of the nationalist discourse which, by its very nature, insists on presenting national claims as unique, a product of each nation's distinct identity. Nationalists prefer to justify their claims by reference to the particular culture, history, and religion of their nation, rather than by relating them to a broad theory that could fit other national groups. On this count, nationalism differs from other schools of thought. Whereas liberals, for instance, often go out of their way to demonstrate that their specific policies, however remote, correlate with a general theory, nationalists consistently attempt to disguise the universality of their arguments and emphasise the particularistic aspects of their claims and policies. This tendency to emphasise the particular is a universal characteristic, shared by all nationalist claims. Only after we realise this can we begin to search for a general theory hiding behind the multitude of national arguments.

This search is valuable for several reasons. First, a general theory of nationalism could provide the conceptual tools required for a critical evaluation of a broad variety of social phenomena grouped under the generic rubric of nationalism. This evaluation could lead to the conclusion that, at least in some cases, the term "nationalism" has been misused, and could also help us understand the temptation to misuse it. Second, a theoretical framework will enable distinctions between a theory of nationalism and nationalistic policies, similar to the differentiation we make between communism and liberalism as political theories and the specific policies of certain Communist or liberal parties. Last but not least, a comprehensive theory might reveal a different, and possibly more favourable, interpretation of nationalism than is commonly accepted, and underscore the importance of nationalism for the understanding and evaluation of a broad range of social and political phenomena.

Theories of Nationalism:
A Search for a Common Ground

A theoretical clarification is in order to begin with. The term "theory" is used here in a programmatic, normative context. It is therefore to be distinguished from other theoretical approaches concerned with the historical development of nationalism, its economic, political, and cultural roots, or its various manifestations. The purpose is to outline a justification of nationalism, that draws attention to its normative aspects, rather than to explain its emergence and development.

Contrary to the ethnocentric nature of nationalistic discourse, which extols the virtues and singularity of one particular nation, a *theory* of nationalism is, by nature, polycentric. It necessarily recognises and cherishes the plurality of the national phenomenon. Its arguments develop in reference to features shared by all nations, rather than on justifications resting on the specific history, cultural traditions, religious beliefs, or particular values of any one nation. The claim that the Jews are God's chosen people thus *cannot* be justified with reference to a *theory* of nationalism, although it is certainly a nationalist claim.

Similarly, Mickiewicz's claim that "the Slavs were a chosen people because they were the 'new barbarians,' a people without a heritage, with a virgin soul ready to accept a new revelation,"[8] which is an integral aspect of the Polish nationalist discourse, *cannot* find support in a *theory* of nationalism. Cruise O'Brien claims that virtually every Christian nation took the idea of a chosen people in the promised land and applied it to itself. Although unsure of the full number, O'Brien observes that "writers of the following nations explicitly refer to their people as chosen and to their land as promised: England, France, Germany, Spain, Poland, Russia, Sweden, Switzerland, Ireland, and especially and insistently the United States, for both whites and blacks took up this theme."[9] Other nations, such as Israel, Iran, and Egypt, could be added to this list. But no nationalist would ever describe the pretension to be a chosen people living in a promised land as part of a general pattern, as this would invalidate the claim. Being chosen is only meaningful if others are not.

It is clear why the nationalist discourse often deliberately attempts to mask latent overarching arguments, but the similarities between the different national claims are too obvious to ignore. It is precisely this tension between praise for the particular and the awareness of universality that makes nationalism, as a political and social phenomenon and as a theory, so attractive and complex. It is attractive because it captures the importance of context, of cultural affiliations, of the need for roots, for belonging, for human development and self-fulfillment, thereby illuminating a broad range of issues that liberal theory tends to brush aside. It is complex because it forces the realisation that there are two different and incompatible discourses embedded in each national claim. One tends to describe the particular sequence of events through which a nation has evolved by referring to what is unique to the group, thus developing arguments that are only meaningful to the group's members. The other emphasises the universal dimension of politics, places the national story within a framework, and relates it to that of other nations, thus developing arguments that are also meaningful within a general context.

The complicated relations between these two layers of discourse could be exemplified by following the claims raised by both sides in the Israeli-Palestinian conflict. Israelis tend to view the establishment of the state of Israel in light of their personal and painful history of expulsion and persecution, from the days of the destruction of the Second Temple through the horrors of the Holocaust and present-day anti-Semitism. This narrative is told in ways that necessarily lead to one conclusion: Due to the tragic sequence of events that marks Jewish history, Jews need a state of their own to secure their existence and to ensure a public sphere where Jewish life can prosper. The story told by the Palestinians follows a similar path of sorrow, expulsion, and mistreatment, and reaches the same conclusion: Palestinian history teaches that in light of their long oppression and in order to ensure their self-protection, Palestinians need a state of their own. The Israeli and Palestinian claims are both grounded in their past suffering. Other nations struggling to ensure their national rights, such as the Kurds, the Basques, or the Armenians, also offer a history of suffering and subjection as grounds for their entitlement to such rights. But suffering and persecution are *not* suitable grounds for bestowing national rights. Many groups, such as religious sects, women, homosexuals, or members of opposition parties, share a history of suffering, and discrimination. These might entitle them to compensation but not to national rights. By the same token, it would be unreasonable to claim that national groups that have never suffered persecution are therefore less entitled to national rights.

A historical account of the nation's past may explain how the nation came about, its present condition, the collective fears and traumas that motivate it, its attachment to a particular territory, or its adoption of a particular religion, but it cannot, as such, justify granting it national rights. National rights can only be consistently justified on universal grounds by referring to the value individuals find in the existence of nations, and by assuming that human beings care as much about the national environment in which they implement their life-plans as about the specific content of these plans. The notion of the contextual individual and its concomitant implications, which rely on the right of individuals to be self-determining, on the acknowledgment of the importance of cultural membership, and on the assertion of a general right to culture and national self-determination, must therefore be at the center of any theory of nationalism.

Cultural Nationalism and Liberal Values

The version of nationalism that places cultural commitments at its center is usually perceived as the most conservative and antiliberal form of nationalism. Kohn, for example, used the term "cultural nationalism" to describe East European nationalism and distinguish it from its Western counterpart. Cultural nationalism, Kohn argues, preaches the establishment of closed societies, favours the authoritarian uniformity of state and faith, and fosters xenophobia. Its goals are "narrow, self-centered, antagonistic"; it sees the nation as "a political unit centering around the irrational pre-civilized folk concept," lending itself "more easily to the exaggeration of imagination and excitation of emotions." In short, Kohn's cultural nationalism is on the verge of the pathological and doomed to culminate in catastrophe.[10]

Liberal nationalism bears no resemblance to Kohn's description. In fact, it is mainly characterised by the features Kohn had assigned to the Western nationalism modeled on the Enlightenment: It is pluralistic and open, sees national groups as not only a product of history, but also of human will, and broadly follows humanistic tradition. It is structured in line with the assumptions of ethical individualism, stating that "the only way to justify any social practice is by reference to the interests of those people who are affected by it."[11] Accordingly, it rules out appeals in the name of God, Nature, History, Culture, the Glorious Dead, the Spirit of the Nation, or any other such metaphysical entities, unless these claims can be justified in terms of human interests.

Guided by this view of ethical individualism, it places strong emphasis on the possibility and the importance of choice. However, the strong communal dimension of all forms of nationalism is undeniable, and liberal nationalism indeed assumes that living within one's national community is of value to individuals. The first two chapters considered the instrumental dimension of national membership, namely, its ability to provide a set of beliefs, interests, and behaviours, as well as a coherent, transparent, and intelligible environment in which individuals can become self-determining. It was suggested that in the open and ever-changing modern world, life in a cultural environment that is familiar, understandable, and thus predictable is a necessary precondition for making rational choices and becoming self-governing.

Life within one's nation has a further advantage. It offers the possibility of being acknowledged by significant others, be it peers or superiors: "they understand me, as I understand them; and this understanding creates within me a sense of being somebody in the world."[12] Agreement with this statement does not imply subscribing to an illusion of perfect harmony or mutual understanding, but rather suggests the presence of certain intangible links among members of a national entity.

Yet, one of the most significant aspects of a "national life" is to be found in an altogether different sphere. A national life allows individuals to enjoy a degree of self-fulfillment they cannot experience on their own. Liberal nationalism does not claim that individuals can find true freedom and expression only through complete identification with the community. It does not endorse claims such as those voiced by Fichte, that only by completely identifying with the whole can man become really man, realising himself in utmost plentitude, and it is this realisation that is the perfect freedom. Membership in a national community is not viewed in perfectionist terms, although it is still assumed that it allows individuals to lead a more meaningful life.

In what way is life within one's nation better and more meaningful? Two terms require clarification in this context: "meaningful" and "within one's nation." The term "meaningful" refers to the nationalist belief that every action taking place within the boundaries of a national entity is endowed with additional meaning. In every field of human activity—music, theatre, literature, sports, the army, or the economy—every action performed within a national context counts both as a contribution to that particular field and as a contribution to the national endeavour. For example, Andy Warhol's pictures represent an artistic contribution, but they are also a stage in the development of American culture. Lines such as

> I travelled among unknown men,
> In lands beyond the sea;
> Nor, England! did I know till then
> what love I bore to thee.
>
> (William Wordsworth, "Lucy" II)

have entered the pantheon of Western poetry, but are also pillars of English culture. In the 1936 Berlin Olympics, Jesse Owens not only won four gold medals and set three world records but, through these achievements, attained a national victory for his country (and for black people everywhere). From a national perspective, the painter working in the solitude of his atelier, the poet writing to his loved one, or the athlete competing in a sports event, strive for the pinnacle of their own individual achievements but, willingly or unwillingly, they are also contributing to the advancement of their own particular nations. If we accept Williams' claim that "culture is the ordinary," then the meaning of most of our daily actions transcends their particular and direct function. The ability to turn an everyday act into a source of national pride is one of the most appealing aspects of nationalism. It contextualises human actions, no matter how mundane, making them part of a continuous creative effort whereby culture is made and remade. Insofar as every action within a national entity is endowed with this additional dimension, individuals living within national frameworks enjoy options unavailable to those outside them. It is in this sense that national frameworks can be said to bestow extra merit on social, cultural, or political acts, and to provide individuals with additional channels for self-fulfillment that make their lives more meaningful.

But living within one's own community could make life more meaningful in other respects. Living within a community where members share an "imagined" sense of togetherness engenders mutual responsibilities. The development of human relationships, the ability to strive together with others to achieve shared goals, enriches human life. Moreover, the respect for continuity inherent in national membership enables individuals to place themselves in a continuum of human life and creativity, connecting them to their ancestors as well as to future generations and lessening the solitude and alienation characteristic of modern life.

We still need to clarify the use of the term "living within one's nation." This could sound like a territorial claim, suggesting that individuals must live in physical proximity to other members of their group, but in the modern world this is not necessarily the case. We should here distinguish between two distinct claims.

The first is that in order to lead a prosperous cultural life, a nation needs a public sphere. As the phenomenon of modern diasporas proves, a national community could in fact have more than one public sphere and need not occupy a continuous territory. For example, Said draws our attention to the fact that Cubans in Florida remain Cubans setting up their own Havana in Miami:

> Having come to the New World in an age of rapid travel and communication no longer means that you have to give up the old country, since it turns out that you can bring it with you. A century ago, the implacable realities of geography meant that, over time (though, of course, a longer time than most people can recall), most immigrants began to forget the old country in much the same way that even the most bereaved of lovers eventually ceases to be able accurately to picture a loved one's face. Now the simple accessibility of the entire world makes such forgetfulness all but attainable.[13]

The second claim is that in order to be able to enjoy the additional national dimension ascribed to an individual achievement, the latter need not take place within one's national community. Although written far away from Dublin, *Ulysses* is part of the Irish culture it portrays. While writing Ulysses, Joyce was in a metaphysical sense, "living within his community," and could have claimed he never left home. It is therefore wrong to reduce the concept of "living among one's people" to the concrete, physical place where a person is living at the moment of creation. We should understand this concept in more abstract terms.

This discussion demonstrates that there is more than one way to live a national life and contribute to the prosperity of one's nation. This approach demands that we reinterpret the concept of national obligations, taking into account this variety.

National Obligations

The liberal view of national membership presented here could be attacked on the grounds that it leads to the disintegration of precisely those frameworks it values most dearly. It is commonly argued that the preservation of national frameworks does not require choice or creative skills, but rather loyalty, commitment, and a readiness for self-effacement, and that the existence of nations depends on the fact that membership in them is not elective but dictated by fate. National obligations are therefore frequently portrayed as imposing on individuals, regardless of their consent, a duty to follow the rules, to be faithful rather than innovative.

Liberal nationalism takes issue with both these claims. It argues that membership in a nation is elective, since individuals can leave the nation of their birth and create new national affiliations, and that this turns the adherence to a culture and the assumption of national obligations into voluntary acts rather than inevitable consequences of fate. But claiming that national obligations could be seen as voluntarily assumed says nothing about their nature. Individuals can, voluntarily, choose to become subservient to a person or an idea. So what is the liberal-nationalist view of the content of national obligations? Are they best defined as conscious obedience, or is it possible to arrive at a more open interpretation of this concept that will make it compatible with a liberal understanding of nationalism?

In the literature on nationalism—Anderson, Deutsch, Gellner, Hertz, Smith, Snyder—the term "obligation" is rarely found. Instead, we usually find terms such as "duty" and "loyalty." The use of these terms is meant to allude to the involuntary, ultimate nature of national affiliations, to portray them in radical terms as a commitment to support the nation unconditionally, to accept blindly all its cultural and social features, to be ready to sacrifice one's life to protect it and ensure its continued existence. According to this interpretation, loyalty means nothing less than a *total commitment*, an *effacement* of the individual vis-à-vis the nation. But this is only one possible interpretation of loyalty in general and of national loyalty in particular. We are supposed to be loyal to our family and friends, to the values we hold as well as to our nation. Under very extreme and extraordinary circumstances, these loyalties could indeed demand that we sacrifice our lives. We are not, however, usually required to take our displays of loyalty to such extremes.

87

If the only determining feature of national obligations is the readiness for self-sacrifice, then the relations between individuals and their nation are fundamentally different from all other types of social relations. On the other hand, if self-sacrifice is only demanded in rare and extreme cases, but is not the one and only defining characteristic of national obligations, then these obligations share a great deal with other associative commitments.

A social body can only generate those obligations logically derived from its ends, and national obligations must therefore refer to what we might term "the national goals." There are several general aims every nation is likely to pursue: assuring its continued existence, the well-being of its members, the flourishing of its culture. To assume national obligations thus means acquiring special responsibilities toward fellow nationals, contributing to the ongoing existence of the national unit, partaking in the continuous re-creation of its culture, learning and respecting its traditions, and engaging in a political struggle that will ensure the nation a public sphere of its own. All these obligations can be pursued in a more or less extreme way.

The struggle for the revival of Hebrew as a living, modern language might provide a good illustration of the range of options in the fulfillment of national obligations. Eliezer Ben-Yehuda (1858–1922) led the effort to turn biblical Hebrew into a living language. He was a "lingual zealot." Although Hebrew lacked many words necessary for life in a secular, mundane, and prosaic context, Ben-Yehuda insisted on speaking only Hebrew and invented new words as needed, which he registered in his dictionary. For Ben-Yehuda's supporters, speaking any language but Hebrew meant betraying their national duties. Much later, during the 1970s and 1980s, Jewish dissidents in the Soviet Union were ready to risk imprisonment for teaching Hebrew. Today, Hebrew is the mother tongue of several million people for whom speaking Hebrew is no longer part of a conscious and deliberate effort. Many Israelis today feel safe enough to incorporate English words when speaking or writing in Hebrew. They are no longer purists of their own language but are open to learning others as well as incorporating foreign expressions. By using the language, they fulfill their national obligation and contribute to the process of re-creating their own culture. Nevertheless, were they ever threatened or forbidden to speak their language, they too might be ready to risk their liberty and their lives for it.

Individuals have a choice. They can refuse to speak the language of their community, reject their culture, and assimilate into a different culture. They can also stay within their culture, develop special mutual responsibilities, and retain and foster a sense of exclusiveness, thereby contributing to the preservation of the nation as a lively social unit. This does not entail that nationalists are culturally conservative or that they revere their own particular culture. They can be critical of it; they can aspire to change it, develop it, or redefine it. They may be deeply disappointed by it, believing it to be in decline and inferior to other cultures. Plamenatz emphasises this point when he suggests that calls to devote oneself to the flourishing of one's culture are usually voiced when a culture is felt "to be inadequate or lacking."[14] Fichte's *Address to the German Nation* was indeed delivered in this spirit. Fichte saw the Germany of his times as corrupt, on the verge of disintegration and annihilation. This age, he said, is like a shade that stands weeping over its own corpse. Germans must therefore make a choice:

> If you continue in your dullness and helplessness, all the evils of serfdom are awaiting you; deprivations, humiliations, the scorn and arrogance of the conqueror; . . . until, by the sacrifice of your nationality and your language, you have purchased for yourselves some subordinated and petty place, and until this way you will die out as a people. If, on the other hand, you bestir yourselves and play the man, you will continue in a tolerable and honorable existence, and you will be growing up among and around you a generation that will be the promise for you and for the Germans of most illustrious renown.[15]

Understood in this way, the assumption of national obligations implies the reflective acceptance of an ongoing commitment to participate in a critical debate about the nature of the national culture, suggesting that individuals have a reason to adhere to their national obligations even after the establishment of a nation-state. Hence, contrary to Seton-Watson's claim that independent nations, which are territorially satisfied and nationally conscious, no longer need nationalism, this interpretation views a commitment to the nation as a sustained, enduring project. This project involves encouraging individuals to remain, by choice, within their national group, to actively participate in the continued re-creation of their national culture, and to contribute to the well-being of their fellow members. In this sense, nationalism has a permanent role. Therefore, it seems that the most common way of fulfilling national obligations is not through self-sacrifice, or by subordinating one's well-being and interests to the welfare of the collective, but rather by participating in a cultural dialogue. The language we teach our children, the bedtime stories we tell them, and the lullabies we sing to them, are as good a way of satisfying our national obligations as a declaration of readiness to die for the sake of the nation.

Pluralistic Nationalism

Liberal nationalism requires a state of mind characterised by tolerance and respect of diversity for members of one's own group and for outsiders. Contrary to widespread perceptions, national communities might, in some respects, be more open and pluralistic than communities in which social bonds rely on a set of shared values. When membership is based on an overlapping consensus of shared values, those outside the consensus can be marginalised, and their membership questioned to the point of turning them into outcasts, as was the fate of Communists in the United States. But in a society where social cohesion is based on national, cultural, and historical criteria, holding nonconformist views does not necessarily lead to excommunication. All through the bitter confrontation between de Gaulle and Sartre concerning the independence of Algeria, de Gaulle never doubted that Sartre was a respected member of the French nation. Or, mark the difference, the English public never saw Kim Philby or Antony Blunt as anything but Englishmen, and the Israeli public still sees Uri Davis, an Israeli affiliated with the PLO, as an Israeli. The national bond is not broken even in cases of extreme normative disagreements. Since the roots of unity in national communities are outside the normative sphere, they can accommodate normative diversity, and in this sense be more pluralistic than groups held together by shared values.

Since it is predicated upon a universal commitment to the existence of national groups as such, liberal nationalism is polycentric by definition. It thus falls under the rubric of what Walzer calls "reiterative universalism."[16] Reiterated acts of self-determination create a world marked by differences. A theory of nationalism grounded in the assumption of reiterative universalism is necessarily polycentric, that is, it presupposes that there is one civilisation but many nations and views particularistic national struggles as variations on a theme. Every national struggle thus represents an attempt to re-create the particularity of each nation, but also reflects the aspiration to join the "family of nations, the international drama of status equals, to find its appropriate identity and part."[17] Reiterative universalism thus implies a moral lesson, since it is "a moral act to recognize otherness in this way"; it teaches modesty, and suggests that there is something to be learned from others.[18]

Some might claim that nationalist movements tend to become entrenched in their own particularistic concerns and ignore those of others. Indeed, in the heat of the battle, most national movements will deny the national rights of their opponents. Yet, at the same time, they will rely on the universal right of all nations to self-determination articulated in the United Nations' charter in order to gather support and justify their own particularistic struggle.

The first version of reiterative nationalism appeared in the aftermath of the French Revolution. The Girondins had advocated promoting "sister" revolutions in the territories that France had conquered, or expected to take over. In the First Propagandist Decree, dated November 19, 1792, the National Convention declared in the name of the French nation that "it will grant fraternity and aid to all people who wish to recover their liberty." The Second Propagandist Decree, dated December 15, 1792, went one step farther and issued a document headed as follows: "[From] the French People to the _____ People." This document was sent to all revolutionary generals, who were asked to fill in the blank with the name of the appropriate country, as it was conquered and/or liberated. The document opens with the following words: "Henceforth the French nation proclaims the sovereignty of the people of _____. You are henceforth, brothers and friends, all equal in rights, and all equally summoned to govern, to serve and defend your Patrie."[19] The idea that all national liberation movements should model themselves on French nationalism was accepted by other nations too. For example, the 1792 Convention of Irish Patriots declared that it contemplated with joy the spectacle of the "grand nation" giving liberty to Europe.

Supporters of the French Revolution described themselves as patriots of their own countries and claimed that, by following the French example and accepting French guidance, they were serving the best interests of their own nations. "Blank-space patriots" were henceforth to devote themselves to two nations: *la grand nation* and their own. It is quite obvious that the "blank-space patriots" and the *soeur republiques* were favoured only due to their potential value as supporters of the French ambition to eventually rule Europe, and the cynicism underlying this idea was later a source of bitter disillusionment. In fact, it was also partly responsible for the emergence of the ethnocentric German nationalism expressed by Fichte in his Adresses to the German Nation (1807), which were delivered in French-occupied Berlin. But despite these drawbacks, the idea of reiterative nationalism played a significant role in European nationalism up to the end of the nineteenth century. One harbinger of the Jewish national revival that led to the emergence of the Zionist movement was Aaron David Gordon. Gordon urged the Jewish nation to struggle against assimilation. Jews should tap their creative sources, but without setting themselves apart from other nations. Nations, he argued, are organic entities, and in the process of mutually activating each other, they resemble celestial bodies and create relations of mutual solidarity."[20]

Another illuminating example appears in the writings of Kazimierz Brodzinski, who credited the Poles with being the first to realise that the principle of national egoism had to be replaced with a polycentric perspective. Formerly, he argues, each nation had regarded itself as the goal and centre of the universe, and

> the Polish nation alone (I say it boldly and with patriotic pride) could have a foreboding of the true movement of the moral universe. It has recognised that every nation is a fragment of the whole and must roll on its orbit and around the centre like the planets around theirs.[21]

This passage reflects the extraordinary combination of particularistic pride and universal commitment typical of the progressive-romantic version of liberal nationalism prevalent in mid-nineteenth-century Europe. This approach promoted the idea of the brotherhood of nations, which share a sacred duty to be mutually helpful in the struggle for freedom and international justice.[22]

This fellowship of nations fighting for their independence is a major feature of liberal nationalism. It is in this spirit that Mazzini addresses his fellow Italians and asks them,

> What is it that makes our heart beat when hearing the story of battles for national liberation taking place in far and remote places? . . . A people, Greek, Polish, Circassian, raises the banner of the fatherland and of independence, fights, conquers, or dies for it, what is it that makes our heart swell with joy at its victories, and sorrow over its defeats? . . . And why do you eagerly read the miracles of patriotic love recorded in Greek story, and repeat them to your children with a feeling of pride, almost as if they were stories of our own fathers?[23]

Even Treitschke, from his extreme ethnocentric position, recognises that all nations, like all individuals, have their limitations, but it is exactly in the abundance of these limited qualities that the genius of humanity is exhibited. The rays of the Divine light are manifested, broken by countless facets among the separate peoples, each one exhibiting another picture and another idea of the whole. Every people has a right to believe that certain attributes of the divine reason are exhibited in it to their fuller perfection.[24]

Beyond its obvious moral virtues, polycentric nationalism has a methodological advantage: It is free from the theoretical limitations inherent in particularistic nationalism. Ethnocentric nationalists, by relying on arguments exclusively related to one particular nation, rule out a universal justification of national rights and lose the ability to hold a meaningful dialogue with members of other nations.

The polycentric nature of liberal nationalism helps to distinguish it from other movements that have often been associated with nationalism—imperialism, racism, fascism, and nazism.

Imperialism, according to Smith, is nationalism's closest relative since

it fits perfectly with the sense of superiority inhering in 'ethnocentric nationalism,' [however] imperialism is essentially a derogation, even a contradiction, of the main tenet of 'polycentric nationalism'—the right of each nation to realise itself in perfect autonomy, so as to be able to contribute to mankind.[25]

Fascism is also a reversal of the trend of "polycentric nationalism." It introduces additional elements "which in themselves contradict 'polycentric' tenets, and substitutes the State for the Nation, as the prime object of collective allegiance and identification."[26] Racism again reverses the "polycentric" trend, although it could be regarded as a post-Darwinian aberration of "ethnocentric" nationalism.

Nazism, Smith claims, is the purest contradiction of nationalism *in toto*. At first glance, nazism would indeed appear to be the final culmination of "ethnocentric" nationalism, "a sentiment that Hitler knew only too well how to exploit." Yet, if we trace the course of Nazi ideology, we shall find that

the original vertical division of the world, envisaged by even 'ethnocentric' nationalism, gets gradually subverted by radical imperialism into this diametrically opposed racial casteism on global scale, using pseudo-scientific 'Darwinian' notions of domination through struggle.

There is as much connection between nationalism and nazism, Smith argues, as between nationalism and communism; the convergence between both pairs of ideologies is to be sought in the particular social contexts, not in ideological affinity or structural similarity.[27]

"Racism," "sexism," and "chauvinism" are, respectively, a ranking of races, sexes, and states, but "nationalism," claims Walzer, works differently. It is entirely compatible with a theory of incommensurability or with mere agnosticism about ranks and orders. "Nationalists are more like patriots, in that they can respect and value commitments similar to their own in other people—and they can do so, unlike egoists, without viewing the others as competitors and antagonists."[28]

We have so far argued that nationalism could be more pluralistic and less ethnocentric than is commonly assumed, and in this sense, it is not hard to dissociate it from its supposedly close ideological relatives. Differentiating between nationalism and its more notorious associations, however, requires a detailed discussion of its ethical implications.

Beginning with the idea of the contextual individual and proceeding from cultural to national rights, a certain notion of the necessity of cultural and national life emerges, suggesting that individuals are better off when able to share their lives with some particular others they care about and see as their partners in a life-project. This partnership creates not only special human relations, but also special rights and obligations that affect our understanding of the moral sphere. The ethical implications of nationalism, which will be developed in the next chapter, are closely related to this understanding of the importance of national membership and the particular ties it creates.

F I V E

THE MAGIC PRONOUN "MY"

Recall the face of the poorest and the most helpless man whom you may have seen and ask yourself if the step you contemplate is going to be of any use to him, will he be able to gain anything by it? Will it restore him to a control over his own life and destiny? In other words, will it lead to 'swaraj' or self-rule for the hungry and spiritually starved millions of our countrymen? Then you will find your doubts and yourself melting away.   —*Gandhi*

The reputation of nationalism has been most notorious in the ethical sphere. Nationalism has been blamed for promoting intolerance, communal egoism, arrogant patriotism, racist tyranny, and genocide. Dunn argues that nationalism is the

starkest political shame of the twentieth century, the deepest, most intractable and yet most unanticipated blot on the political history of the world since the year 1900. . . . Nationalism does violate so directly the official conceptual categories of modern ethics, the universalist heritage of a natural law conceived either in terms of Christianity or of secular rationalism.[1]

In this chapter, the pervasive view of the ethics of nationalism as necessarily objectionable is rejected. Nationalism, it is argued, offers a set of moral values worthy of respect and serious consideration.

A discussion of the ethical implications of nationalism will enable us to trace the connections between feelings of belonging and moral obligations, which are not unique to membership in a nation but also to membership in other constitutive communities. The ethical approach presented in this chapter will, therefore, be referred to as "the morality of community."

The morality of community is not meant to replace liberal morality, and ties of membership are obviously not the exclusive source of moral duties. Rather, it is argued that both these approaches, in a puzzling entanglement, shape our thinking on moral issues.

There are four ways in which the morality of community deepens our thinking on moral issues. First, rather than promoting rational egoism and mutual disinterestedness, it encourages members to develop relations based on care and cooperation. These relations are crucial for the functioning of a liberal state in general, and a liberal welfare state in particular. Second, it can account for our intuition that we have a reason, at least in some cases, to favour those who share their life with us, and about whom we care deeply. Third, the morality of community demonstrates that it is possible for individuals who care about particular others and who are well aware of their specific affiliations, to agree on principles of justice. Fourth, notwithstanding prevalent views, the implications of the morality of community regarding attitudes toward nonmembers are no more and, in fact, probably less self-interested, than those derived from liberal theory. In fact, developing the morality of community leads to a much greater commitment to global justice than that advocated by most liberal writers.

The Morality of Community

One of the distinctive features of membership in a constitutive community is that members view their self-esteem and well-being as affected by the successes and failures of their individual fellow members and of the group as a whole. Consider, for example, the pride and excitement Israeli-Jews felt when the writer S. Y. Agnon became the first and only Israeli ever to win a Nobel Prize, the elation in the streets of Tel-Aviv when the Israeli basketball team defeated the Soviet team in the 1970s, and the country's delight when the Israeli representative became Miss Universe.

Members of a constitutive community are also affected by the personal achievements of their fellows in deeper ways: The achievements of others allow them to enjoy qualities that they cannot develop in themselves and profit from the results of activities they cannot pursue. The richness of their culture, the range of opportunities open to them, the norms, patterns of behaviour, and the values they hold, all are influenced by the activities of their fellow members, whose accomplishments influence their chances of living a full, satisfying, and stable life. You are men, Mazzini tells his fellow Italians, "that is, rational and social creatures capable, *by means of community only*, of a progress to which no one may assign limits."[2]

Both the development of individuals and that of humanity at large depend, according to Mazzini, on the existence of mediating associations that enable the development of a rich and meaningful life and the cultivation of personal attachments without which "there would not be enough substance or convictions in man's life to compel his allegiance to life itself."[3]

From a moral perspective, a more crucial advantage of communal life is that it allows individuals to develop and abide by "a sense of justice." According to Rawls, the development of a sense of justice is conditional on being situated, on having special relations, on fostering active sentiments of love and friendship, on witnessing the manifest intentions of others to act for our welfare. Our sense of justice is a generalization of "wanting to be fair with our friends and wanting to give justice to those we care for."[4]

Informal human communities cannot be maintained, let alone flourish, unless their members develop some sense of mutual responsibility toward each other. Were individuals not ready to dedicate time and effort, and perhaps even occasionally set aside their own interests for the sake of their friends, they would have no friends. Were diaspora Jews to stop caring for Israel and Israel for them, the communal bonds between these two parts of the Jewish people would be considerably eroded. Hence, a sense of mutual care and mutual responsibilities among members can be seen as a precondition for the personal enjoyment of all goods derived from communal life.

It could be claimed that this argument is a variation on rational egoism suggesting that, since individuals derive personal benefits from the success of their fellow members, they tend to support them in the hope of securing egoistic gains. This type of self-centered justification would still be in agreement with the general lines of the argument, presented here, as long as it is predicated on the premise that, having internalised the principle that they personally benefit by caring for their fellow members, individuals consistently endorse this mode of thinking and do not, in each particular case, reconsider their position. This position enables us to bypass the controversial question of whether, "by nature," individuals are rational egoists or sympathetic cooperators. If both positions have similar ethical consequences then, no matter how interesting this debate might be, it is of limited practical significance.

The assumption that individuals care for members of their community does not imply that they are naturally altruistic, that they have close and loving relations with every member of their community, that they are equally committed to the welfare of all others, or that they always act with the good of others in mind. I make no

attempt to idealise communities or to rely on implausible assumptions about the purportedly harmonious nature of social relationships. The truth is that we might dislike other members of our community, or disagree with them. What, then, is the basis for our relationships? It is neither love nor sympathy but connectedness, the
belief that we all belong to a group whose existence we consider
valuable. Feelings of shame or anger reflect this connectedness as
much as feelings of pride and love. "We are only ashamed of people
we are akin to—members of a particular community to which we
feel we belong," says Berlin. "We are ashamed of what our brothers
or our friends do; of what strangers do we might disapprove, but we
do not feel ashamed."[5] This discussion therefore departs from a
rather modest premise: Individuals consider it beneficial to protect
the particularistic interests and welfare of their fellow members.
Consequently, even though this endeavor might entail sacrifices,
their overriding experience will not be one of personal loss but
rather of self-fulfillment.[6]

In light of the importance that many liberal writers ascribe to
membership in constitutive communities, we would expect particular attachments and feelings of belonging to play a central role in
moral theory. In line with modern liberal philosophy, however,
Rawls argues that the "morality of association" (in many respects
similar to the morality of community), is merely a stage to be transcended in the course of our moral development. What does "tran-
scendence" mean in this context? Does it imply that we ought to act
as if personal commitments are of no moral importance, or rather
that the morality of association does not cover the whole of the
moral realm and we should view some of our moral concerns as
transcending its scope and extending beyond our fellow members to
include humanity at large? The morality of community is premised
on the latter interpretation. Rather than restrict moral duties to
members only, it argues that personal attachments intensify general
moral duties and create new ones. Even at the most developed stage
of moral thinking, that of the morality of principles, Rawls assumes
that associative ties serve to highlight moral feelings, thus making
deception and betrayal by our fellows particularly odious:

> To be sure, deceit and infidelity are always wrong, being con-
> trary to natural duties and obligations, but they are not always
> equally wrong. They are worst whenever bonds of affection and
> good faith have been formed, and this consideration is relevant
> in working out the appropriate priority rules.[7]

Although Rawls' example of the duty to refrain from committing immoral acts leaves open the question of positive duties, his argument nevertheless seems to lead to the following conclusion: When faced with an exclusive choice of alternatives between helping strangers or members of my group—be it my family, my community, or my nation—I have a stronger moral duty to help those to whom I feel close than to help strangers. It would then appear that even individuals who have reached the final stage in the development of their sense of justice, who desire to act out of a conception of right and justice shaped by parties ignorant of their own particularities ought, at times, to prefer their fellow members. Obviously, this need not imply that because our personal attachments lead to an intensified moral duty to care for the well-being of our fellow members, this duty can never be overridden by others. When the needs of strangers are significantly more urgent than those of members, our obligation to help them might indeed be greater than our communitarian obligation to prefer fellows.

Constitutive Ties—Associative Obligations

Expressions such as "How could he do that to his parents?" or "How could she not support women's rights?" illustrate well the popular perception of constitutive ties as generating special obligations. We are far more disturbed by someone who neglects his own children than by someone who fails to support someone else's children, by a person who deserts a friend in need than by one who does not help a stranger, by individuals who are indifferent to starving members of their own community than by those who do not care for starving people in faraway countries. These examples are *not* designed to suggest that we have no obligations to nonmembers in need. Rather, they stress our intuitive belief that it is particularly cruel to overlook the suffering and hardships of those we have a particular reason to care about—our fellow members.

This intuitive belief is grounded in the assumption that deep and important obligations flow from identity and relatedness. Dworkin refers to them as associative obligations, and views them as obligations that social practice imposes on members in biological or social groups, such as the responsibilities toward family, friends, or neighbours. These responsibilities can only count as genuine fraternal obligations when they are viewed as "*special*, holding distinctly within the group, rather than as general duties its members owe equally to persons outside it," and as *personal*: [that] they run directly from each member to each other member, not just to the group as a whole in some collective sense."[8]

The concept of associative obligations is often suspected of serving to cover up a desire to restrict the scope of obligations incumbent on individuals, but this is not necessarily the case. In fact, recognising the binding power of associative obligations increases rather than lessens the scope of our obligations to help others, as the following analysis will show.

When only nonmembers are in need of help the question of favouritism does not loom large, and our motivation for action stems from general moral principles. When members are involved, we are obliged to weigh their needs against those of others, and favour them only if the gap between their needs and those of nonmembers is not too wide. But there is a third category of cases, in which we are under no obligation to help others, unless they are our fellow members. Even though others may need our assistance, our circumstances at the time may be such that helping them would entail too much of a personal sacrifice. Yet the others in question may be of such importance to us that we might be willing to help them without concern for the hardships involved.

Let us look at a specific example. Ethiopians, like many other Africans, live in conditions of extreme deprivation. This gives all human beings who are better placed a reason to attend to their needs. Israel is troubled by considerable economic difficulties but is still in a better situation than Ethiopia, and is therefore under a general obligation to extend help to the best of its ability. But Israel felt it had an additional obligation to attend to the needs of a particular group of Ethiopians to which it is bound by communal ties—Ethiopian Jews. Israel, as the Jewish nation-state, embarked on a concerted effort to help Ethiopian Jews move to Israel and integrate in their new home, despite the high costs involved in such a venture. In the absence of an additional communitarian obligation, it is unlikely that such additional steps would ever have been taken. The fact that Israelis might not be ready to make a similar sacrifice for the sake of non-Jews does not negate the moral value of this act, which is still motivated by genuine concern for others.[9]

This kind of favouritism might be suspected as necessarily grounded in the idea that what is mine is more valuable than what is yours. But this conclusion would be misleading. When I claim that charity begins at home I do not intend to imply that the poor of my town are better but merely that, for the reasons mentioned above, *I* have a greater obligation toward them than to strangers because they are members of *my* community. Similarly, when *I* claim that the preservation of *my* national heritage is more important to *me* than the preservation of other national cultures, I am merely claiming that this is the case for *me*, while recognising that for members of other cultures, the preservation of *their* culture is more important to *them*. These claims do not hide a chauvinistic agenda, nor do they imply an objective hierarchy among different forms of life. They merely suggest that, based on the discussion developed in Chapter 2 regarding cultural choices, individuals will not participate in a communal life unless they assume that, for their intents and purposes, it represents the best of all viable possibilities.

Associative obligations differ in their nature, since they are contingent on the particular character of the association in question. Different types of communities—families, unions, neighbourhoods—thus generate different associative obligations, reflecting the range of issues characteristic of this type of associative tie. Consequently

> I need not act towards my partner as if I thought his welfare as important as my son's. . . . My concern for my union 'brother' is general across the economic and productive life we share but does not extend to his success in social life, as my concern for my biological brother does.[10]

Even when derived from the same type of associative ties, associative obligations arising from membership in each particular union, neighbourhood, or state, may vary depending on the particular terms of membership and on the nature of each association. Hence, we shall encounter different definitions of what it means to be a devoted friend, a loyal comrade, or a good citizen. Moreover, the intensity of associative ties varies among different cultures. In some societies family ties will generate the most important commitments, while in others they will be overshadowed by ideological, professional, civic, or national attachments.

One last feature characterises associative obligations: Since they grow from relatedness and identity, they are independent of the normative nature of the association. There is no reason to assume, as Dworkin does, that only membership in morally worthy associations can generate associative obligations. For example, members of the Mafia are bound by associative obligations to their fellow members, meaning that they have an obligation to attend to each other's needs, to protect each other, to support the families of those killed "in action," and the like. These obligations are not ultimate, and there are obviously sound moral reasons that could override them, but we cannot rule out their very existence. Similarly, citizens of a state involved in an unjust war may be torn between the feeling that they have an associative obligation to serve in the army together with their enlisted fellows, and their commitment to a moral code dictating they should refuse. In these cases, individuals face hard moral dilemmas: Should a person tell the truth or be loyal to friends? Should a Palestinian hand over to the Israeli military police a fellow national who committed a crime? Should a student tell his teacher that his best friend cheated on an important exam? There are no clear answers, and individuals may make different decisions on the merits of each case, but a moral person will be aware of the moral loss entailed by each alternative. Individuals who approach these decisions unaware of the dilemmas implied by them misunderstand the complex range of moral obligations incumbent on them.

If only morally valuable communities could generate associative obligations, the latter would become a meaningless concept. Our obligation to sustain just associations is not contingent on our membership in them but rather on the justice of the association's actions. Conversely, our obligation to help fellow members derives from a shared sense of membership rather than from the specific nature of their actions. Hence had we been born in a community of "villains" we might, nevertheless, be bound by associative obligations, although the latter could be overridden by moral obligations.

We may belong to more than one association, and some of our associative obligations could conflict. Members of national minorities often experience such dilemmas, as could also be true for women who find that an organisation they belong to endorses sexist policies, or for vegetarians who are members of a community gathering for an annual barbecue. Individuals whose multiple loyalties conflict can only consider the obligations raised by their membership in each group, weigh them fairly, and decide on a course of action.

The argument has so far dealt with associative obligations binding fellow members, but are there any guidelines prescribing how members should be treated?

On the Need for Moral Principles

Many communitarians have suggested that, in a truly communitarian society, there is no need for rules and principles, which are replaced by empathy and care. Sandel's description of an ideal community, where principles are superfluous, is a good illustration of this tendency:

> In a more or less ideal family situation, where relations are governed in large part by spontaneous affection ... individual rights and fair decision procedures are seldom invoked, not because injustice is rampant but because their appeal is preempted by a spirit of generosity in which I am rarely inclined to claim my fair share.[11]

In an ideal community of this type, one may get even less than what his "official" dues entitle him to, but this is acceptable since "the question of what I get and what I am due do not loom large in the overall context of this way of life."[12]

Liberals also tend to idealize social relations, portraying them as equal and systematic. Although clearly advantageous theoretically, this distorts their real structure. Human affections are never equally distributed, and even within their own families individuals may not be on equally intimate terms with all members. A social theory that relies on a false assumption of symmetry is bound to neglect the need for protecting those who are less liked. A vision of community in which all members love each other to the exact same degree and all relations are perfectly systematic and reciprocal is as frightening as a vision of a community without love. Furthermore, when communal relations are reduced to reciprocity, fairness, or gratitude, there is nothing special or interesting about them; they fail to add any new dimension to our moral thinking and merely become a special case of contractual relationships.

If it is not the case that affections are or should be equally distributed, however, then a human community exclusively grounded in affection will only generate fears and uncertainty. Being aware of the unequal and inconsistent nature of human emotions, it would be rational for members concerned about "not getting their due," to rely on a set of agreed principles rather than on the feelings others may harbour toward them. Only then might they agree, out of care or love, to share with others what they are rightfully entitled to receive. Following principles may not be the richest, most interesting, or most morally rewarding way to live, but they provide society with "a fall-back position and security in case other constituent elements of social relations ever come apart."[13]

Strangely, communitarianism and liberalism converge in the attempt to place all communities other than states beyond the realm of principles. Communitarians offer a view that expresses the priority of culture and tradition over justice. Moreover, since their view of community is far too harmonious, it tends to foster the illusion that principles of justice are made redundant by love and mutual care. For their part, liberals ignore the need for principles to guide communal behaviour, since they tend to play down the importance of particular communities and view the state as the only significant player in the political domain. Consequently, their main concern is to restrict the potential misuse of power by the state, while remaining almost indifferent to possible abuses of power within particular communities. Liberals assume that freedom of association entails granting voluntary communities the right to manage their affairs. Nozick, for instance, argues that "individual communities may have *any* character compatible with the operation of the framework. If any person finds the character of a particular community uncongenial, he needn't choose to live in it."[14]

This approach seems to imply that striving for a more just community is redundant. This conclusion is both misleading and dangerous. Membership in national communities affects individuals in much more important ways, than liberals tend to assume, and could become even more important in light of the model outlined in Chapter 7.

The claim that principles of justice should feature prominently in the communitarian discussion might seem to conflict with the approach to self-determination suggested in Chapter 3, which granted each community the right to manage its affairs in line with its own tradition and culture. These, nevertheless, are two separate issues. The first is whether the right to national self-determination is to be restricted only to just communities. The answer to this question is negative. Self-determination implies respect for the right of each nation to define its rules of conduct with as little intervention as possible. The second is a theoretical issue: Can liberal nationalism as a theory offer a consistent set of principles of justice valid both within and among communities? The next two sections attempt to justify a positive answer to this question.

Agreeing on Principles of Justice

Two reasons might be adduced for the view that the assumptions of liberal nationalism preclude the possibility of reaching agreement on a set of just principles by which society should be governed.

First, the concept of the contextual individual, which is the basic underlying assumption of liberal nationalism, portrays a person who, by nature, belongs to a particular community (or to several ones) and has a variety of attachments and ties. Although contextual individuals share feelings of belonging with all members of their social group, their degree of affection for each member differs—they have close and loving relations with some, and object to others. The argument that individuals have a reason for preferring those who are close to them would seem to preempt the possibility of reaching agreement on principles of justice.

Second, this task could be hindered even further by another inherent feature of liberal nationalism, namely, its basic assumption that morality is to be grounded on care rather than on mutual disinterestedness. Because of this basic assumption, liberal nationalism cannot endorse Rawls' thought experiment. According to Rawls, individuals can reach agreement because they think about justice from behind a veil of ignorance that masks their particular ties and commitments, implying that communitarian values and beliefs should be transcended in the process of thinking about justice. Ignoring communal ties is not only justified on instrumental grounds, but also by claiming that communal ties are contingent and therefore morally irrelevant.

This is the main point of contention between Rawls' position and the model suggested by the morality of community. Rawls acknowledges that individuals belong to particular communities and that these memberships are highly significant to them, or else he would not have suggested the veil of ignorance as a major feature of his model. Yet Rawls refuses to grant any moral importance to these memberships. This seems particularly odd in light of his argument that in order to develop a sense of justice individuals must be nurtured in a loving, caring community. If our understanding of the need for generalised, impartial principles can only emerge through a commitment to partiality, namely, if the former cannot be attained without experiencing and practicing the latter, then justice cannot become a permanent feature of our moral lives unless we recognise the importance of the morality of community. We pay a price for being trained to act according to principles and—strangely enough—the price is a license to be partial.

It is quite obvious that Rawls' model can only persist over time if parents, friends, and members of particular associations act partially when expressing their concern for some particular others, thus providing the conditions for a constant regeneration of the sense of justice. Impartiality would then only be required from formal institutions but not from individuals in their everyday lives. Can we detect here the remnants of a Hegelian claim, namely, that the most developed moral life is the public one, and that within the family and civil society we are doomed to experience either particular altruism or universal egoism? If this is the case, then the parties are placed behind the veil of ignorance so as to enable them to transcend the less worthy moral features characteristic of the first two stages. Yet this interpretation contradicts Rawls' own claim that, even at the stage of the morality of principles, particular relations intensify moral duties. If particular relations are morally inferior, why take them into account at all? Alternatively, Rawls could be said to place the parties behind the veil of ignorance merely as a prudential measure, without which it is feared that no arrangement would be possible. This section suggests that this complex and counterintuitive measure is redundant, and suggests ways of reaching agreement from a contextualized position.

The morality of community allows individuals to think about justice from their own, partial viewpoints. It rejects the view that to reason ethically, to consider things from a moral point of view, means to rely exclusively on an *impartial* standpoint, and argues that the essence of morality does not concern the ways in which an impersonal, disinterested self acts toward impersonal and equally disinterested others, but rather the ways in which moral agents, bound by ties and relationships, confront other, no less situated persons. It thus presupposes that, in moral behaviour, it is "not the Kantian leap from the particular and the affective to the rational and the universal that makes all the difference; it is rather the Humean step—from the self to someone else."[15] And this step cannot and should not be transcended, but should rather be at the heart of our moral thinking.

Yet, unless we can suggest a process whereby individuals can agree on principles of justice without having to transcend their particularity, extol self-interest and mutual disinterest, all that is left is a choice between a liberal model that disregards the moral importance of particularities, and a national model that precludes the possibility of attaining agreement on principles of justice. In the course of this process, individuals will not be required to redirect their motivations when thinking about justice and to view themselves as mutually disinterested, at

> great costs to those loyalties and convictions whose moral force consists partly in the fact that living by them is inseparable from understanding ourselves as the particular persons we are—as

members of this family or community or nation or people, as bearers of this history, as sons and daughters of that revolution, as citizens of this republic.[16]

This book offers a model by which contextual individuals may come to agree on a set of principles of justice, thereby challenging two of Rawls' basic assumptions: (1) that it is either irrational or immoral for individuals to consider the welfare of particular others when deciding on the moral principles that will govern their community; and (2) that individuals who are aware of their social position, their status, their communal affiliations, and their personal attachments, will inevitably act to secure their own narrow interests and will therefore be unable to reach agreement. The need for the complex restrictions assumed by the veil of ignorance is, therefore, questioned, and another model, grounded in the following assumptions, suggested below:

1.   The parties are aware of being situated and of their own particular conception of the good, as well as of a broad range of such conceptions prevalent in their community; moreover, they are aware of their own interests and preferences and appreciative of their particular ties and commitments.

2.   The parties are mutually interested and act rationally but empathetically, that is, they take into account the needs of some particular others as well as their own needs and interests.

3.   The parties are risk-averse; they do not calculate probabilities. Accordingly, they endorse the "maximin rule," ranking alternatives by their worst possible outcome and adopting "the alternative the worst outcome of which is superior to the worst outcomes of the others."[17]

4.   The parties take into consideration the fact that the agreement they reach will govern their society in the foreseeable future, although future generations may be granted the right to make changes. Hence, when deciding on principles of justice, they will take into account present as well as future interests, or what Hare calls "now for now" preferences and "then for then" preferences.[18] This does not mean the parties should think of their "then for then" preferences as having equal influence on their decision-making as their "now for now" preferences. Rather, the model assumes that it is rational for risk-averse individuals to be concerned about their future, and to attempt to protect themselves even against situations they are unlikely to occupy. Consequently, in the process of agreeing on principles of justice, it would be rational for the parties to

distance themselves from their particular ends and interests as presently conceived, thus widening their focus of concern.

5. The parties are aware of the basic structure of their society and conscious that mobility is an inherent feature of it. They understand that they may come to occupy different roles in the course of their lifetime, live in different communities, and acquire new associates, friends, and families. It is therefore rational for them to take into account the opportunities and risks entailed by the fact that social circumstances change—wealthy people may become destitute, workers unemployed, houseowners homeless, the married divorced, and the ruling party defeated. Consequently, when planning for the future, they attempt to ensure not only the position they occupy now but other hypothetical positions they may occupy in the course of their lifetimes, especially the worst ones.

6. As a result of their emotional ties with a small number of close individuals—relatives, friends, colleagues, employees—the parties are committed to consider not only their own welfare but also that of others they care about. Hence, the parties will act as if mutually interested, taking into account the preferences and interests of others. The ability to recognise and consider different points of view is a necessary stage of moral development. Throughout our childhood and youth, we develop the ability to look at reality from the perspective of others:

> First of all, we must recognize that these different points of view exist, that the perspectives of others are not the same as ours. But we must not only learn that things look different to them, but that they have different wants and ends, and different plans and motives.[19]

We are then aware that the preferences and interests of others differ from our own. Because we care about some relevant others—our children, parents, spouses, some other relatives, close friends, and colleagues—we wish to take their preferences and interests into account. We therefore find that we care to defend a much broader range of interests than our own immediate and present ones. Moreover, in the course of their lifetime, those "others" we care about may occupy many roles and social positions, hold different conceptions of the good, and have a variety of interests. It would then be rational for any party trying to secure the welfare of others to defend the variety of interests and positions these "relevant others" might hold.

The parties do not have to be able to identify completely with the whole range of interests and desires cherished by all others. It might be true, as Hare suggests, that

> I cannot know the extent and the quality of others' sufferings and, in general, motivations and preferences without having equal motivations and preferences with regard to what should happen to me, were I in their places, with their motivations and preferences.[20]

The model does not propose that the parties should adopt the position of "archangel"—that they could or should incorporate and accurately evaluate all the preferences and interests of those they care about. In their commitment to defend the interests and preferences of others, individuals may misrepresent wishes and preferences. But by taking them into account, they enlarge the scope of positions, conceptions of the good, and interests that they take into consideration.

Suppose I wish to defend a minimal number of ten different positions, which I believe I might occupy in the course of my lifetime. Moreover, suppose I am also interested in ensuring that the ten individuals closest to me find themselves in the best possible position, and they themselves could also be placed in ten different positions during their own lifetimes. Furthermore, the welfare of these ten individuals depends on the welfare of others. For instance, I care about my daughter and I know that her happiness is closely related to the welfare of her spouse, their children, and maybe that of her parents-in-law. I care for the welfare of some of my colleagues, and their welfare is closely related to the welfare of their own families and friends. Obviously, there are cases in which this type of transitivity does not work. If my spouse, whom I love, has an affair with another woman he loves, it seems reasonable to assume that my feelings for him will not extend to her. Even though this example shows that there are limits to transitivity, for the purposes of my model it is enough to show that it is valid in a significant number of cases.[21] I thus find myself concerned about many individuals who enter my range of care through my interests and concern for some closely related others.

The spread of care thus looks like a set of concentric circles—individuals care most about those in the circle closest to the centre, but are not indifferent to the welfare of those who occupy farther positions. Hence, although they begin by caring for ten individuals, they find themselves caring about many more, and may therefore be involved in protecting the interests and well-being of numerous others who could occupy a multitude of positions in the course of their lives. Since they are not "archangels," individuals are unable to estimate with any certainty what positions they should defend. Forced to take into account a wide range of interests and conceptions of the good, individuals soon discover that it is irrational for them to protect any one particular position or interest. In fact, they find themselves in a position similar to that of being ignorant of their own interests. Being risk-averse, it would be logical for them to protect the interests of the worst off and to favour the equitable distribution of those primary goods needed for the pursuit of any particular conception of the good or life-plan that they or those they care for may choose to adopt.

But what if most of the others they know are very much like them and occupy similar social and economic positions? Were this the case, would it not be rational for the parties to protect only the interests of their own ingroup? This might indeed be the case in highly polarised and rigid societies, where memberships seldom overlap. The rigid nature of their social structure, however, places these societies beyond the scope covered by this model, in which mobility, within and between societies, is a central feature. Moreover, the definition of a nation as an "imaginary community" held together by feelings of belonging and connectedness, rules out the possibility of total isolation and indifference among various subgroups. Were such cleavages deep enough, the national community would eventually collapse.

It would also be rational for the parties in this model to protect the welfare of future generations, an impossible task for the disinterested parties in the Rawlsian position. In an attempt to protect the right of future generations, Rawls found it necessary to change his principles and rely on associative obligations. Each generation, he argues, should care for its immediate descendants as fathers would care for their own children. The parties in the original position are thus advised to "imagine themselves" fathers, and if uncertain about how much they should set aside for their children, they should consider "what they would believe themselves entitled to claim from their fathers."[22] Clearly then, Rawls recognises that, at least in some cases, the parties in the original position must acknowledge the power of family attachments and of particular ties, or else the question of justice for future generations cannot be answered. Rawls is therefore forced to impose on the parties two conflicting motivations. The model presented here avoids the need for this duality since the motivations of the parties support rather than hinder the attempt to extend principles of justice to include future generations.

The parties will end up choosing principles of justice similar to those endorsed by Rawls. These principles will guide the conduct of social institutions vis-à-vis their members, namely, institutions will be bound to be impartial when it comes to the different conceptions of the good, interests, and preferences held by their members. But knowing that their first duty is to their members, these institutions will act to promote the latter's well-being and give preference to the interests of their members over those of nonmembers. Partiality and impartiality may therefore be justified in different contexts.

According to this view, the relevant distinction is not between the public and the private sphere but between attitudes toward members and nonmembers. We can now reformulate the central claim of the morality of community that members should come first, and re-define it as follows: Whereas partiality toward members is justified, one ought to be impartial among members. The model offered here regarding the formulation of principles of justice could be ap-plied in any large community with similar results, namely, imparti-ality among members would be endorsed as the valid rule of conduct.

The relevant group should thus be defined in each case. For exam-ple, one of the implications of the right to culture discussed earlier was that different cultural groups have a right to establish schools that cater to their specific needs. It is justified for these schools to favour children who belong to the group they are meant to serve, but it would be unjustified for them to discriminate in any way among these children. When hiring workers for an Afro-Caribbean community centre, it might be justified to prefer Afro-Caribbeans, but it would be unjustified for the Afro-Caribbean director to prefer her sister over all other candidates.

These examples illustrate how overlapping memberships compli-cate the picture and might lead to moral dilemmas. Suppose I am a member of a municipal committee selecting candidates for a munici-pal program, and my best friend is among the applicants. Do I have a reason to prefer him? In my capacity as a member of this commit-tee, my reference group is the community at large, and I must there-fore act impartially toward all the candidates who meet the resi-dence requirement. Only after the committee has ruled on this issue, do I have reason to speak to my friend, and to my friend only, and sympathise with his disappointment, or share his delight for getting the job.

At times, dual loyalties might lead to personal tragedy. Suppose that a general has to decide which of three battalions will be sent into a dangerous battle, and he knows that his son is serving in one of them. As a father, the general has a duty to protect his son, but as a military commander he should send the best battalion and disregard his personal concern. By doing the right thing, the general could indeed find himself in the very tragic position of being forced to send his son to an almost certain death.

The morality of community thus assumes that to be just normally presupposes not only that

> an agent is attached to certain abstract concepts and ideals, but also more fundamentally that he is attached to and cares for his community, and that he has a sense that his own good and that of those he cares for most is associated with the general adherence to [some] ideals.[23]

It thus ignores neither the power of particular attachments nor the need for principles. It recognises the binding force of membership and the particular duties derived from it, although without granting them ultimate priority. It therefore argues that, knowing what is the right thing to do in each case demands that we weigh a wide range of considerations, some mutually incompatible and incommensurable. Untidy compromises do not merely reflect difficulties in the implementation of moral principles but the deeper, inherent complexity of the moral sphere.

Caring for Nonmembers

Why are we so troubled by the idea that charity begins at home? Why is it so morally disturbing to think that we have special relations with our fellow members, and that these relations require us to attend to their needs before we attend to the needs of nonmembers? In short, why are partiality and favouritism so morally worrisome?

It seems that our aversion to favouritism is not so much related to the notion of caring for particular others as it is to the idea of conferring legitimation on an attitude that disregards the needs of nonmembers. It is for this reason that even those who accept some measure of favouritism as justified, tend to restrict it as much as possible. Dagger, for example, suggests that compatriots take priority only in the case of "other things being equal."[24] This view tends to minimise the significance of membership, by implying that we are only justified in providing for the welfare for our fellow citizens if all other noncitizens are needy to the same degree. But this is never the case. Most of us believe that we should first attend to the needs of our own citizens, allowing for a much greater deviation from universal principles than the one justified by the notion of "other things being equal." This implies that we tend to grant membership, as well as the obligations that follow from it, a much more substantive role in our moral thinking than Dagger would care to admit.

Gewirth attempts to justify ethical particularism on universal grounds, and argues that the right of individuals to establish voluntary communities derives from universal principles of human rights. Voluntary associations have special collective purposes which, in turn, "justify the particularistic, preferential concern that members have for one another's interests."[25] This preferential concern, however, cannot "extend to violate the moral rights of other persons."[26] This approach thus focuses the discussion on the rights of others and its scope depends on the understanding of these rights. "Rights" can be interpreted in negative terms, namely, as the right to act freely and without external intervention. This interpretation leaves very broad scope for particularistic rights; in fact, the only duty to outsiders would be to refrain from interfering with their lives, "to leave foreigners as we found them."[27] This approach makes allowances for extensive preferential treatment, and turns any form of support for nonmembers into supererogatory acts. But if nonmembers are also supposed to enjoy positive rights, such as the right to be sheltered, fed, and educated, it becomes very difficult to justify any form of partiality. In these circumstances, distributing resources among members would be justified only if it could be proven that, in doing so, we are not depriving nonmembers of their rights. Therefore, the license to favouritism within Gewirth's argument might be either too restricted or too broad. In fact, the problem with most liberal justifications of favouritism is that they imply much greater favouritism toward members then they care to admit.

Let us assume that the parties in Rawls' original position were to decide on their attitude toward nonmembers. Since they are aware of their membership in a particular society, and since they are self-interested, it would be rational for them to refuse to share *any* of their resources with nonmembers. While this argument is developed in greater detail in the next chapter, its conclusions are also relevant to the present discussion: If liberal morality indeed endorses a more radical form of favouritism and social egoism than that advocated by the morality of community, then some of the strongest objections against the moral implications of nationalism are misplaced.

But the morality of community has another advantage, deriving from the nature of modern membership. Modern individuals belong to a complex network of memberships, which is conducive to allaying fears about nonmembers. After all, the same people who are not members of one community we do not belong to—say a church—could be members of another community we are affiliated with—say a union. Hence, those we consider our fellow members do not necessarily belong to one closed and homogeneous group. If each individual has different circles of membership, and if there is no one ultimate membership that includes all others, the distinction between members and nonmembers becomes blurred. Given the nature of memberships in the modern world, the morality of community need not be as xenophobic as would appear at first glance. I see myself as an Israeli, but I am also a member of the academic community and therefore committed to the notion of academic freedom. I therefore have a duty to support Palestinian colleagues in their struggle to reopen the universities closed by the Israeli army in the West Bank. Obviously, the duty to defend academic freedom is a general duty, but the fact that I am a member of the academic community and share this membership with members of other nations intensifies my duty to defend their interests. Hence, I am less troubled by the fact that brokers at the Israeli stock exchange failed to organise a sit-down strike in solidarity with Palestinian academics, than by the fact that no Israeli university has officially done so.

In the previous section we concluded that the morality of community justifies favouritism, implying that in each particular case it is justified to favour members, namely, those who belong to the group relevant to the action in question. The answer to the question of who is a member will, however, vary in line with the activity being considered. When considering whether to contribute money to a political campaign, one should take into account one's political loyalties rather than one's family ties. I need not support a member of my family who upholds a political position I oppose. But when deliberating whether I should contribute a kidney to my sister, her political opinions will be irrelevant.

The morality of membership is often assumed to lead not only to xenophobia, but also to extreme communal egoism. Berlin forcefully attacks egoistic memberships of this kind:

Finally, by a development which need cause no surprise, full-blown nationalism has arrived at the position that, if the satisfaction of the needs of the organism to which I belong turns out

114

to be incompatible with the fulfillment of the goals of other groups, I, or the society to which I indissolubly belong, have no choice but to force them to yield, if need be by force. If my group—let us call it nation—is freely to realise its true nature, this entails the need to remove obstacles in its path. Nothing that obstructs that which I recognize as my—that is, my nation's—supreme goal, can be allowed to have equal value with it.[28]

This is an adequate description of the moral implications of national theories providing ultimate justification for the absolute priority of the needs of fellow members. The integration of liberal and national values inherent in the morality of community, however, precludes the possibility of granting ultimate value to national goals. We should be careful not to obscure the difference between the selfishness characterising the ultimate versions of nationalism Berlin speaks of, and the individualistic liberal nationalist approach, which justifies the right of individual members of every nation to give preference to the shared pursuit of common interests. This distinction resembles that drawn by Barry between selfishness and individualism. Selfishness, argues Barry, is "the pursuit of one's own interests without regard to the interests of others," while individualism is "the doctrine that it is legitimate to pursue one's own interests on the same terms as those on which others are free to pursue theirs."[29]

While liberal nationalism suggests that individuals have a reason to be concerned with the welfare of their fellows before they are concerned with the interests of nonmembers, it places this argument within the framework of a universal theory. Participants in communal struggles, patriots, and devoted nationalists, suggests Mazzini, are not to be freed from asking themselves the Kantian question:

You must ask yourself whenever you do an action in the sphere of your country, or your family . . . if what I am doing were done by all and for all, would it advantage or injure humanity? And if your conscience answers, it would injure humanity, desist; desist, even if it seems to you that an immediate advantage for your country or your family would ensue from your action.[30]

Communal membership will be meaningless unless individuals learn to see it as tied up with their own identity, and perceive fellow members as partners in a shared way of life, as cooperators they can rely on. Having developed this attitude, they cannot but care for

115

other members, wish them well, delight in their success, and share in their misfortune. These feelings provide individuals with a reason to attend first to the needs and interests of their fellows. If the moral force of such feelings is denied, ruling out any special attention to fellow members, the social structure might collapse and we shall be left with isolated individuals and an abstract humanity.

SIX

THE HIDDEN AGENDA:
NATIONAL VALUES AND
LIBERAL BELIEFS

Recent versions of nationalism seem to lend little credence to the liberal nationalist position offered in previous chapters. Witness the bloody struggles in Yugoslavia, the violent clashes between Sikhs and Hindus in India, and the frequent outbursts of ethnic hatred within and between the new republics of Eastern Europe. A cursory glance at the surrounding reality could easily lead to the conclusion that liberal nationalism is a rather esoteric approach.

Nevertheless, there is a long-standing though much denied, alliance between liberal and national ideas that might explain the inconsistencies pervading modern liberal theory: Why is citizenship in a liberal state more commonly a matter of birthright and kinship rather than choice? Why do liberals believe that individuals owe political loyalty to their own government—as long as it acts in reasonably just ways—rather than to the government that is demonstrably the most just of all? Why does the liberal welfare state distribute goods among its own citizens, while it largely ignores the needs of nonmembers? The answers to these questions direct us to the national values hidden in the liberal agenda.

The Restricted Scope of Distributive Justice

Questions about distributive justice play a central role in modern liberal theory. Yet, the fact that the liberal welfare state is necessarily predicated on certain "national beliefs" is often overlooked. Its conception of distributive justice is only meaningful in states that do not see themselves as voluntary associations but as ongoing and relatively closed communities whose members share a common fate. Within such communities, members develop mutual attachments that supply the moral justifications required for assuming mutual obligations, without which the idea of a "caring state" is unsustainable.

According to Sandel, the liberal welfare state is based on a paradox, that is, it pursues policies predicated on social care in a state based on individualistic values:

It is a striking feature of the [liberal] welfare state that it offers a powerful promise of individual rights, and also demands of its citizens a high degree of mutual engagement. But the image that attends the rights cannot sustain the engagement.[1]

Willingness to assume the burdens entailed by distributive justice, therefore, rests on an assumption that liberal theory cannot itself provide, namely, a feeling of relatedness to those with whom we share our assets, "some way of seeing ourselves as mutually indebted and morally engaged to begin with."[2] The "other" with whom we share the fruits and burdens of cooperation must be identifiable and familiar.

Liberal theory also fails to give a convincing account of another element crucial to the functioning of the welfare state, namely, the roots of social union, the social forces that keep society as a distinct, separate, and more significantly, a continuous framework. Rawls suggests that social unity and the allegiance of citizens to their common institutions are founded on an agreement regarding some guiding principles of justice.[3] But this agreement is too thin, and is insufficient to ensure the continued existence of a closed community in which members care for each other's welfare, as well as for the well-being of future generations.

A justification of inward-oriented distributive policies is dependent on the notion of communal ties and loyalties. Indeed, liberals have no choice but to presuppose the existence of such ties and "treat community as prior to justice and fairness in the sense that questions of justice and fairness are regarded as questions of what would be fair or just within a particular political community."[4] Although granting priority to the community and restricting distributive policies to members can hardly be considered a self-evident liberal tenet, there have been no serious attempts to justify this approach, and liberal philosophers have seldom addressed this issue. Rawls might seem to be deviating from this tendency when he claims that the last stage of our moral development is "the morality of principle." After grasping the importance of acting fairly, we accept the rationality of the two principles and develop a desire to act justly. This desire commands us to adopt a moral behaviour that recognises no boundaries. Clearly, says Rawls, a sense of justice and a love of humankind are two closely related sentiments, largely defined by the same conception of justice: "If one of them seems natural and intelligible, so is the other."[5]

But if the move from the morality of association to universal morality is so natural, why not advocate one global system of distributive justice? Why does the principle of equal respect and concern apply only within rather than across political frameworks?

Supported by an obscure use of terminology, Rawls' theory of justice indeed appears to be universally applicable, while in fact it is not. A just society, Rawls argues, should adopt the following two principles:

1. Each person has an equal right to a fully adequate scheme of equal basic rights and liberties, which scheme is compatible with a similar scheme *for all*.

2. Social and economic inequalities are to satisfy two conditions: first they must be attached to offices and positions open *to all* under conditions of fair and equality of opportunity; and second, they must be to the greatest benefit of the *least advantaged* members of society.[6]

Although the usage "for all" could be construed as pointing to a universal context, it nevertheless refers only to members. If, however, the "morality of principle" rests on a claim of universality, it is unclear how are we to justify the particularisation of distributive justice, or why we should give priority to the welfare of the "least advantaged members of our society" over that of starving children in Ethiopia.

Rawls does not justify the particularisation of distributive justice, but several arguments could be advanced in support of this view. For instance, it could be suggested that it is logical for the parties placed in the original position to adopt the principle that "charity begins at home." As claimed in the previous chapter, contractarian arrangements inevitably lead to social egoism. Social egoism could be avoided if, and only if, the contract is made to include all human beings. Unless liberal theory can satisfactorily explain why a social contract should include only certain individuals while leaving others out, a global contract seems the only possible option, making "the life prospects of the globally least advantaged the primary standard for assessing our social institutions."[7] Rawls does not choose this option and prefers, like other liberal writers, to "start from what is and grope towards the ought."[8] The "is" in this case is a world divided into nation-states. But a coherent liberal theory should either endorse this world order and explain its virtues, or reject it and suggest ways of changing it. Accepting it without explaining it seems unjustified.

Another approach to the question of why distributive policies should only consider the needs of members is to argue that distributive justice apportions the fruits of social cooperation: Only those who have participated in one way or another in the production process deserve a share of the goods. But those most in need are frequently those who have not participated in the production process—the "worst off" could be unemployed, seriously handicapped, ill, drug addicts, minors, or old. It seems safe to assume that at least some of them have not contributed to the production of goods, yet most liberal philosophers would suggest that these very groups should be the first to benefit from welfare policies. Therefore, entitlement needs to be justified on grounds other than the contribution to the production of goods to be distributed.

The notion of "charity begins at home" could also be justified on instrumental grounds: In practical terms, we are simply better equipped to promote the welfare of the members of our own society, and these attempts should therefore be given priority. In and of itself, however, the instrumental argument cannot cancel the principle that we are still bound by a duty to attend first to the needs of those who, by some agreed global standard, are worst off. In fact, the instrumental argument merely suggests that, after we have classified "all" those in need, when "all" is defined as a global category, we should examine our ability to help them in terms of a costs and benefits estimate. Preferring members of our own society would only be justified if it could be proven that our ability to help them far exceeds our chances of helping nonmembers. The availability of modern technologies and of means of communication and transportation suggests that such cases are relatively few and far between. In the context of the present argument, what is even more significant is that liberal writers seldom offer this argument—the duty to help nonmembers is not ruled out due to specific difficulties, but is rarely raised at all.

The contractarian approach to distributive justice could pursue an altogether different line of argument to justify the idea that we owe special duties to the members of our own society. In a society based on contract, members could be said to enjoy special rights and duties by virtue of this contract. On this basis, we could claim that fellow citizens bestow and impose on each other reciprocal rights and duties.[9] But if we indeed have a moral duty to help those who are worse off on a global scale, contracting among ourselves to overlook this duty and give priority to our own needs would be a strictly immoral act.

The notion of the morality of community developed in the previous chapter, sustained by the concept of the contextual individual, suggests a solution to this problem. The "others" whose welfare we ought to consider are those we care about, those who are relevant to our associative identity. Communal solidarity creates a feeling, or an illusion, of closeness and shared fate, which is a precondition of distributive justice. It endows particularistic relations with moral power, supporting the claim that "charity begins at home." Moreover, the morality of community can serve as grounds for justifying the allocation of resources to the well-being of future generations, and to the study and preservation of the communal past. Consequently, the community-like nature of the nation-state is particularly well suited, and perhaps even necessary, to the notion of the liberal welfare state.

Terms of Membership

The terms of membership prevalent in liberal states reinforce the view of the state as more than contingent associations held together by a formal contract, which individuals can enter or leave at will. Two major issues involving terms of membership force liberals to resort to national ideas:

Demarcation: Since liberalism cannot provide a theory of demarcation, it has adopted for this purpose the national ideal of self-determination.

Continuity: In order to sustain its character as a law-abiding and caring community, the liberal state must view itself as a continuous community rather than as a casual association of parties to a contract that could be rescinded at any time.

Surprisingly, liberal literature hardly deals with membership. It would appear that, on the basis of liberal premises, it is hard to say much about appropriate criteria for distinguishing between members and nonmembers. Barry indeed criticises individualist tradition for its neglect in developing criteria appropriate for the determination of membership in a state. The three traditional positions on this issue are so weak, he argues, as to be "a serious embarrassment to anyone sympathetic to the general individualist enterprise." The first attitude is "simply a refusal to take the question seriously, [as] is Locke's contract of association: people somehow got together to form a political society and this society then set up a particular form of government."[10] The contractarian tradition takes the existence of the group for granted. It can help us understand the type of social arrangements and moral principles agreed upon, but this explanation can only begin after individuals have gathered together in order to form a group. In itself it cannot, however, account for any of the principles leading to the creation of groups in the first place.[11]

Since the contractarian approach takes society as a given, the voluntary nature of membership becomes hypothetical. Rawls outlines the nature of this claim very clearly:

> No society can, of course, be a scheme of cooperation which men enter voluntarily in a literal sense; each person finds himself placed at birth in some particular position in some particular society, and the nature of his position materially affects his life prospects. Yet a society satisfying the principles of justice as fairness comes as close as a society can to being a voluntary scheme, for it meets the principles which free and equal persons would assent to under circumstances that are fair. In this sense its members are autonomous and the obligations they recognize self-imposed.[12]

Accordingly, hypothetical voluntarism assumes that rational human beings who relate to their membership in society as a given, could be persuaded to agree to the terms of a social contract that will further their own interests. But can we also assume that they are likely to agree to their position as members? Taking this issue for granted might seem to imply that individuals do not care to which society they belong as long as it is governed by principles of justice. The importance of national identity, the effect of cultural membership on individual preferences, and the ability to become an equal member of a political unit, do not loom large in this type of argument.

The second approach Barry refers to is a purely instrumental one. It suggests that it is possible to specify in universal terms the interests that states exist to protect, and that appropriate state boundaries could be derived from these principles:

Boundaries in this view, are to be determined on a technical basis, and not with any reference to the desires of the inhabitants to be associated politically with some people and not others. Such theories are characteristic of market oriented economists whose only use of the state is as a remedy for "market failure."[13]

But this technical view of the state obviously contradicts the voluntary nature of the association, and could not be acceptable to liberals.

The third approach to the issue of demarcation is predicated on notions of culture, communal identity, and self-determination. Barry points to the limitations inherent in this view:

If [self-determination] is put forward as a right of each individual, it hardly makes any sense, except as an alternative way of expressing the Lockean consent theory: and it breaks down in just the same way wherever there is a lack of agreement because some people want one boundary and the others want another— which is of course, the only context in which there is any problem in the first place.[14]

It seems that Barry dismisses this option far too quickly, however, because he confuses two separate questions: the justification for establishing a separate political entity on the one hand, and agreement on the territory this entity should occupy on the other. In some instances, the notion of self-determination is indeed not sufficient to solve territorial disputes. Obviously, if two groups are deeply attached to a particular territory for historical, national, and religious reasons, and they demand to realise their right to self-determination in the same territory, appeals to this right are not conducive to a solution, but they could be useful regarding a deeper type of demarcation. They can justify our respect for the wishes of a group to preserve its distinct nature by separating itself from all others. Why should we—Jews, Palestinians, Basques, or Irish—establish our own separate political entities? Because there is something distinct about us that we wish to preserve and the best, although not the only, way of doing this, is ensuring for ourselves a public sphere imprinted with our own cultural and political institutions.

Although a national group can preserve its uniqueness in ways other than the establishment of an independent state, states can only justify their separate existence on national grounds. State boundaries might be the result of wars, conquests, secessions or peace agreements. If there is no morally acceptable justification of these events, however, the integrity of these boundaries might be repeatedly questioned: If they are neither natural nor justified, why should they be respected? If the state is nothing but the product of a human contract, why not put this contract to a new test? Why not ask nonmembers to join in, and respect their wishes when they do? Liberal theory cannot give adequate answers to these questions. Modern states have, therefore, chosen to adopt national self-determination as their justifying principle, even when their members do not constitute a nation. This serves two purposes: It provides them with a principle of demarcation, and it strengthens the claim that members of the state share something more than coordinating institutions, something that evokes in them feelings of solidarity and fraternity. Terms of membership set by the liberal state thus reinforce the view of the state as a distinct historical community rather than as a voluntary association.

The Priority of Birthrights

Unlike natural communities, which are shaped by history and destiny, liberal associations are voluntary; individuals are free to join them or opt out of them at will. The liberal tradition views states as voluntary associations of this type, while relating to nations and ethnic groups as communities of fate.

But this is a false distinction, as states and nations belong to an intermediate category; strictly speaking, they are neither voluntary associations nor communities of fate. In the modern world, most individuals are born into a nation and a state, thus making membership in these associations a matter of destiny rather than choice. Nevertheless, although the usual way of acquiring membership in both the state and the nation is by birth, membership remains elective as long as individuals can join or leave.

Citizenship is indispensable for the well-being of modern individuals. Stateless persons are deprived of protection, lack civic and welfare rights, have no passport, and officially belong nowhere. Without a country, Mazzini tells his fellow Italians,

> you have no name, token voice, nor rights, no admission in the fellowship of the peoples. You are the bastards of Humanity. Soldiers without a banner, Israelites among the nations, you will find neither faith nor protection; none will be sureties for you.[15]

124

Citizenship is therefore a primary good that all individuals deserve. The Universal Declaration of Human Rights states in Chapter 15 that "each person is entitled to citizenship." But in which state? Are people entitled to acquire citizenship in any state of their choice? If states were strictly voluntary associations, the answer to this question would indeed be yes. So why is this not so?

All associations draw boundaries between members and nonmembers, and establish terms for acquiring and foregoing membership. These terms reflect the nature of the association and the way in which its members understand their mutual affiliations. If liberal states are seen as based on a covenant between free individuals who have contracted among themselves to create a political framework meant to defend their rights and serve their interests, it would seem reasonable to assume that membership will be granted to all those who actively consent to share in this covenant. Preference would then be given to those who are most committed to the agreed upon principles and ends, and who are best qualified to further the aims of the association. A liberal state resting on these assumptions would grant citizenship only to informed adults who actively request it, thereby expressing their willingness and consent.

Nevertheless, even though self-professedly voluntary associations, liberal states have preferred birthright over choice as a criterion of membership. For example, most liberal states automatically grant citizenship to their citizens' descendants, even if the latter never visited their parents' state and never explicitly declared a wish to become members of it. At the same time, outsiders who appreciate liberal values and wish to become members of a liberal state have to apply for membership and face the risk of rejection. Why not limit the right to obtain citizenship to those who actively ask for it? And why are not all applications considered on equal grounds? In fact, why place restrictions on membership at all? Instead, why not accept all those who wish to join?

Liberals could perhaps claim that restrictions on membership are a necessary condition for fulfilling the purposes of the association, claiming that a voluntary association may legitimately restrict membership in order not to harm the interests it was meant to protect. Suppose a group of individuals decides to establish a club for the purpose of playing bridge once a week. At the club there is room for only twenty tables; after accepting 500 members, the club rejects all further applications. It would seem unreasonable to suggest that members are morally obliged to agree to play only once a fortnight in order to enable others to join the club, as this would hinder the interests the association was established to serve.

Let us look at another example. A group joins together to create an operatic society. They decide to meet once a week to listen to operas. If an outsider committed to change the musical repertoire of the society were to request membership, she could justifiably be rejected on the grounds that the society was formed in order to foster a particular kind of activity, and members wish to preserve this aim.

But why do the existing members of a voluntary association have a right to exclude others who wish to join it? Is it morally right for them not to consult nonmembers, at least regarding decisions that significantly affect the latter's future, such as terms of membership? These questions are even more significant when what is at stake is the right to acquire citizenship. Membership in a state differs in two major respects from membership in voluntary associations of the kind we mentioned. First, the allocation of rights and services in the modern world depends on membership in a state, turning the latter into a necessity. Second, in the case of a bridge club or an operatic society, those who are refused membership can easily create an alternative association, but new states are not so easily established. Is it then justified to refuse citizenship to certain individuals on the grounds that members desire to protect their interests—as in the case of the bridge club—or on the grounds that members desire to retain the particularistic nature of the association—as in the case of the operatic society?

A state can claim that it is justified in restricting membership on the grounds that it can only accommodate a limited number of members if it desires to serve their interests and provide them with a modicum of welfare. For example, it appears rational for risk-averse individuals placed behind the veil of ignorance to agree to let go of those wishing to leave, while restricting, or even banning altogether, the entrance of new members, unless they bring with them their own resources or can, in some way, contribute to the society at large and particularly to the welfare of those worse off. Consequently, we could reject requests of membership submitted by poor and unqualified individuals on the grounds that those members of society who are presently worst off are the most likely to be hurt by their immigration. Note, however, that when a society decides to allow entry only to those who might contribute to the welfare of those worst off, it is attending to the needs of its own members rather than to those of nonmembers. Such extreme restrictions on membership might seem exceedingly unfair, not least because those who make them are precisely those most likely to enjoy their outcome, but also because the resources that members distribute among themselves are often obtained through factors not directly contingent on them. These factors could include luck, strategic and geographic advantages, certain valuable resources, or worse still, the past exploitation or appropriation of others' wealth, land, or manpower. Why should those who, by a stroke of luck or due to a historical process, are fortunate enough to belong to a prosperous society, continue to enjoy their good fortune without sharing it with others?

If demarcation can only be justified on contractarian grounds, and if we have no right to contract among ourselves to disregard the needs of others, then a consistent liberal argument should advocate the removal of restrictions on membership. All those who wish to become members should be accepted, irrespective of the possible deleterious effects of an influx of new members on the welfare of the present ones. If liberal theory is unable to justify a situation in which "noncitizens must depend upon the policy choices of *citizens* if they are to acquire rights on their own behalf,"[16] it should advocate that barriers be pulled down and allow the market to control immigration.

A different situation emerges, however, when the state is not merely viewed as a gathering of individuals striving to improve their lot, but rather as a community struggling to preserve its distinctive character. Assuming that individuals have a right to preserve the uniqueness of their communal life, it would make sense to place some restrictions on membership and claim that we, who already belong, should do the choosing "in accordance with our own understanding of what membership means in our community and of what sort of a community we want to have."[17] This view of immigration laws, as designed to preserve the unique nature of the state, is the official policy of many nation-states. Hence, Turkey was ready to absorb Turkish refugees fleeing Bulgaria; Israel regards every Jew as a potential citizen; and before unification, West Germany granted automatic citizenship to East Germans or to anyone defined as part of German culture. It is worth noting that this national approach does not imply that members of affluent nation-states are free to disregard the needs of others who are not members of their nation, but only that we should differentiate between attending to the needs of nonmembers and accepting them as members.

Ackerman is one of the few liberal theorists who grapples with the problems raised by the concept of citizenship in a liberal state. He claims that liberal states should not be regarded as private clubs but as the arena of a public dialogue, so that "in an ideal theory *all* people who fulfill the dialogic and behavioral conditions have an unconditional right to demand recognition as full citizens of a liberal state."[18]

Should the liberal state then open its borders to all those, but only to those, who are able to participate in the liberal dialogue? Ackerman thinks it should. The only qualification required for membership is the ability to participate in an intelligible way in the social dialogue of justification. However, in order "to be intelligible, one's utterance must be translatable into a language comprehensible to other would-be participants. It is this chain that links the theory of citizenship to a theory of translation."[19] This definition is truly puzzling. It implies that, beyond an ability to understand the terms of participation, and beyond the willingness to take part in a liberal discourse, membership in a liberal state demands an ability to share in the ruling culture; it demands that members share certain cultural features that facilitate a deeper type of understanding.

Ackerman himself sustains this interpretation of his view in the following statement:

> The relationship between the theory of translation and the theory of politics has, I think, been ignored in recent liberal writings. Indeed, one often gets the impression that only the "sciences" of human choice—like economics and decision theory—are central to the concerns of liberal political philosophy. And since I will also call upon such techniques at later stages in the argument, it is important to emphasize that we are lost without the sciences of culture as well as the sciences of choice.[20]

This passage would seem to suggest that, in order to engage in a fruitful dialogue, citizens of a liberal state must agree not only on the principles of their discourse, but must also share some sort of cultural and social background. Mill endorses a similar position when he argues that linguistic homogeneity is a necessary condition for democratic politics to work, since it is only through this homogeneity that citizens can take part in the same political debate.[21] Unfortunately, these suggestions were never fully elaborated, and the cultural dimension of membership in a liberal state has remained practically unexplored.

It would appear then that there are two requirements for membership in a liberal state:

1. General civic competence—the readiness and the ability to communicate, argue, and discuss matters with fellow citizens, and to form judgments on the basis of this dialogue
2. A shared culture and identity—the competence to act as a member of *this* particular society.

Prospective citizens must be able and willing to be members of this particular historical community, its past, its future, its forms of life and institutions. "In a community that values the autonomy and judgment of its members, this is obviously not a requirement of pure conformity. But it is a requirement of knowledge of the language and the culture."[22] A state that views itself as a community is justified in offering citizenship only to those committed to respect its communal values, collective history, and shared aspirations for a prosperous future.

But what if one is part of the culture but rejects the rules of the game? If the state were indeed an association based on contract as much as it is a community based on culture, it would be reasonable and justified for it to proclaim at the outset that those who do not intend to follow the "rules of the game" will fail to qualify as members. No contract, either public or private, should be signed with an individual or a party that, a priori, announces an intention to break it. Hence, a militant anarchist or a religious fundamentalist who openly declares an unwillingness to follow the agreed social code, should not be accepted as a member.

But here again we have an example of a liberal state following a communal rather than a contractarian approach. Suppose that someone who is a citizen of a state by birthright becomes a militant anarchist or a religious fundamentalist. Should the state consider withdrawing that person's right to citizenship? Liberals would probably not agree with the suggestion that there could be circumstances under which the state would be justified in denying citizenship. Breaking the law deserves punishment, but in no case could a declaration of intention to break the law serve as grounds for withdrawing citizenship. The native anarchist would then remain a citizen while others, sharing his views but not born in the state, would fail to qualify for membership. In this case, birthright overpowers the most elementary terms of membership required by a contractarian theory. The notion of the state as a freely entered social contract is discarded in favour of feelings of kinship and belonging typical of community-like associations. In a community of this type, it would be natural for members to show more concern for self-perpetuation than for adherence to the rules of the game. Those born and educated within the state, who were trained to see it as their own, are therefore preferred as future members.

This discussion makes clear that the liberal assertion that "it seems best to regard the state as an association rather than a community" is misleading.[23] Modern states, even liberal states, have adopted the conception of the nation-state, and therefore see themselves as communities rather than as associations based on contract. The perception of the state as a community will become even clearer when we turn to a discussion of political obligations. In line with the main argument of this chapter, the next section discusses the inevitable "nationalist assumption" behind the liberal conception of political obligations.

A Question of Obligation

This section applies the notion of associative obligations developed in the previous chapter to the political sphere. It is argued that the only way of justifying a central role for political obligations in liberal philosophy is to adopt the description of the liberal state as a community that generates a particular type of associative obligations, namely, political obligations.

The concept of political obligations has been widely discussed in liberal theory.[24] Liberal philosophers define political obligations as obligations voluntarily assumed by free and rational agents, thereby implying consent and offering grounds for the legitimation of state authority. Nonetheless, political obligations in a liberal state are not assumed in as free and rational a process as is commonly argued. This process entails free and rational considerations as well as emotional and intuitive elements. Alongside national obligations, political obligations thus belong to the wider category of associative obligations, that is, obligations rooted in feelings of membership in a particular association. These obligations are generated by social associations that induce among their members feelings of membership and belonging, as well as the belief that the preservation of their society is a worthy endeavour. Members thus see themselves as partners engaged in a shared and ongoing effort, which generates mutual responsibilities and obligations, care for future generations, and respect for the communal past.

Dworkin indeed suggests that political obligations could count as associative obligations, but liberal philosophers have ignored this possibility for two main reasons:

First, communal obligations are widely thought to depend upon emotional bonds that presuppose that each member of the group has a personal acquaintance of all the others, which of course cannot be true in large political communities. Second, the idea of special communal responsibilities holding within a large, anonymous community smacks of nationalism, or even racism, both of which have been sources of very great suffering and injustice.[25]

The fear of nationalism, however justified, is hardly a reason to over-look the importance of a category of obligations which, according to Dworkin, most people believe themselves bound by. Although Dworkin clarifies the liberal reluctance to place political obligations under the rubric of associative ones, this is nonetheless a necessary step.

A political obligation is a requirement to support and maintain political institutions, obey the laws, participate in the political pro-cess, defend one's country, and the like. The voluntaristic approach embodied in the liberal claim that political obligations are assumed by free, rational agents, runs into several difficulties.

In most of the literature on political obligations it is taken for granted that all citizens enjoy—or are burdened with—the same po-litical obligations. One argument alone, however, cannot possibly serve to justify the assumption of political obligations by all the in-habitants of a liberal state.[26] If explicit consent were the only possible basis for political obligations, then members of the state who do not actively declare their agreement should be released from political obligations. Since most of the population, or at least large segments of it, fail to express such explicit consent even through the minimal act of casting a vote during elections, it would appear that they have no political obligations. But the presence of large groups of citizens unencumbered by political obligations would cast doubts on the view of the state as a voluntary association whose authority is grounded on consent. Liberals must therefore find ways of dealing with the difficulties caused by the reluctance of most citizens to per-form acts that could be taken as indications of their consent.

Tussman suggests that only those who have consciously agreed assume an obligation; all others—"non-consenting adult-citizens"—

should be treated as minors who are governed without their consent. This argument bases the authority of the government on the consent of an active elite, and overlooks the fact that the silent majority did not explicitly consent to delegate its authority. Pitkin points out that this argument renders the notion of general consent irrelevant to the obligation to obey the government:

> You are obligated to obey a government that is legitimate authority, whether you personally consented to it or not. If you have consented, you are obliged as a member; if not, as a child. . . We are all obliged to obey a government based on the consent of the aware elite, the true members, whether or not we have consented. A government is legitimate when those who are aware consent to it, and it then becomes legitimate for all its subjects.[27]

Pitkin's criticism sheds light on the problems entailed by Tussman's interpretation of the consent theory: Either obligations are restricted to a small elite, or most of the citizens must be treated paternalistically.

A second group of arguments suggests that political obligations should not be based on consent but on gratitude: Obligations are a way of paying the debts one owes the state, following the enjoyment of benefits and services one has received from it. But this is a very problematic basis for political obligations.

Let us examine these two options in the application of this approach. The first argues that, following the acceptance of certain services or goods and *regardless* of our awareness of what this acceptance implies, we assume obligations. According to the second, we can only assume an obligation if, before we receive certain goods or services, we are aware that accepting them entails an obligation. If I borrow a book from a fellow student while unaware that she takes this to imply that I thereby consent to help her with her studies, it can hardly be claimed that I have assumed an obligation to help her. But if, prior to my taking the book, she makes it clear that her condition for lending it to me is that I help her with her exams, then my accepting the book creates an obligation, even without an explicit promise. This obligation is based on consent to the terms of the exchange:

> In the absence of consent, one might indeed claim that the enjoyment of certain social goods and benefits might provide a reason for supporting the state and enable others to enjoy its

benefits too, but having a reason is different from having an obligation. If accepting goods or services from the state would automatically create obligations, there would be no voluntarily assumed political obligations—by the time one is capable of rationally considering one's willingness to assume them, one would already be in debt for all the numerous goods and services already received. Disregarding the fact that these goods and services were usually accepted at a stage when we could neither reject them nor evaluate their meaning, renders the notion of freely assumed obligations meaningless. We are thereby deprived of our ability to reflect on, evaluate, and at times reject the obligations imposed on us by the mere fact that, from birth, we have enjoyed certain benefits from the state. But if receiving a benefit or accepting a service only creates obligations when accompanied by conscious consent, the benefit theory is reduced to the consent theory, and we are back to the initial problem.

This argument does not deny that gratitude can indeed influence the willingness to assume obligations, but rather suggests that gratitude, in and of itself, is not a conclusive and binding reason for doing so. Suppose state A sends special forces to save the survivors of a sinking ship, who are citizens of state B. It would be odd to claim that these survivors, who are probably very grateful to the state that saved them, now owe political obligations to state A rather than to state B. On its own then, the gratitude argument cannot be a basis for political obligations.

Another justification for assuming political obligations could rely on a normative evaluation of the political framework—given the moral obligation to support just institutions, if one regards a government as advancing justice then one has a moral obligation to support it. But these terms raise a new difficulty: "It is not so much your consent nor even the consent of the majority of the aware few in your society that obligates you. You do not consent to be obligated, but rather are obligated to consent if the government is just."[28] If the obligation to obey a just government is not a political obligation but a moral one, why do we owe political obligations to our own state unless it is ruled by the fairest of all governments? Consider the suggestion that we are bound to support or obey just, beneficial, fair, and efficient governments. The fact that we regard a state, any state, as worthy of support, is obviously relevant to the question of how we ought to act toward it. As this evaluation cannot be "particularised," however, it cannot be used to sustain the notion of political obligations to a particular state, unless we compare different governments and obey the fairest of all.[29] But this leaves open the most essential question related to political obligations: Why do I have obligations to my own state, assuming that it is reasonably just, but not to the fairest of all states? If we cannot answer this question by reference to the normative argument, then we must admit that the attempt to ground particular political obligations on universal, moral justifications has proven unsuccessful.

The process by which we assume political obligations to a particular state, *our* state, can only be understood in light of their nature as associative commitments, whose moral importance is derived from the notion of membership rather than from general moral duties. In what way does our membership in a specific state affect our moral ties with it and turn it into the object of our obligations?

The Associative Nature of Particular
Political Obligations

If the concept of political obligations is to become meaningful in the real world, it must address the following question: Do we have any reasons for assuming political obligations to our own state? We may feel we owe an obligation to a state where justice and fair play have attained perfection, but it would be hard to define this as a political one. By contrast, we might feel we owe a political obligation to our own state, which is not completely just. Having said that, the claim that we are free from assuming political obligations to a perfectly just state that is not ours clearly cannot imply that members of that state should be released from their political obligations, but only that justice, by itself, is not sufficient reason for assuming political obligations.

When seeking justifications for particular political obligations, the question cannot be addressed from the neutral standpoint of a detached self, but rather from the position of a contextual individual. Justifications for assuming political obligations must therefore be grounded, at least partly, on the way in which individuals understand their own social position. The fact that we are citizens of a particular state, however, is a necessary but not a sufficient condition for creating obligations. Citizenship is a formal concept, based on legal criteria rather than on feelings of membership, but formal attachments cannot, in and by themselves, sustain such obligations.

If citizenship in a particular state could explain the nature of obligations owed to it, the discussion about consent would be meaningless.

We must differentiate here between the two aspects of membership described by the following two statements:

Formally X is a member.
X feels that he is a member.

The second statement is the one that carries the thrust of the associative argument, suggesting that one is bound by obligations because one sees oneself as a member. Suppose that a child is born to Israeli parents living in the United States, and automatically acquires Israeli citizenship. The child may not even be aware of the fact that he carries Israeli citizenship, has never visited the country, and has no interest in it. His formal possession of Israeli citizenship is meaningless to him and cannot possibly generate any obligations. Similarly, people who are aware of their formal membership but have consciously rejected it cannot be presumed to be encumbered by obligations. If someone aquires, by birth, citizenship in a state he despises, his formal membership cannot serve as grounds for generating obligations to that state.

Associative obligations must therefore be based on some sense of belonging, on an active and conscious discovery of one's position, and on an affirmation of this position. One may have acquired associative membership in a particular social group by birth rather than through voluntary choice, but unless one identifies with this membership, it cannot generate obligations. In this restricted sense, we could approach associative obligations as voluntarily assumed.

The assumption of associative obligations thus depends on feelings of belonging and identification with the association. The associative approach to political obligations thus suggests that individuals assume such obligations because they see the state as *their* state, its laws as *their* laws, and its government as *their* government. As Raz claims, it is mistaken to dismiss these views as a blind and groundless acceptance of authority. Individuals assume such obligations because they

identify with their society and hold themselves to be under an obligation to obey the law which they regard as expressing that attitude. This attitude is not consent. It is probably not something initiated by any specific act at any specific time. It is likely to be the product of a gradual process as lengthy as the process

135

of acquiring a sense of belonging to a community and identifying with it.[30]

Although these obligations are acquired in the course of a socialisation process, they are "as valid as an obligation acquired through consent and for precisely the same reasons."[31]

But the process of socialisation is relatively independent of the moral nature of the society. A sense of membership in a state is established well before individuals are able to make normative evaluations. Furthermore, it is possible to feel alienated from a just and moral society and develop a sense of membership in an unjust society, which is precisely what worries the liberal philosopher and leads him to rule out belonging as a criterion for political obligations.

Raz assumes that consent to obey the laws of an unjust government is not a morally appropriate expression of identification with one's society.[32] But what is the meaning of the phrase "morally appropriate expression of identification"? It seems as if Raz is arguing that it would be appropriate to identify only with morally virtuous societies, a claim that probably suits a liberal viewpoint but misses the essence of the associative thesis, which is that we are affiliated and therefore morally obligated, rather than morally obligated and only then affiliated.

It is now clear how the morality of community, by insisting on a relationship between membership and obligatins, has a bearing on the present argument. Let us consider the following case. An Israeli who is firmly committed to the existence of the state of Israel might view the Israeli occupation of the West Bank as an extremely immoral act. When called up for military service in the occupied territories he faces a moral dilemma, torn between his desire to act justly and his obligation to the state. Whatever his personal decision, the fact that he faces a dilemma suggests that, although aware of the state's immoral policies, he still feels an associative obligation to it. He may in the end decide not to serve, but this would merely suggest that, when balanced against other obligations and against the particular circumstances of the case, particular associative obligations may be overridden by more general moral ones.

This example also illustrates the claim that feelings of belonging, on which associative obligations rely, emerge independently of the moral nature of the state. In fact, even members of groups who feel that they themselves have been wronged, such as members of deprived classes, or women, may still feel they have a reason to support the state that has mistreated them. As long as, despite their victimisation, they retain a feeling of belonging, they will feel obliged. This sheds light on the true essence of associative obligations: They are not grounded on consent, reciprocity, or gratitude, but rather on a feeling of belonging and connectedness.

Two conclusions can be drawn from this view of political obligations as a type of associative obligation. The first and most important is that individuals assume obligations to a state not only because it is effective as a mechanism of coordination and as a protector of their rights and interests, but rather because it serves as an object for their identification. They comply with its rules, support its institutions, and are willing to defend it to their death, because they see it as their own.

Second, if their state issues laws and policies they see as unjust, they will have to reflect and decide whether to obey them or not but, in so doing, the fact that they owe associative obligations to the state will be considered and weighed along with other arguments. Hence, the associative nature of political obligations does not imply unconditional obedience and loyalty to the state, but rather suggests that feelings generated by membership and identification play a central role in shaping one's decision concerning obligations to a particular state.

Simmons claims that we should reject the requirement of singularity of ground, namely, the requirement that there be one and only one set of grounds for political obligations, as well as the demand of the "universality of political obligations over some range of persons (e.g., over all men, over all citizens of a particular state, etc.)."[33]

Four ways of assuming political obligations can be construed as the basis of this argument:

1. Assuming *particular* political obligations. Some individuals will assume political obligations solely on the basis of their feeling of belonging. The fact that the political system represents the social group with which they identify will suffice to evoke their consent, and they will support their country "right or wrong." For members of this group, feelings of belonging will act as a necessary and sufficient condition for assuming an obligation. This need not be an unreflective process: Individuals can reflect on the notion of membership and adopt it only after critical deliberation but still believe that, once they have assumed membership, their loyalty and obedience to their group must be unconditional.

2. Assuming *justified particular* political obligations. Members of the second group will assume political obligations on a dual basis—

a sense of belonging coupled with a moral and functional evaluation of *their* state. Justified political obligations are assumed in two stages: While at the initial stage individuals acquire a sense of belonging to a particular political system, the second stage entails the moral evaluation of the system itself. Moral judgment is thus reintroduced into the realm of political obligations. Individuals in this category will only assume obligations to a state after judging it worthy of their moral support, but they will not seek out the most just state of all in order to turn it into the object of their political allegiance.

Feelings of belonging thus act as a preliminary condition, necessary but not sufficient for assuming justified political obligations. It is a preliminary condition because it emerges before the question of political obligations arises, and it is necessary because it provides a guideline as to which political framework is a relevant object of evaluation. It is insufficient, however, because it could lead one to assume political obligations to unjust states.

3. The assumption of *justified* political obligations. In this third group, individuals will assume obligations solely on the basis of a moral and functional evaluation of the state's policies and activities. For members of this group, moral evaluations are a necessary and sufficient condition for assuming obligations. These are the rare and unusual individuals who will only feel obliged to the most just state of all.

4. A fourth group includes individuals who neither feel a sense of belonging to a state nor evaluate it to be reasonably just, and therefore see themselves free from all political obligations. They may still recognise the government's authority to perform a broad range of acts and may feel committed, in the name of fair play, to obey a broad range of laws and policies. The absence of political obligations does not necessarily imply the justification of disobedience or revolution.[34] A state, however, can only accommodate a limited number of individuals who think of themselves as unencumbered by any political obligation since, in any substantial numbers, such individuals would threaten its stability.

Acknowledging the associative aspect of political obligations may help explain why certain individuals develop obligations to a particular state without formal citizenship in it, on the basis of feelings of belonging, as is the case for members of diaspora groups. It can also help explain why members of national minorities, notwithstanding their formal citizenship in it, may feel alienated from a state and consequently released from any obligations to it. It is thus clear why the state has greater authority over certain individuals than over others.

The main advantage of the approach presented here is its ability to place normative evaluation within a context. It can explain why most of us assume, and rightly so, that our obligations are not to the state that is the most just of all, but to our own state, as long as it is reasonably just.

The associative nature of political obligations can explain why, in a world made up of nation-states perceived as playing not only a coordinating but also an expressive role, most citizens feel they owe their state obligations. Ironically then, the liberal notion that the legitimacy of a state's authority is to be grounded on the consent of most, if not all citizens, can best be accomplished in the modern world of nation-states, a reality presenting liberals with a serious dilemma: They can either disregard associative ties as not important, thereby failing to explain why most individuals owe political obligations to their own states, although these states are less than perfectly just, or be forced to admit that associative obligations are morally significant, thereby supporting some version of the morality of community.

The perception of political obligations as associative reinforces the national view of the state as a locus of identification rather than as merely a formal mechanism for the just allocation of resources and the protection of rights.

It was argued that modern liberalism has incorporated certain national ideals, a development that has enabled it to retain its dominant position in a world of nation-states. By absorbing national concepts, liberalism has been able to take for granted the existence of states inhabited by specific populations, and discuss notions like distributive justice, consent, obligations, participation, and social responsibility in reference to this reality. Liberals were thereby able to circumvent such thorny issues as membership and immigration, as well as the more general question of how groups are structured. These moves have made modern liberal theory dependent on national ideals and a national world order, thus leaving liberals little choice. Except for some cosmopolitans and radical anarchists, nowadays most liberals are liberal nationalists.

S E V E N

MAKING A VIRTUE
OUT OF NECESSITY

There are parts even of Europe, in which different nationalities are so locally intermingled, that it is not practicable for
them to be under separate governments... There is no
course open to them but to make a virtue of necessity, and
reconcile themselves to living together under equal rights
and laws. —*John Stuart Mill*

The modern concept of the state draws inspiration from both liberal
and national ideas. These two schools of thought could have joined
in an ideal marriage: Nationalism could have supplied parameters
for demarcating state boundaries, buttressing the view of the state as
a community characterised by the mutual responsibility and the internal cohesion required by a welfare state, while liberalism could
have provided the moral principles needed to guide personal and
institutional behaviour. Indeed, many nineteenth-century liberals
believed that "individual liberty and national independence or unity
would go together,"[1] and that liberal principles could best be implemented within a homogeneous nation-state. "Free institutions are
next to impossible in a country made up of different nationalities,"
argues Mill. "Among a people without fellow-feeling, especially
if they read and speak different languages, the united public
opinion, necessary to the working of representative government,
cannot exist." Thus, Mill thought it necessary that "the boundaries
of the government coincide in the main with those of nationalities."[2]

So why did this promising engagement come to a bad end? Why
are today's liberals so averse to nationalism? One obvious answer
relates to the history of nationalism in the twentieth century, when
it broke away from the tradition of Herder, Mazzini, Mill, Naumann
and others, and assumed the distorted features of fascism, nazism,
and racism. The horrendous results of this unholy alliance drove

postwar liberals to adopt a strictly universalistic approach and adhere to principles that were formulated without regard for colour, race, sex, or religion. As Kymlicka has accurately pointed out, the struggle of blacks and women for equal rights has contributed to the intensification of this trend; any deviation from universalist arguments on grounds of national or cultural rights was henceforth objected to, fearing it would legitimise "separate but equal" discriminatory policies.[3]

The liberal state thus emphasised its role as a neutral mediator and as an honest broker of individual interests, forbidden to promote or express any particular life-plan or conception of the good, and ensuring all members an equal chance to pursue their individually defined goals. The state was not only supposed to act as if it had no bias toward one particular colour, culture, gender, or religion, but was indeed supposed to be free of all identifying characteristics or associations with particular groups or individuals. The state was therefore seen as an embodiment of abstract humanity, representing those universal human qualities that unite all human beings. All dividing features were to be removed from the public sphere. Family affiliations, religious alliances, and professional ties were all viewed as private matters inconsequential to political life: The true nature of political agents was their citizenship, equally shared by all.

But the liberal state has in practice continued to operate within the constitutive assumptions of the modern nation-state and to see itself as a community with a distinctive culture, history, and collective destiny. The growing dissatisfaction of ethnic groups and national minorities living within liberal states lends persuasive support to this claim. Members of these minorities feel excluded from the public sphere because they realise that it achieves an appearance of disinterest in cultural issues by exclusion, namely, by rejecting all those who do not belong to the dominant culture.

The continued existence of national minorities attests that the national ideal of "a state to each nation," despite its wide acceptance, has never been implemented. Why this gap between the ideal and its realisation? Why was the principle of national self-determination implemented in ways leading to the creation of states that were nationally heterogeneous and perpetuated the problem of national minorities? On what grounds can one justify the persistent adherence of modern politics to the concept of the nation-state, an obviously utopian ideal that could never be implemented? What moved liberal states to shy away from the recognition of their national premises? This chapter is concerned with these questions.

A State to Each Nation—An Unattainable Ideal

The fundamental principles underlying the establishment of nation-states after the First World War closely resembled Mill's liberal nationalism. In the spirit of Wilson's Fourteen Points (1918), these principles stated that a new European order should be based on the right to national self-determination, and it was this belief that guided the participants at the Paris Conference when they redrew the map of Central and Eastern Europe and replaced the old dynastic borders with new ones. Wilson therefore demanded changes in the Italian border, autonomy for the ethnic groups within Austro-Hungary, independence for the Balkan states, autonomy for Turkey and for the ethnic groups living there, the liberation of Rumania and Montenegro, and independence for Serbia and Poland.

Yet, as Mill had already noted in 1861, there were major difficulties in implementing the national ideal of a state for each nation, the most prominent being the geographic one. There were (and still are) areas in Europe where members of different nations are so closely intermingled that it is impossible to grant each an independent nation-state. This is particularly true in light of the interpretation of national self-determination prevailing at the time, namely, as a stage in the social evolution of human units developing "from family and tribe to county and canton, from the local to the regional, the national and eventually the global."[4] As long as national self-determination was expected to be part of a linear process of historical evolution leading to increasingly larger social units, the idea that it should also be granted to groups wishing to secede and create their own small, homogeneous national units was a priori ruled out.

In the Wilsonian era, this tendency to prefer unifying national movements was reinforced even further. The prevailing belief at the time was that only large states could be free and progressive, while small ones were doomed to dependence and oppression: The ideal state was nationally and culturally homogeneous, politically centralised, economically and technologically developed, and militarily powerful, namely, self-sufficient, and thus free. Consequently, only nations in sovereign states able to attain economic, strategic, and political autonomy were considered capable of enjoying self-determination.

The borders of the new states established in the Paris Agreement were drawn with these aims in mind. As far as possible, every state received a variety of agricultural areas, industrial resources, and access to the sea. Hence, Poland gained access to the Baltic Sea through German-populated areas, and industrial Bohemia, agricultural Slovakia, and Ruthenia were combined to create the multinational state of Czechoslovakia. Sudetenland, a mountainous area endowed with what was considered an easily defensible border, was annexed to Czechoslovakia, despite the fact that most of its population was German-speaking.

But the belief that only viable independent states could ensure national self-determination in the end hindered the implementation of the national vision. Whenever considerations of independence and viability conflicted with aspirations for national homogeneity, the former took precedence. As a result, most of the successful struggles for independence in the postwar era were led by movements striving for unification rather than for secession. This was true for Germans, Italians, Poles, Rumanians, Yugoslavians, Bulgarians, and Greeks. The supremacy of the viability principle, combined with the desire not to harm the integrity of existing states is crucial for understanding why, in many cases, rather than solving the national problem, the newly drawn boundaries sowed the seeds of national unrest. Stateless nations that had hoped to secede and establish their own state, and nation-states whose fellow nationals were scattered over several states and aspired to annex these territories found no support for their demands. These separatist and annexationist movements could, indeed, find legitimation in the ideal of national self-determination, but advocates of national liberation were in no rush to support them. The fear of Balkanisation, of the fragmentation of existing states into small, antagonistic, and nonviable units, was much too strong. In fact, since the acceptance of Bangladesh, the international community has not granted recognition to any secessionist movement until the breakdown of the Soviet Union.

Let us take a brief look at the result of these policies in Western Europe, the cradle of nationalism. Although their numbers are hard to estimate, many citizens of Western European nation-states see themselves as members of national minorities living in a state that does not fly their flag. Are the Scots, the Welsh, the Lombards, the Bretons, or the Corsicans national minorities? If this is so, then a large percentage of Europe's citizens could indeed count as members of national minorities.

Modern nation-states have attempted to blur the fact that they are composed of different national groups by fostering a liberal-democratic definition of the nation. According to this definition, all those who inhabit a particular territory and live under the rule of the same government are members of the same nation, but modern history has time and again refuted the claim that citizenship and membership in a nation are one and the same. No amount of conceptual manipulation could do away with the problems aroused by the presence of minorities.

National minorities had lived under foreign rule long before the emergence of nation-states, but "the problem of national minorities" surfaced in full force only in the aftermath of the First World War, following the dissolution of empires. The establishment of nation-states did increase the number of people who came to be ruled by their fellow nationals. It also resulted in a considerable number of national minorities left to be ruled by others, and feeling deprived and threatened due to their failure to accomplish their national aims. In a world of nation-states, being a minority not only entails subjection to foreign rule, but also forfeiting recognition as a distinct national group. The most palpable expression of disregard for stateless national groups was, and still is, that international institutions such as the League of Nations or the United Nations, in spite of their names, accept only states as members.

National minorities found subjection to the nation-state more oppressive than imperialistic rule for a further reason. Empires had indeed been perceived as a foreign ruling power, but had left cultural matters to the discretion of national groups. By contrast, the nation-state was not only assigned administrative, economic, and strategic functions, but also adopted a particular cultural and national identity. Consequently, in order to be considered full-fledged citizens, individuals had to identify not only with the state and its institutions but also with the culture of the ruling nation. State involvement in cultural issues deeply affected the self-image of national minorities, which came to feel that the effort to shape all the citizens of the state into one homogeneous nation destined them for erosion. Mobilization of the masses, socialization, cultural uniformity, nation-building, assimilation, all the magic words of modern nation-states, became the national minorities' nightmare.

The new European nation-states were forced to pledge respect for the religious, linguistic, cultural, and political rights of the national minorities remaining within their borders. Poland, Rumania, Czechoslovakia, Greece, and Yugoslavia committed themselves to respect the rights of minorities, and the League of Nations established a commission to oversee the implementation of these agreements, but arrangements proved unsuccessful. Their weakness lay in the fact that these provisions had been designed to comply with the demands of minorities as these had been formulated in the era of large empires. At that time, national minorities could have been satisfied with a limited measure of economic and political rights and a modicum of cultural and religious autonomy, but in the era of nation-states, this was no longer enough.

Homogeneous nation-states were revealed as a pipedream, and the illusion that liberal and national ideals could be fully accommodated within one political framework could thus be expected to fade away. Although many national movements continue to entertain this dream, present reality demonstrates that attempts to make it come true inevitably lead to bloodshed. Renouncing the ideal of a homogeneous national state allows us to explore a new set of options. One option that liberals might view as the most plausible is a state that is nationally and culturally neutral. This ideal cannot be implemented, however, since cultural differences are part and parcel of the political reality rather than merely private matters. Liberal nationalism advocates taking cultural and national differences into account, acknowledging that members of national minorities, even within the most liberal of states, have legitimate grievances, and formulating ways of alleviating them.

The Illusion of Neutrality

Historically, neutrality has not been a prominent feature of liberalism. For as long as liberalism supported the minimal state and was mainly concerned with negative freedom, it could be claimed that "the *sine qua non* of liberal states, in all its varieties, is that governmental power and authority be limited by a system of constitutional rules and practices in which individual liberty and equality of persons under the rules of law are respected."[5] But as soon as the state assumed a more active role, extending far beyond nonintervention, liberalism could not do without a notion of state neutrality. For welfare liberals, or left liberals as they are at times called, equality came to mean distributing the fruits of social cooperation so that members could enjoy equal opportunities in the pursuit of their life-plans and conceptions of the good. A liberal political entity is thus to be recognised not only by the freedoms it protects but also by the neutral distributive principles it adopts.

A minimal state, because of its "thinness," could be viewed as neutral even when endorsing a particular conception of the good, as long as it refrained from interfering in the lives of all its members to the same extent. All that was needed was for the minimal state to

L

show tolerance and forbearance toward those holding different conceptions of the good. But for the welfare state, which is committed to act in ways that will ensure all its members equal chances in the pursuit of their life-plans and conceptions of the good, neutrality must mean more than forbearance and toleration. It would appear that the welfare state can choose to endorse only one of two available versions of neutrality. The first and more modest one is defined by Mendus as "causal neutrality," namely, neutrality regarding reasons for action. This form of neutrality implies that the government should not aim at disbenefiting certain groups simply because they hold a particular conception of the good. The second and more strict form of neutrality concerns not only reasons but also outcomes, and suggests that "no laws should be passed or policies adopted which make it easier to pursue one conception of the good rather than another. . . . Where the reason based argument precludes only actions *designed* to bring about disbenefit, this principle rules out actions which will *in fact* bring about disadvantage."[6] But it is impossible to be neutral in this second sense. The state is forced to take a stand on social, political, moral, and economic questions, and those who agree with state-advocated policies have a better chance of pursuing their own life-plans and conceptions of the good. For instance, even barring any formal restrictions on communist activities in the United States, the chances Communists have to pursue their life-plans will obviously be considerably smaller than those of individuals who identify with the American ethos. Under these circumstances, granting members equal rights is not enough to ensure them equal opportunities, since the worth of these rights is higher for those who identify with the ethos of the governing institutions. Hence, ensuring that all members enjoy an equal chance to pursue their own conceptions of the good requires that the state refrain from endorsing any particular conception of the good and act solely as a coordinating apparatus. But restricting the role of the state so severely would be of no help, since even the most general procedural principles reflect beliefs about what is fair and efficient. Views about the fairness of procedures express a certain conception of the good, as views about efficiency cannot be fully developed unless ends are assigned, and the assignment of ends necessarily reflects a view about personal well-being and the preferred social order.[7] This is particularly true in welfare states, which cannot avoid taking a stand regarding distributive policies. Any attempt to implement a strict interpretation of neutrality in a welfare state is therefore doomed to failure.

In the neutralist position, the state has a secondary role in the lives of its citizens: "the state is not itself to pursue the good life—whatever that may be—; it is simply to establish and maintain the ground rules within which others can engage in that pursuit."[8] The state is viewed as an abstract and impersonal entity, above and distinct from both the government and the governed, different from society both in terms of its special functions and in terms of the peculiar character of the authority it exerts. State institutions are therefore assumed to reflect the strength of legalism and codification, show concern for formalisation and depersonalisation, and emphasise the universal nature of the state, thereby making it equally accessible to all its members. But this attempt to portray political institutions as aloof from all interests and desires is both illusory and oppressive,[9] since it confers on the particular values guiding state actions the status of universal, impartial rationality, and projects anyone opposed to state policies as advancing a particularistic, self-serving stand that challenges impartial, rational judgments. This perception places political dissidents, be they women, members of minority nations, or opposition parties, at a disadvantage. This leads to a paradoxical result: The attempt to relate to all members equally culminates in an ideal discriminating against anyone outside the consensus, opposed to state policies, or protesting its actions.

Welfarism led the modern liberal state in two conflicting directions—while forcing the adoption of distributive policies that necessarily reflect a certain set of values, it also fostered the ideal of neutrality. The result was a morally biased state, unwilling to acknowledge its own inclinations and deluding itself into believing that it was free from any particular conception of the good.

The Cultural Origins of Politics

Welfarism has not only led to a normative, but also to a cultural bias. Inspired by the ideal of welfare, liberals abandoned the notion of the minimal state and replaced it with that of the caring state. The need for justifying mutual responsibilities and fostering support for redistributive policies brought the welfare state to present itself as a community, sharing an ethos of a common past and a collective future, including notions of closure and strict demarcation between members and nonmembers.

It could still be claimed that, in spite of its communal features, the welfare state can adopt a neutral standpoint regarding culture thus allowing all its members an equal chance to pursue their particular cultural allegiances. This claim entails a fallacy, as the chances of members of minority groups to promote their cultural life are more restricted than those of the majority. Continued adherence to the notion of cultural neutrality prevents the modern welfare state from acknowledging the disadvantages suffered by minorities, and the need to ensure them special rights and protection.

Political sociologists view the modern nation-state as culturally biased for reasons much deeper than the instrumental grounds suggested so far. The political structure of every state, argues Pye, is inevitably rooted in the native genius of the ruling nation. This is the very essence of the notion of political culture:[10]

> The concept of political culture assumes that each individual must, in his own historical context, learn and incorporate into his own personality the knowledge and feelings about the politics of his people and his community. Each generation must receive its politics from the previous one, each must react against that process to find its own politics.[11]

One thing that everyone knows but no one can quite demonstrate, says Geertz, is that "a country's politics reflect the design of its culture."[12]

> Between the stream of events that makes up political life and the web of beliefs that comprise a culture it is difficult to find a middle term. . . . Culture, here, is not cults and customs, but the structure of meaning through which men give shape to their experience; and politics is not coups and constitutions, but one of the principal arenas in which such structures publicly unfold.[13]

The cultural essence of the state comes to the fore in its political institutions and in the official language, as well as in the symbolic sphere, in the selection of rituals, national heroes, and the like. Attitudes toward the political system, the psychological orientation toward social objects, political norms of behaviour, the interpretation of history promoted by the governing institutions, all unavoidably reflect a particular culture. For example, the Israeli parliament is called the Knesset, after the "Great Knesset," a central religious and political institution in the period of the Second Temple. Modeling itself after "the Great Knesset," the Israeli parliament has 120 members. Its symbol, the seven-arm candelabra, was a traditional ritual object. Hebrew is one of the official languages of Israel (alongside Arabic); the Sabbath is the day of rest.

Could this be avoided? Could a state develop a totally neutral political structure, equally unconnected to the culture of any one of its citizens? Perhaps, but at the risk of alienation and irrelevance. Geertz uses the example of Indonesia to illustrate this point. As a result of 200 years of Dutch occupation, the patterns of official life became disjointed from popular culture and sentiments. Indonesia suffered from a fragmented party system, the enfeeblement of formal law, and the marginalisation of government activities. States, claims Geertz, can acquire legitimacy only if their acts are seen as "continuous with the selves of those whose state it pretends it is, its citizens—to be, in some steeped-up, amplified sense, *their* acts." Citizens do not have to agree with what the state does in order to see its acts as "theirs"; "it is a question of immediacy, of experiencing what the state 'does' as proceeding naturally from a familiar and intelligible 'we.'"[14] This claim sheds further light on the view of political life developed in the course of this work, as extending far beyond the procedural sphere and as an expression of cultural identification.

As those who create the political system, legislate its laws, occupy key political positions, and run the state bureaucracy have a culture that they cannot avoid bringing into the political domain, the separation between state and culture is revealed as an impossible endeavour. Members of minority groups thus feel alienated from the public sphere, less able to understand its cultural origins, less capable of playing according to the "rules of the game." They can, of course, decide to become acquainted with the culture of the ruling nation, but this demands that they devote time and efforts that members of the majority culture can invest elsewhere. Furthermore, members of minority groups, argues Kymlicka, can be outbid or outvoted on a range of issues crucial to the survival of their communities, a threat that members of majority cultures simply do not face. As a result "they have to spend their resources on securing the cultural membership which makes sense for their lives, while members of the majority culture get theirs for free."[15]

If the liberal pretenses of neutrality at large and of cultural neutrality in particular are indeed only pretenses, and if belonging to a minority group unavoidably carries with it social, political, and frequently economic disadvantages, we might conclude that no national group should be forced to live as a minority. But why should only national minorities have a right to a place of their own, where they can constitute the majority, while Communists or vegetarians are not entitled to similar rights? It is certainly as hard to pursue a communist way of life in the United States as it is to pursue an Inuit life-style in Canada. One answer could be that members of the Communist party or vegetarians have no desire to isolate themselves, but instead wish to persuade the majority to adopt their views, while members of national minorities have no such desire. They consider their way of life appropriate to them, but only to them, and it is for this reason that they seek segregation from the rest.

This discussion makes clear that although it cannot be ensured that each nation will have its own state, all nations are entitled to a public sphere in which they constitute the majority. The ideal of the nation-state should therefore be abandoned in favour of another, more practicable and just.

Global Responsibilities, Regional Organisations, Local Autonomies

Abandoning the ideal of a state for every nation requires us to redefine concepts like sovereignty, independence, and national self-determination, and reevaluate their mutual links. The distinction suggested in Chapter 3 between the right to self-rule and the right to self-determination could inform an alternative perspective.

Were we willing to accept that the right to self-rule and the right to national self-determination need not be fulfilled within the same framework, we would have to ask what the proper scope of implementation for each one of these rights is. The most probable answer is that the scope should correspond to their purpose. The right to self-rule is meant to allow individuals to participate in the making of those decisions that have a major influence on their lives. Defining the relevant framework thus requires us to define the political structures in which such decisions are likely to be taken. Since the end of the Second World War, independent states have agreed to restrict their autonomy, and cross-national economic cooperation—involving the development of joint policies, effective regulations, and continuous coordination—seems to have become the order of the day. What is true in the economic sphere is certainly true at the strategic level: Only large, regional organisations can develop the military power required for adequate defense. Ecological problems also require regional, maybe even global, cooperation. In their attempt to ensure security and prosperity, modern states have become increasingly dependent on each other. The need for cooperation requires them to delegate authority for significant decisions to a regional level including, for instance, taxation brackets, production quotas, quality control, and the like, not to speak of the placement of ballistic missiles and nuclear plants. Due to the growing influence of regional institutions on the life-prospects of individuals, implementing their right to self-rule requires them to organise in order to affect the character and the function of regional bodies. (The term "regional" as used here indicates organisations above state level.) This does not suggest that local authorities, or even neighbourhoods, should have no power to make economic or ecological decisions, but rather that such decisions should be guided by principles decided at the regional level. Clearly then, self-rule implies that individuals should affect all levels of the decision-making process.

By contrast, implementing the right to national self-determination leads in the opposite direction. National identity is best cultivated in a small, relatively closed, and homogeneous framework, which neither wishes nor needs to reach beyond the members of the nation. This is, therefore, a process motivated by the need for cross-national alliances on the one hand, and by the persistent strength of aspirations for national segregation on the other.

Conventional wisdom suggests that this leads to two excluding options: either to a postnational, integrated, and peaceful world, or to a Balkanised world of small states involved in relentless war. Were this the case, it might indeed be logical to surrender national aspirations in favour of peace. But a third option emerges from the discussion so far, whereby nations might enjoy the right to national self-determination together with the benefits accruing from membership in broader political alliances. We saw in Chapter 3 that only by replacing the aspiration of an independent state for each nation with more modest solutions such as local autonomies, federative or confederative arrangements, could all nations come to enjoy an equal scheme of national rights. Ensuring the ability of all nations to implement their right to national self-determination would then lead to a world in which traditional nation-states wither away, surrendering their power to make economic, strategic, and ecological decisions to regional organisations and their power to structure cultural policies to local national communities.

Sheltered under a regional umbrella, all nations, regardless of their size, resources, geographical position, or economic viability, can acquire cultural and political autonomy and secession no longer constitutes a problem. Indeed, many of Europe's small nations, which failed to establish independent nation-states, look forward to European unification. The Corsicans, Basques, Catalans, and Irish nationalists rightly assume that, as a self-professed multinational entity, the EC will not seek to shape a homogeneous cultural commu-

nity, nor will it follow the undesirable tradition of international organisations to include only states. The EC could become a community of nations that openly recognises the diversity of its constitutive
units. An instance of the respect and recognition shown by the
emerging EC for particularistic sentiments as long as these do not
threaten the union, is the creation of an office for "languages in
lesser use, to encourage the preservation and revival of ethnic
languages."

The fact that a regional organisation is more likely to foster conditions that will enable smaller nations to prosper suggests a further
justification for the creation of such bodies. Contrary to the usual
justification adduced for regional cooperation, namely, that it allows
individuals to transcend their national attachments, the merits of
cooperation can now be couched in terms of its value to the free
pursuit of national life.

Indeed, not all nations will be equal within a regional organisation. Some will probably be stronger than others and the use of some
languages will be more widespread; one or two will probably be
chosen as the lingua franca, but this agreement will express a technical need for communication rather than an attempt to identify the
whole region with a particular culture. Viewing this as an instrumental decision rather than as a way of promoting assimilation has
important psychological advantages. One can provide a justification
for a lingua franca on instrumental-utilitarian grounds, namely, that
it will facilitate communication, broaden professional prospects,
open a wide range of occupational and political roles, and set all
members of the regional organisation on an equal footing, whereas
it would be unjustified to attempt to assimilate members of minorities in order for them to achieve these same benefits. The simultaneous move toward cooperation on the one hand and segregation on
the other thus grants small nations benefits denied to them in the age
of nation-states.

Regional cooperation is also advantageous for members of large
nations which, no matter how big and prosperous, could never offer
their members the benefits they can obtain through a regional organisation. Nations should also take into account long-term considerations, and recognise that power and prosperity are unstable factors: One nation finds oil, another has access to the sea, a third has
fertile lands. But markets change, oil prices fluctuate and wells dry
up, air transport has made some of the benefits of sea access obsolete
and lowered the price of imports, strategic considerations and ecological conditions constantly change. But, above all, old nations can

split and thereby lose their relative advantage as big, unified entities. Western Europe, which was assumed to be beyond nationalism, is a good example of this type of instability. Separatist tendencies now prevail in Western European nations, which have become aware of the fragile and tenuous nature of their unity. The English realise that they may one day find themselves divorced from the Welsh, the Scots, and the Irish; the Lombardian league makes a united Italy a questionable proposition; the Corsicans do not wish to define themselves as French, and no one can assure the French that the Normans or the Bretons will not follow in their footsteps. Although Germany is reunited, there is no assurance that Prussia, Bavaria, or Saxony will not wish to see themselves as distinct national entities in the future. Since no nation can assume it will remain united forever, nations have a reason to join political arrangements in which such splits will cause them minimal harm.

Regional organisations will enable nations to cooperate as equal partners rather than support one's nation domination over others. Nations, argues Walzer, do not compete for members as some religions do:

> When they freely celebrate their histories, remember their dead, and shape (in part) the education of their children, they are more likely to be harmless than when they are unfree. Locke may have put the claim too strongly when he wrote that "there is only one thing which gathers people into seditious commotions, and that is oppression," but he was close enough to the truth to warrant the experiment of radical tolerance.[16]

A regional organisation, which takes the equality of nations for granted, is therefore more likely to foster toleration and diversity than political arrangements based on oppression and domination.

The Moderating Power of Interlocking Relations

Regional cooperation is gradually developing in various parts of the world, with the EC as the best-known example. This cooperation, however, has usually been justified on grounds different, and perhaps even contradictory, to the ones suggested here. Rather than stressing the national perspective, supporters of national cooperation emphasise economic and military advantages, hoping that the latter will enable individuals to forego their national attachments. The argument suggested here is motivated by radically different reasons. From a liberal-nationalist viewpoint, encouraging cooperation among nations is advantageous on three counts. First, it allows members of small nations to lead a full and satisfying national life. Second, it contributes to individual freedom by relieving pressures to assimilate as a way of improving the economic or occupational prospects of members of minorities. Cooperation aims, as far as possible, to equalise the prospects of all national communities regarding their chances of becoming objects of choice. Third, it fosters the idea that developing a prosperous national life is not contingent on closure and isolation but rather on the development of transnational ties, serving to allay the more ethnocentric and xenophobic aspects of nationalism.

The last two points call for further clarification. Chapter 2 discussed the conditions under which we can assume that an individual has *chosen* his way of life. Clearly, making choices implies that individuals have an adequate range of options to choose from, namely, that these options are relevant to their lives and that none of them entails unreasonable costs that would condemn them to marginalisation and destitution. A powerful, although unofficial, way of motivating individuals to assimilate (or to emigrate) is to present them with a forced choice between two unequal options: either to join a stronger, wealthier nation and share in its sense of security, its economic prosperity, and, at times, its feelings of superiority, or to remain closed within their own culture, doomed to marginalisation and very often poverty. When faced with a cultural choice, individuals are thus obliged to take into account considerations found beyond the realms of culture and communal membership. One advantage of the model proposing a regional organisation and national local autonomies is that it allows individuals to make these decisions on the basis of "the relevant reasons alone," solely on the basis of their cultural and communal preferences. The procedure of conversion to Judaism illustrates an attempt to ground choice on "relevant reasons alone." People wishing to convert to Judaism must couch this desire in strictly cultural and religious terms. No extrinsic reason, including the wish to marry a Jew, is considered valid ground for conversion.

As the separation of church and state was meant to ensure freedom of religion by enabling individuals to assume only those religious commitments that reflected their religious beliefs, separating the pursuit of a national life and the ability to achieve strategic, economic, and ecological gains through cooperation with other nations is meant to enable individuals to express their national affiliations

while free from alien constraints. It allows individuals to differentiate their preferences rather than to cluster all of them in one insepa-
rable sheaf.

A necessary condition of this separation, is that no national community be significantly better off than others, namely, that regional
organisations will, as far as possible, be communities of equals, both
on the individual and the national levels, lest individuals be motivated to join it for reasons other than national-cultural ones.

The third advantage points to the positive moral effects of cooperation. Cooperation forces individuals to realise that they belong to
different communities and share preferences with members of various groups. Those with whom they share their national affiliations
may not necessarily share their class, gender, or ideological preferences, and those who share their strategic or ecological preferences
may include, but also exceed their national group. As shown in
Chapter 5, these interlocking memberships cannot be placed in a
hierarchial order. For some, belonging to a social class is a more
important locus of identification than being members of a church,
whereas identification with a political party or with a gender support group will, for others, mean more than affiliation with a particular nation. What makes this picture even more complicated is that
the same individuals assign different values to membership in distinct groups at various stages of their life. The awareness that we are
entangled in a series of complex webs of membership blurs the line
between members and nonmembers and promotes cross-group
affiliations.

The present model contends with some of the fears evoked by the
morality of community. Individuals may indeed prefer members of
their community on a certain issue, but their simultaneous membership in several nonoverlapping groups turns those who are nonmembers from one perspective into potential fellow members from
another. Arguments that demonise nonmembers or call for the pursuit of members' interests at the expense of outsiders will find it
harder to get attention. Overlapping memberships stimulate moderation and cooperation:

> When individuals belong to a number of different organized or
> unorganized groups with diverse interests and outlooks, their
> attitudes will tend to be moderate as a result of psychological
> cross-pressures. Moreover, leaders of organizations with heter-
> ogeneous membership will be subject to the political cross-pres-
> sures of this situation and will also tend to assume moderate,

155

middle of the road positions. Such moderation is essential to political stability.[17]

Lijphart claims that most group theorists support this view. Truman, for example, states that "if a complex society manages to avoid revolution, degeneration, and decay [and] maintains its stability . . . it may do so in large measure because of the fact of multiple memberships." Lipset similarly argues that "the chances of a stable democracy are enhanced to the extent that groups and individuals have a number of crosscutting, politically relevant affiliations."[18]

Lijphart suggests "consociational democracy" as a way of reducing tensions in a cleavaged society. A consociational democracy is a political system that comprises numerous segments, each enjoying a high degree of autonomy in the running of its own affairs and governed by a "grand coalition" that includes representatives of all the different groups. The electoral system ensures all groups, except for very small ones, proportional representation in all political organisations, as well as a proportional share of the public expenditure and of all civic appointments. The different groups have mutual veto power and can veto decisions they view as vital, a mechanism meant to overcome the problems of simple majoritarianism. Since no nation is likely to attain a simple majority in a regional organisation, and since it cannot be assured that its particular interests will be protected unless it agrees to a mutual veto system, all are encouraged to endorse this arrangement.

In a consociational democracy, all segments have a say in matters of common interest, with the extent of their influence roughly corresponding to their representation. Decisions and policy implementation in all other matters are left to each segment. Rather than attempting to weaken or do away with segmental cleavages, consociationalism grants them explicit recognition and turns them into constructive elements within a larger political framework. It aims to allow every segment autonomy, either through a territorial arrangement or, when the nation is spread within others, to attain partial autonomy by establishing schools, cultural and communal centres, publications in its own language, and the like:

> Where the segments are geographically too interspersed, segmental autonomy has been established on the personality principle: in the Netherlands, Austria, and as far as the religious-ideological subcultures rather than the linguistic communities are concerned, in Belgium. It should be noted that, although it is easier to delegate governmental power and administrative

responsibilities to territorially concentrated segments, autonomy has proved to be compatible with both approaches.[19]

The model suggested here tries to equalise life-prospects for members of all nations, be they weak or powerful. It allows every nation representation, an equal share in the distribution of goods, and a fair chance to occupy official positions, pursue its life-plans, and adhere to its culture. Indeed, the chances for members of larger nations to pursue their shared goals will always be better, because their "buying power" will inevitably be greater. But the fact that one is affiliated with a small nation is a matter of bad luck rather than of unfairness. This unavoidable inequality at times leads to conflict, and consociational democracy is not a magic panacea for all ills. We have seen it end in disaster, as the Yugoslavian and Lebanese experiences painfully attest. These failures could be explained in various ways, by pointing to demographic changes in Lebanon (a problem discussed later as an example of the "de facto principle") and to the uneven economic development, coupled with the abrupt collapse of an authoritarian regime, in the Yugoslavian case. These are sobering reminders that good ideas do not always succeed and may even lead to human suffering. Barry is right in claiming that adopting the consociational model cannot guarantee that a state will become as peaceful and prosperous as Switzerland or Holland and that, in fact, consociational arrangements reinforce national cleavages:

It is sometimes possible to maintain a system of party alignments cutting across a line of communal cleavage. It is usually possible to shift from this to a system where parties articulate the communal cleavage. But it is extremely difficult if not impossible to move in the reverse direction, because of the primitive psychological strength of communal identification and the effects of social reinforcement on maintaining the political salience of communal identification.[20]

The consociational model is indeed meant to give full expression to national differences, but attempts to lessen hostility among different national groups by emphasising the importance of shared, transnational interests. Such arrangements are likely to encourage all members of a particular nation to present a united front, in some cases, and promote transnational unions or corporations in others.

Notwithstanding these problems, Barry claims he cannot offer "an alternative panacea." Nor can I.[21] Two critical shortcomings of this model merit, however, special attention, as they touch on issues of great theoretical and practical concern. The first is the "Russian doll phenomenon," namely, the problem posed by the fact that every "national territory," however small, includes among its inhabitants members of other nations. Hence, granting local autonomy to a national group might reduce, but will not eliminate the problem of minorities. The second relates to problems of immigration. Liberal nationalism is committed to the liberal ideal of freedom of movement as well as to the right of national communities to preserve their distinctiveness. But attempts to accommodate both these ideals within a consociational setup is extremely problematic, as free immigration might threaten the national character of each segment. The following discussion offers several reasonable compromises aimed at coping with these problems. These compromises are not merely part of an ideal model, but are suggested as concrete guidelines for reflecting on some of the most pressing issues of our times:

Defining a political entity as a national community is only justified if a substantial majority of its citizens has consented to this definition. This implies that the national character of a political entity is to be determined de facto not de jure. Hence, attempts such as that of Israeli law to bar parties that deny the Jewish character of the state from standing for election is unjustified. Moreover, decisions about the national character of a particular government should only reflect the interests of those governed by it. Members of diaspora communities should not be allowed to participate directly and formally in the decision-making process, whereas all formal members of the political entity, irrespective of their national membership, have a right to participate in this process. Jews, Irish, or Italians living in the diaspora should not be party to decisions concerning the national character of their respective national homelands, although these decisions significantly affect their lives, but the Palestinian citizens of Isreal, as well as the Pakistani citizens of the United Kingdom, or Algerian citizens of France, should participate in this process. In this light, the decision to allow Estonians living in Sweden to vote in a referendum on the nature of the emerging Estonian state while excluding inhabitants of Russian origin, is unjustified. Although Estonians need not accept individuals of Russian origin as members of the Estonian people, they are not justified in depriving them of citizenship rights.

This approach suggests a dynamic view of the national nature of political entities. The most obvious source of change would be demography. A national entity can find it has become binational, or

158

multinational, and that it must consequently change its official definition. This being the case, it seems justified for members to fear that immigration will change the future character of their society. On these grounds, would it be justified for a liberal national entity to place restrictions on the immigration of nonmembers? This is one of the hardest challenges that liberal nations face today.

The following guidelines might be helpful in dealing with this problem. Although they cannot bridge the gap between the ideal of free immigration and the ideal of national self-determination, together they may lead to a reasonable balance between them.

First, a clear distinction should be drawn between the rights of refugees and the rights of immigrants. Although certain restrictions on immigration could be justified, they could never rescind the *absolute* obligation to grant refuge to individuals for as long as their lives are at risk.

Second, after individuals have entered a certain territory under the justified impression that they will qualify for citizenship, it is unjustified to change these terms retroactively. This is a crucial issue for many republics established after the collapse of the Soviet Union. For example, out of Estonia's 1.5 million inhabitants, 600,000 are Russians who entered the country after 1940, while out of Latvia's 2.5 million inhabitants, Latvians are only 52 percent and in Riga they are a minority. Naturalisation laws have thus evoked serious disputes. The Estonian parliament, striving to secure the Estonian character of the new state, has passed a law that deprives Russians of their Estonian citizenship. Automatic Estonian citizenship will only be granted to anyone residing in the country before June 1940, when the Soviet Union annexed Estonia, and to their next of kin. All those who are not entitled to automatic citizenship but have lived in Estonia for at least two years, are allowed to apply for citizenship, which might be granted if—and this is the law's stumbling block—they have never served or were never affiliated with the occupying Soviet forces, and on condition that they master the Estonian language. While the language restriction could be justified as a rather standard requirement of citizenship, as it is, for instance, in the United States, the wording of the first restriction is sufficiently vague to allow the Estonian government to reject most of the applications submitted by individuals of Soviet origin, even when born in Estonia. While the Estonian rage over the Soviet occupation is understandable, creating another wrong will not right the first one. Estonia and Latvia must face the fact that the injustices inflicted on them have turned them into binational states, and there is no way of turning the clock back.

Third, liberal democratic principles dictate that, if a majority of its citizens so wishes, a national entity is justified in retaining its national character. On these grounds, a national entity might be seen as entitled to restrict immigration in order to preserve the existence of a viable majority. Kasher claims that Article 1 of the United Nations' Convention on the Elimination of All Forms of Racial Discrimination, can be interpreted as agreeing with this kind of favouritism. The article states the following:

> Special measures taken for the sole purpose of securing adequate advancement of certain racial or ethnic groups, or individuals requiring such protection as may be necessary in order to ensure such groups or individuals equal enjoyment or exercise of human rights and fundamental freedoms shall not be deemed racial discrimination, provided, however, that such measures do not, as consequence, lead to the maintenance of separate rights for different racial groups and that they shall not be continued after the objective for which they were taken have been achieved.[22]

Kasher understands this to imply that special measures intended to preserve the status of a group as a majority are only justified until a viable majority has been achieved.[23] This seems to be a plausible solution, although it is not easy to define what is meant by "a viable majority."

Restrictions on immigration constitute a violation of the right of national minorities to equal treatment, as they only serve the needs of the majority. Therefore, they can only be justified if members of the minority have materialised their right to a national entity of their own, to which they could immigrate if they desired to live as members of a majority, and as long as family reunions are allowed. Hence, the Israeli "Law of Return," which actively encourages the immigration of Jews and grants them automatic citizenship and financial assistance on their arrival in the country, would only be justified if the largest minority in the state, namely, the Palestinians, would also have a national entity in which they could enact a similar law. Even if a Palestinian state was established, however, it would not be justified to expel the Palestinian citizens of Israel to that state, just as the existence of a Russian political entity cannot justify expelling citizens of Russian origin from the Baltic republics. Restrictions placed on the entry of future members differ significantly from injustices inflicted on present members, which can never be justified.

Once individuals have formally joined a political community they should be treated as equals. Nationality should not be the basis for distributing goods, rights, or services. The political culture should be open to all and members of national minorities ought to be encouraged to participate and integrate into the political sphere. It is true that entering the political culture requires members of minorities to join a political process reflecting a national culture not their own. Their difficulties on this count should be recognised, and it would be unjustified to use them for promoting assimilation into the national culture. Pragmatic reasons once again support moral ones: As a political entity becomes more tolerant of cultural differences, it lessens the risks of national unrest.

Another principle that derives from the nature of liberal nationalism concerns the obligation of every nation to respect the rights of other nations to self-determination. But some nations might be too poor to reach any reasonable level of prosperity, and this could hinder their ability to lead on autonomous national life. It is cynical to assume that the people of Bangladesh or of Ethiopia, or of Egypt or Turkey for that matter, enjoy their right to national self-determination to the same extent as the people of Norway or the United States. The implications of the distinction between equal liberties and equal worth of liberty should be considered in this context. The worth of liberty to a person or group is proportional to their capacity to advance their ends by means of the liberty granted. Individuals in poor countries are often forced to make a choice between living with their own people or improving their life-prospects in a society in which they will be a minority. If when choosing the latter option individuals were mainly motivated by instrumental considerations, their decision cannot be seen as expressing a cultural choice, it would be misleading to see it as waiving the right to national self-determination and expressing a desire to assimilate into a new culture.

This point underscores one of the most important implications of a theory of liberal nationalism: Restricting immigration in order to retain the national character of a certain territory, is only justified if all nations have an equal chance of establishing a national entity, in which its members will be given a fair chance of pursuing their personal and collective goals. The right to preserve cultural homogeneity is therefore contingent on the welfare of other nations. Liberal nationalism thus implies that it is justified for a nation to seek homogeneity by restricting immigration only if it has fulfilled its global obligation to assure equality among all nations.

Wealthy nations, concerned with avoiding pressure to open their gates to immigrants who are apt to change the national and cultural status quo, should, therefore, embark on efforts to improve standards of living in poorer countries, on both moral and prudential grounds. This, in fact, entails a restricted implementation of Rawls' second principle on a global scale. But without the claim that individuals are entitled to lead fulfilling lives within their own national and cultural environment, Rawls' argument could lead to the conclusion that the best way of ensuring members of poor nations a modicum of well-being would be to spread them among other, more prosperous communities. In fact, neither nationalism nor liberalism can, in and of themselves, justify support for the rights of individuals to prosper within their own communities, a claim that can only be sustained through liberal nationalism.

The argument justifying closure on the one hand and global responsibility on the other could be manipulated cynically, and used to justify the deportation of immigrants or *Gastarbeiter* back to their countries of origins. Le Pen in France, the Neo-Nazis in Germany, and supporters of white Australia or white California, indeed rely on similar claims when urging the deportation of existing populations. Note, however, that they not only demand a retroactive change of terms, but most important, call for deportation first and the redistribution of resources later. Their popularity lies in the fact that they tie a promise of economic benefits—better job prospects and salaries, lowered housing prices, and the like—with the attainment of cultural homogeneity. It is doubtful that these policies could have gained such wide support had they entailed the economic sacrifices implied by the liberal nationalist argument. A further difference between the liberal nationalist argument and its cynical "translation" is that the latter uses the language of race rather than choice, and the policies it advocates in fact prevent individuals from assimilating, even when they choose to do so. An important conclusion to be drawn from these examples is that ideological movements flying only one flag, be it equality, liberty, or national liberation, are to be viewed with suspicion. Human beings have a wide range of interests, preferences, and needs, and a sound political philosophy will attempt to balance all of them rather than pursue one at the expense of all others.

The attempt to create a synthesis sometimes results in a diluted version of both poles. Nevertheless, the attempt to integrate liberal and national ideals leads to a scheme of international justice that is less egoistic than the liberal one, entails genuine respect for different ways of life, and extends the limits of toleration, thus emphasising central liberal values without losing sight of national ideals.

We can now summarise the characteristics of a liberal national entity. This entity will endorse liberal principles of distribution inwards and outwards; its political system will reflect a particular national culture, but its citizens will be free to practice different cultures and follow a variety of life-plans and conceptions of the good. The political entity described here differs from the traditional liberal entity in that it introduces culture as a crucial dimension of political life. Its unity rests not only on an overlapping consensus about certain values essential to its functioning, but also on a distinct cultural foundation. Membership in this entity will be more accessible to certain individuals, capable of identifying the political entity as their own, than to others. Consequently, even if governing institutions respect a wide range of rights and liberties and distribute goods and official positions fairly, members of minority groups will unavoidably feel alienated to some extent. Alienation rather than a deprivation of rights is to be acknowledged as the main problem affecting members of national minorities.

The openness of the political culture and the readiness to compensate culturally disadvantaged members of minority groups may lessen the hardships faced by cultural minorities. Yet, minorities "may vote and enjoy all the formal-legal privileges of citizenship, and still be functionally excluded from the political process, and thus effectively excluded from the life of the 'true' political community."[24] This tension is endogenous to any liberal national entity and cannot be resolved.

The Return of Cultural Nationalism

In light of the preceding analysis, it is surprising to find that, notwithstanding its shortcomings, the concept of the nation-state still prevails. The popularity of this concept rests on several widely held fallacies, namely, that free institutions can only operate within a homogeneous nation-state, that a state can mobilize its citizens only by invoking the power of national ideals, and that economic development and modernization require cultural homogenization.

The first assumption suggests that members of different nationalities and various cultural backgrounds can hardly be expected to act harmoniously in the same state since

163

the same books, newspapers, pamphlets, speeches do not reach them. One section does not know what opinions, or what instigation, are circulating in the other. The same incidents, the same acts, the same system of government, affect them in different ways; and each fears more injury to itself from the other nationalities, than from the common arbiter, the state.[25]

Internal mistrust will either result in prolonged internal conflict or in despotic rule.

Furthermore, Mill assumes that a multinational state will not succeed in galvanising its population into political, economic, or military action. Only national feelings can be relied on to recruit an army resting on a liberal raison d'etre, that is, protecting the people against their government. Mill considers a national army in sympathy with the people as "the grand and only effectual security in the last resort against the despotism of the government," while in an army composed of several nationalities

soldiers to whose feelings half or three-fourths of the subjects of the same government are foreigners, will have no more desire to ask the reason why, than they would have in doing the same things against declared enemies. . . . The sole bond that holds them together is their officers, and the government which they serve; and their only idea, if they have any, of public duty, is obedience to orders.[26]

Mill consequently fears that such an army is more likely to serve the interests of the ruler than those of the nation, thus turning from a source of national pride and confidence into a source of instability and danger.

Gellner turns our attention to political and economic aspects and suggests that modern states can only function under conditions of cultural and linguistic uniformity, without which citizens cannot participate in the political process or become involved in technological development and economic growth:

The mutual relationship of a modern culture and state is something quite new, and springs, inevitably, from the requirements of a modern economy. . . . All this—mobility, communication, size due to refinement of specialization—imposed on the industrial order by its thirst for affluence and growth, obliges its social units to be large and yet culturally homogeneous.[27]

VIRTUE OUT OF NECESSITY

As Gellner makes clear, nationalism had indeed been conceived as providing the impetus for progress and modernisation. But both Mill and Gellner speak for the needs of another era.

It is now believed that the economic future lies in cross-national cooperation. Economic considerations are expected to overcome linguistic and cultural differences and provide the momentum for a regional system that is both multinational and multicultural. In this system, industrialisation and technological development will be achieved without cultural standardisation, and with growing mobility among cultural frameworks. Nationalism and modernisation indeed nurtured each other during the first stages of the nation-state, but their paths seem to have parted. Today, nationalism is not seen as serving as a vital motivation for economic progress and development and, in fact, it is rather feared that it might constitute an obstacle to both.

A united Europe, if and when the process of unification comes to closure, will offer a concrete model of the consociational democracy suggested here. Although the events taking place in Eastern and Central Europe seem to be leading in the opposite direction, it seems safe to predict that these new states will seek to join regional organisations based on economic, strategic, and ecological cooperation, which are bound to restrain their autonomy. Eastern European states will therefore find that they cannot avoid going though political and economic processes similar to those followed by Western nation-states. Czechoslovakia, Hungary, and Poland have applied for membership in the EC, and the new republics created after the collapse of the Soviet Union will eventually find their place either in the EC or in new federative agreements. Although the exact terms of these agreements are hard to predict, they will probably resemble those on which the EC is based, namely, they will allow the different national groups a broad range of national autonomy, and develop policies of coordination and cooperation on economic, strategic, and diplomatic issues across national lines. The triadic principle of one army, one currency, one passport (implying free movement of goods and individuals within the boundaries of the federative or confederative system and a coordinated trade and immigration policy), will presumably capture the essence of the coordinated policies. Under this union, it will not really matter if the Yugoslav federation is divided into four separate national autonomies, or if Slovaks and Czechs separate.

Accepting the idea that national self-determination might best be

165

attained within a larger regional framework implies that political thought has entered a new age, in which the principle of national self-determination no longer provides the sole justification for political organisation. It also challenges the belief that a stable political framework requires cultural, linguistic, or religious uniformity. Does this lead to a vision of a world without borders? Walzer rejects this ideal and emphasises the need for closure.[28] If we appreciate differences, Walzer claims, we must accept that borders must be placed somewhere, and if we eliminate borders between states, local communities will create their own. Experience shows that, as the borders of the state become more open, communities will set up their own. In the cosmopolitan cities of multinational empires, or in cities where there is a steady influx of immigrants, the neighbourhood that preserves cultural uniqueness becomes a substitute for the political framework.[29]

The concept of "border" appears here in two different senses. Unlike that implied by a distributive framework, preserving the cultural character of a community requires a different kind of boundary. Cultural uniqueness is preserved in Quebec, in Belgium, and in many other places, without an actual geographical border. Scattered peoples like the Jews or the Armenians, and immigrant groups such as Hispanics in Southern California, Cubans in Miami, Algerians in France, and Pakistanis in England, and religious sects like the Mormons in Utah, the Amish in Pennsylvania, or the ultra-Orthodox Jewish community in Jerusalem, also manage to preserve their identity without tangible boundaries. National and cultural groups wishing to preserve their uniqueness thus draw invisible frontiers between themselves and all "others," and create closure by constructing ideological, religious, linguistic, and mainly psychological barriers between members and nonmembers.

The real test of power for cultural and national affiliations has arrived. Technological development and economic prosperity now depend on cross-national associations, and assimilation is, more than ever, a feasible option. Will national groups withstand pressures to melt together into a new regional culture, or will they be motivated to invest in the preservation of their cultural heritage, their language, their distinctiveness? Pye claims that the continuity of separate political traditions imprinted by particular national cultures "constantly resists the levelling forces at work in the social and economic spheres of modern life."[30] Time will tell whether this is true. But a postnational age in which national differences are obliterated and all share in one shallow universal culture, watch soap operas and CNN, eat MacDonalds, drink Coca-Cola, and take the children to the local Disneyworld, is more a nightmare than a utopian vision.

These could appear to be idle concerns in these tragic times, when fanatic versions of nationalism are causing so much anguish and suffering. But it is precisely at such times that individuals are lured by the appeal of cosmopolitan visions, which overlook the importance of national aspirations. The way to confront ethnocentric nationalism is not to suggest that national interests should be denied altogether, but to offer an alternative national view. It seems rather clear that nationalism will simply not go away, and the question that remains open is whether its guise will be some form of virulent ethnocentrism or a sober vision, guided by respect for liberal values.

NOTES

Preface

1. Svensson 1979, p. 432.
2. Ibid., p. 433.
3. External preferences are preferences concerning other individuals. Such preferences, Dworkin argues, should not serve to justify rights, as these rights might restrict the autonomy of others. Thus, while my interest in living a worthy life is grounds for a right and might burden others with some duties that would restrict their freedoms, my interest in others living a particular kind of life cannot be grounds for a right and cannot burden others with duties. (Dworkin, *Taking Rights Seriously* [London: Duckworth, 1978], pp. 234-36.)
4. Taylor 1994, pp. 58–59.
5. Kymlicka 1989, p. 150.
6. Gurr et al. 1993, p. 301.
7. MacCormick 1994, p. 12.
8. Ibid., p. 13.
9. Greenfeld 1994, p. 455.
10. Lucas 1972, p. 360.
11. Ibid., p. 323.
12. Ibid., p. 331.
13. Ibid.
14. Achad Ha'am 1965, p. 401.
15. Ibid., pp. 401, 402.
16. Rousseau 1965, p. 65.
17. Fichte 1968, p. 193.
18. Rousseau 1965, p. 64.
19. Ibid., p. 65.
20. Ichilov 1993, p. 48.
21. Ibid., p. 95.
22. While I take Dinur's words to express the tension between nation and state, for him this tension was a hidden one. He was a firm supporter of the nation-state and saw Israel as a Jewish, rather than a multinational, state.
23. Walzer 1992, p. 54
24. Lucas 1972, p. 470.
25. Walzer 1992, pp. 60–61.
26. Lucas 1972, p. 494.
27. Khon 1966, p. 146.

28. Ibid., p. 174.
29. Walzer 1992, p. 61.
30. Bettes 1961, p. 26.
31. Ibid., pp. 17–18.
32. Ibid., p. 29.
33. In Mendus-Flor and Reinharz 1980, p. 109.
34. Ichilov 1993, p. 85.
35. Okin 1989, p. 255.
36. Ibid.
37. Gutmann 1992, p. 12.
38. Young 1989, p. 267.
39. Ibid.
40. Ibid., p. 265.

Introduction

1. MacCormick 1981, pp. 247–48.
2. Gellner 1971, p. 149.
3. Lukes 1988, p. 4.
4. Berlin 1986, p. 42.
5. Anderson 1983.
6. Raz 1986, p. 207.
7. Jewish nationalism has often been justified in terms of anti-Semitism and the Holocaust rather than through a theory of nationalism. The right of the Jews to a state, however, cannot rest on their painful history but on the fact that they are a nation like all others. Protestants were also persecuted in certain places, but it is not usually assumed that they could, on these grounds, demand the right to self-determination. Homosexuals and handicapped individuals were also victimised by the Nazis, and this might entitle them to compensation but not to national rights.
8. Williams 1985, pp. 163–64.

Chapter One

1. De Maistre, in Berlin 1990, p. 100.
2. Mill 1975, p. 84.
3. See, for example, Taylor 1985a and b, 1989; Carrithers et al., 1985; and Kymlicka 1989.
4. Geertz 1973, p. 35.
5. Ibid., p. 49.
6. Mauss 1938, p. 22.
7. Ibid., p. 3.
8. Lukes 1985, p. 293.

9. Mill 1975, p. 70.

10. Kedourie 1985, p. 37.

11. Rawls 1972, p. 448.

12. MacDonald 1949, p. 82.

13. Ibid. For an excellent discussion of these issues, see Arblaster 1984, chaps. 2–3.

14. Berry 1986, p. 2.

15. Fichte's *Address to the German Nation* expresses this view quite clearly.

16. Berry 1986, p. 4.

17. Gutmann 1985, p. 23, [emphasis added].

18. Gaus 1983, pp. 2–3.

19. Rawls 1972, pp. 522–23.

20. Rawls 1985, p. 241.

21. Ibid., p. 289.

22. Ibid., 1985, p. 299.

23. A similar position is adopted by Lukes 1985, p. 298; and Kymlicka 1988, p. 190.

24. Kymlicka 1990, p. 209.

25. Taylor 1985b, 1:25–26.

26. Ibid., pp. 19–23. The reference here is to fundamental decisions that relate to questions such as the sort of person I wish to be rather than to ordinary mundane decisions, which are often made on the basis of comparisons rather than on evaluations. Decisions such as "Shall I go to the movies rather than to a friend's?" or "Should I play chess or dominos with my children?" will most probably be decided on the basis of contingent compatibilities with other alternatives rather than on the basis of their evaluations of higher or lower, noble or base.

27. Ibid., p. 34.

28. Rawls 1985, pp. 41–42.

29. Collini 1988, p. 427.

30. Friel 1990, p. 47.

31. A comparison between intellectual curiosity about a culture and a potential interest in adopting it may help to clarify this issue. Membership requires more than saying, "It is a splendid language; I love the sound of it," or "I appreciate the manners, the tradition, and the history of this people." It requires a readiness to follow the culture, as well as to create special relations with its bearer.

32. Berlin 1990, p. 10.

33. Perec, in Shiloni 1989, p.106

34. Raz 1986, p. 203.

35. Mulhall 1987, p. 23.

36. Mill 1975, pp. 386–87.

37. Raz 1986, pp. 423–24.

38. Walzer 1989a, p. 41.

Chapter Two

1. I have relied on Raz's definition of right: "X has a right if and only if X can have rights and, other things being equal, an aspect of X's well-being (his interest) is a sufficient reason for holding other person(s) under duty" (1986, p. 166).

2. MacDonald 1949, in Waldron 1984, p. 27.

3. This is a matter of enormous complexity, since we can reject our cultural affiliations while still cherishing certain of the values and habits of the old culture, as we can decide to retain our cultural identity while rejecting some of its values. The important element is that only those values, norms, and cultural practices we judge to be valuable can be adopted as guidelines.

4. Kymlicka 1989, pp. 186–87.

5. Sandel 1991, p. 31.

6. Ibid., p. 37.

7. Luck, therefore, plays a significant role in our ability to satisfy our preferences. When others share our preferences, a certain product may become readily available because popularity may help to increase production. If the product we desire is not readily available, however, the fact that others also want it may reduce our chances of obtaining it.

8. Waldron 1987, p. 21.

9. Ibid., pp. 21–22.

10. For a definition and a discussion of the concept of external preferences, see Dworkin 1977, pp. 234–38.

11. Kymlicka 1989, pp. 148–49.

12. Ranger 1983, p. 261.

13. Ibid., p. 238.

14. Steinberg 1981, p. 63.

15. Walzer 1989b, pp. 25–26.

16. Trilling 1972, p. 115.

17. Stevenson 1974, p. 78.

18. Williams 1971, p. 318.

19. Ibid., p. 322.

Chapter Three

1. Margalit and Raz 1990, p. 440.

2. Dinstein 1976, p. 102.

3. Carr et al. 1939, p. xvii.

4. Weil 1952, p. 95.

5. Deutsch 1969, p. 19.

6. Hertz 1944, p. 7.

7. Ibid., p. 3.

8. Dyson 1987, p. 591.

9. Although a territory could be construed as one of several features included in the definition of a nation, this territory need be neither well defined nor recognised—two indispensable attributes of state territory—in order to be of importance to the formation of a nation.

10. D'Entreves 1967, p. 318.

11. Seton-Watson 1977, p. 1.

12. Geertz 1973, p. 315.

13. Forsyth 1987, p. 506.

14. Sureda 1973, p. 17.

15. Although women were not granted voting rights, they were nevertheless considered part of the national community and were assumed to be indirectly represented through their fathers or spouses.

16. In Kohn 1966, p. 326.

17. Kedourie 1985, p. 14.

18. Smith 1986, p. 129.

19. Hegel 1967, p. 279.

20. Burke, in Waldron 1987b, p. 118.

21. Hegel 1967, pp. 218–19.

22. Ibid., p. 218.

23. Smith 1983, p. xxiv.

24. Ibid., pp. xxx.

25. Anderson cites some fascinating examples of the way in which new nations tie themselves to a fabricated past. For example: "The late President Sukarno always spoke with *complete* sincerity of the 350 years of colonialism that his 'Indonesia' had endured, although the very concept 'Indonesia' is a twentieth-century invention, and most of today's Indonesia was only conquered by the Dutch between 1850 and 1910. Preeminent among contemporary Indonesia's national heroes is the early nineteenth-century Javanese Prince Diponegaro, although the Prince's own memories show that he intended to 'concord [not liberate!] Java', rather than to expel 'the Dutch'" (Anderson 1983, p. 19).

26. Hobsbawm and Ranger 1983, p. 1.

27. Kroeber and Kluckhohn 1952, p. 181, cited by Singer in the *Encyclopedia of Philosophy*.

28. Osterud 1987, p. 379.

29. Cobban 1969, p. 107.

30. Seton-Watson 1977, p. 7.

31. Renan (1882), in Snyder 1964, pp. 26–29.

32. Hampshire 1983, p. 145.

33. Quoted in Gellner 1987a, p. 6: "L'oubli et, je dirais meme, l'erreur historique, sont un facteur essentiel de la creation d'une nation" (Renan 1882, "Que'est-ce qu'une Nation?").

34. Gellner 1983, p. 7.

35. Williams 1961, p. 57.

36. Gellner 1983, p. 7.

37. Anderson 1983, pp. 13, 15.

38. Only in the unlikely case that the whole of Europe should regard itself as one European nation, could self-rule and national self-determination be said to overlap.

39. Thornberry 1989, p. 883.
40. Berlin 1969, pp. 157–58.
41. Donnelly 1989, p. 148.
42. Raz 1986, p. 207.
43. Rawls 1972, p. 60.
44. Walzer 1986, p. 231.
45. Ibid., p. 228.
46. Raz 1986, p. 209.
47. Dinstein 1976, p. 112.
48. Ibid., p. 116.
49. Houser 1971, p. 92.

Chapter Four

1. Elon 1987, p. 33.
2. MacCormick 1981, pp. 247–65.
3. Graham 1986, p. 140.
4. O'Brien 1988, p. 18.
5. Berlin 1972, p. 19.
6. Seton-Watson 1977, p. 445.
7. Popper 1962, p. 49.
8. Walicki 1982, p. 265.
9. O'Brien 1991, p. 29.
10. The terms used here to describe Kohn's position are taken from Snyder 1954, pp. 118–20.
11. Barry 1983, p. 124.
12. Berlin 1969, p. 156.
13. Said 1987, p. 3.
14. Plamenatz 1976, p. 27.
15. Fichte 1968, p. 215.
16. Walzer 1989a, p. 9.
17. Smith 1983, p. 159.
18. Walzer 1989a, p. 38.
19. O'Brien 1988, p. 32.
20. Gordon 1952, p. 252.
21. In Walicki 1982, p. 74.
22. Ibid., p. 76.
23. Mazzini 1907, p. 43.
24. Treitschke 1977, p. 359.
25. Smith 1983, p. 257.
26. Ibid., p. 261.
27. Ibid., pp. 262–63.
28. Walzer 1989b, p. 35.

Chapter Five

1. Dunn 1979, pp. 55, 57.
2. Mazzini 1907, p. 41; emphasis added.
3. Williams 1981, p. 18.
4. Rawls 1972, pp. 570–72.
5. Berlin 1986, p. 42.
6. Norman 1983, p. 249.
7. Rawls 1972, pp. 475–76.
8. Dworkin 1986a, pp. 199–201.
9. This view is explored very convincingly in Blum 1980, pp. 77–79.
10. Dworkin 1986a, p. 200.
11. Sandel 1982, p. 33.
12. Ibid.
13. Waldron 1990, p. 629.
14. Nozick 1974, pp. 323–24.
15. Williams 1985, p. 265.
16. Sandel 1982, p. 179.
17. Rawls 1972, p. 153.
18. Hare 1981, pp. 101–2.
19. Rawls 1972, pp. 468–69.
20. Hare 1981, p. 99.
21. I thank A. De-Shalit for raising this objection.
22. Rawls 1972, p. 289.
23. Flanagan and Jackson 1987, p. 630.
24. Dagger 1985, p. 437.
25. Gewirth 1988, p. 294.
26. Ibid., p. 295.
27. Goodin 1988, p. 675.
28. Berlin 1979, p. 343.
29. Barry 1987, p. 354.
30. Mazzini 1907, p. 50.

Chapter Six

1. Sandel 1984, p. 94.
2. Ibid., p. 90.
3. Rawls 1985, p. 249.
4. Dworkin 1986a, p. 208.
5. Rawls 1972, p. 476.
6. Rawls 1985, p. 227, emphasis added.
7. Pogge 1988, p. 233.
8. Ibid.
9. Dagger 1985, p. 437.
10. Barry 1983, pp. 126–27.

11. Democratic theory faces a similar problem, and can offer no clear guidance on these matters: "controversies regarding boundaries present an important practical limit to the scope of democracy as a method of making collective decisions." It may not be surprising, argues Whelam, that "democracy, which is a method for group decision-making or self-governing, cannot be brought to bear on the logically prior matter of the constitution of the group itself, the existence of which it presupposes" (1983, p. 148).

12. Rawls 1972, p. 13.

13. Barry 1983, pp. 128–30.

14. Ibid., p. 127.

15. Mazzini 1907, p. 53.

16. Ackerman 1980, p. 71.

17. Walzer 1983, p. 32.

18. Ackerman 1980, p. 88.

19. Ackerman 1980, pp. 72–73.

20. Ackerman 1980, p. 72.

21. Mill 1975, chap. 16.

22. Von Gunsteren 1988, p. 736.

23. Raphael 1970, p. 39.

24. For a very good critical discussion of political obligations, see Pateman 1985; and Simmons 1979.

25. Dworkin 1986a, p. 196.

26. Pateman 1985, p. 8.

27. Pitkin 1972, p. 60.

28. Ibid., p. 61.

29. Henry 1970, p. 276.

30. Raz 1986, p. 98.

31. Ibid.

32. Ibid., p. 92.

33. Simmons 1979, p. 35.

34. Ibid., p. 194.

Chapter Seven

1. Seton-Watson 1977, p. 443.

2. Mill 1975, pp. 382, 384.

3. Kymlicka 1989, p. 4.

4. Hobsbawm 1990, p. 33.

5. Gray 1986, p. 75.

6. Mendus 1989, p. 13

7. Raz argues this point very convincingly in his criticism of Rawls. See Raz 1986, pp. 117–24.

8. Jones, in Mendus 1989, p. 118.

9. Young 1987, p. 60.

10. Pye and Verba 1966, pp. 4, 7.

11. Ibid., pp. 6–8.
12. Geertz 1973, p. 311.
13. Ibid., pp. 311–12.
14. Ibid., pp. 316–17.
15. Kymlicka 1989, p. 187.
16. Walzer 1991, p. 7.
17. Lijphart 1977, p. 10.
18. Ibid., pp 10–11.
19. Ibid., pp. 42–43.
20. Barry 1991, p. 146.
21. A very interesting discussion of possible solutions to national conflicts is to be found in Horowitz 1985.
22. Kasher 1985, p. 110.
23. Ibid., pp. 111–12.
24. Hirsch 1986, p. 437.
25. Mill 1975, p. 382.
26. Ibid., p. 383.
27. Gellner 1983, pp. 140–41.
28. Walzer 1983, pp. 38–40.
29. Ibid., pp. 36–39.
30. Pye and Verba 1966, p. 4.

BIBLIOGRAPHY

Achad Ha'am. 1965. *The Collected Essays of Achad Ha'am* (in Hebrew).

Ackerman, B. A. 1980. *Social Justice in a Liberal State.* New Haven, Conn.: Yale University Press.

Akzin, B. 1969. *State and Nation.* London: Hutchinson.

Almond, G. A., and S. Verba. 1963. *Civic Culture.* Princeton, N.J.: Princeton University Press.

———. 1980. *The Civic Culture Revisited.* Boston, Mass.: Little, Brown.

Amery, J. 1986. *At the Mind's Limits.* New York: Schocken Books.

Anderson, B. 1983. *Imagined Communities.* London: Verso Editions and NLB.

Arblaster, A. 1984. *The Rise and Decline of West Liberalism.* Oxford: Blackwell.

Arieli, Y. 1964. *Individualism and Nationalism in America.* Cambridge, Mass.: Harvard University Press.

Barabu, Z. 1956. *Democracy and Dictatorship: Their Psychology and Patterns of Life.* London: Routledge and Kegan Paul.

———. 1971. *Society, Culture and Personality.* Oxford: Blackwell.

Barnard, F. M. 1965. *Herder's Social and Political Thought.* Oxford: Clarendon Press.

———. 1969. *J. G. Herder on Social and Political Thought.* Cambridge: Cambridge University Press.

Barry, B. M. 1973. *The Liberal Theory of Justice.* Oxford: Clarendon Press.

———. 1983. "Self-Government Revisited." In Miller and Siedentop, eds., *The Nature of Political Theory.*

———. 1987. "Nationalism." In the *Blackwell Encyclopedia* of *Political Thought.* Oxford: Blackwell.

———. 1991. *Democracy and Power.* Oxford: Clarendon Press.

Beehler, R. 1978. *Moral Life.* Oxford: Blackwell.

Beetham, D. 1980. *Max Weber and the Theory of the Modern State.* London: Allen & Unwin.

———. 1984. "The Future of the Nation-State." In McLennan, Held, and Hall, eds., *The Idea of the Modern State.*

Bendix, R. 1964. *Nation-Building and Citizenship.* Berkeley, Calif.: University of California Press.

Benn, S. I. 1967. "State"and "Nationalism." In the *Encyclopedia of Philosophy*.

Benn, S. I., and G. F. Gaus, eds. 1983. *Public and Private in Life*. Australia: Croom Helm.

Berger, P. L., B. Berger, and K. Hansfried. 1973. *The Homeless Mind, Modernization and Consciousness*. Middlesex, England: Penguin Books.

Berlin, I. 1969. *Four Essays on Liberty*. Oxford: Oxford University Press.

———. 1972. "The Bent Twig: A Note on Nationalism." *Foreign Affairs* 51:11–30.

———. 1976. *Vico and Herder*. London: Chatto & Windus.

———. 1979. *Against the Current*. Oxford: Oxford University Press.

———. 1980. *Concepts and Categories*. Oxford: Oxford University Press.

———. 1986. Interview. *Israeli Democracy*, pp. 40–43. (in Hebrew)

———. 1990. *The Crooked Timber of Humanity*. London: John Murray Publishers.

Berry, C. J. 1986. *Human Nature*. London: Macmillan.

Betts, R. F. 1961. *Assimilation and Association in French Colonial Theory*. New York: Columbia University Press.

Blum, L. A. 1980. *Friendship, Altruism and Morality*. London: Routledge and Kegan Paul.

———. 1988. "Gilligan and Kohlberg: Implications for Moral Theory." *Ethics* 98:472–91.

Breuilly, J. 1982. *Nationalism and the State*. Manchester: Manchester University Press.

Brownlie, I. 1985. "The Rights of People in Modern International Law." *Bulletin of the Australian Society of Legal Philosophy* 9:104–19.

Buchanan, A. 1987. "Justice and Charity." *Ethics* 97:558–75.

Bullivant, A. 1981. *The Pluralist Dilemma in Education*. London: Allen & Unwin.

Carr, E. H., et al. 1939. *Nationalism, A Report by a Study Group of Members of the Royal Institute of International Affairs*. Oxford: Oxford University Press.

Carrithers, M., S. Collins, and S. Lukes, eds. 1985. *The Category of the Person, Anthropology, Philosophy, History*. Cambridge: Cambridge University Press.

Cobban, A. 1969. *The Nation State and National Self-Determination*. London: Collins.

Cohen, G. A. 1983. "Reconsidering Historical Materialism." In Pennock and Chapman, eds., *Liberal Democracy*.

Cohen, G. A., and W. Kymlicka. 1988. "Human Nature and Social Change in the Marxist Conception of History." *Journal of Philosophy* 75:171-91.

Cohen, M. 1987. *Zion and the State*. Oxford: Blackwell.

Collini, S. 1988. "Speaking from Somewhere." *TLS* (Apr. 15–21):427–28.

Dagger, R. 1985. "Rights, Boundaries, and the Bonds of Community: A Qualified Defense of Moral Parochialism." *American Political Science Review* 79:436–47.

Daniels, N., ed. 1975. *Reading Rawls*. Oxford: Blackwell.

Danielson, P. 1973. "Theories, Intuitions, and the Problem of World-Wide Distributive Justice." *Philosophy and Social Science* 3:331–39.

D'Entreves, A. P. 1967 "The State." In *The Dictionary of the History of Ideas*.

Deutsch, K. 1969. *Nationalism and Its Alternatives*. New York: Basic Books.

Dinstein, Y. 1976. "Collective Human Rights of Peoples and Minorities." *International and Comparative Law Quarterly* 25:102–200.

Donnelly, J. 1984. *The Concept of Human Rights*. London: Croom Helm.

———. 1989. *Universal Human Rights in Theory and in Practice*. Ithaca, N.Y.: Cornell University Press.

Downing, L. A. and R. B. Thigpen 1986. "Beyond Shared Understanding." *Political Theory* 14:451–78.

Dunn, J. 1979. *Western Political Theory in the Face of the Future*. Cambridge: Cambridge University Press.

Dworkin, R. 1977. *Taking Rights Seriously*. London: Duckworth.

———. 1986a. *Law's Empire*. London: Fontana Press.

———. 1986b. *A Matter of Principle*. Oxford: Clarendon Press.

Dyson, K. 1980. *The State Tradition in Western Europe*. Oxford: Martin Robertson.

———. 1987. "State." In the *Blackwell Encyclopedia of Political Institutions*.

Elon, A. 1987. "A Letter from Israel." *New Yorker* (27 July).

Emerson, R. 1971. "Self-Determination." *American Journal of International Law* 65:459–75.

Feinberg, J. 1973. "Duty and Obligations in a Non-Ideal World." *Journal of Philosophy* 70:263–75.

Fennell, D. 1985. *Beyond Nationalism*. Ireland: Ward River Press.

Fichte, G. F. 1968. *Address to the German Nation*. New York: Harper Torchbooks.

Flanagan, O., and K. Jackson. 1987. "Justice, Care, and Gender: The Kohlberg–Gilligan Debate Revisited." *Ethics* 97:622–37.

Forbes, I., and S. Smith, eds. 1983. *Politics and Human Nature*. London: Frances Pinter.

Forsyth, M. G. 1987. "State." In the *Blackwell Encyclopedia of Political Thought*. Oxford: Blackwell.

Frankfurt, H. 1971. "Freedom of the Will and the Concept of a Person." *Journal of Philosophy* 67:5–21.

Friedrich, C. J. 1972. *Tradition and Authority*. London: Macmillan.

Friel, B. 1990. *Dancing at Lughansa*. London: Faber & Faber.

Gaus, G. F. 1983. *The Modern Liberal Theory of Man*. London: Croom Helm.

Geertz, C. 1973. *The Interpretation of Cultures*. New York: Basic Books.

Gellner, E. 1971. *Thought and Change*. London: Weidenfeld & Nicolson.

———. 1973. *Cause and Meaning in Social Science*. London: Routledge & Kegan Paul.

———. 1983. *Nations and Nationalism*. Oxford: Blackwell.

———. 1987a. *Culture, Identity and Politics*. Cambridge: Cambridge University Press.

———. 1987b. "Nationalism." In the *Blackwell Encyclopedia of Political Institutions*.

Geras, N. 1983. *Marx and Human Nature: Refutation of a Legend*. London: Verso.

Gewirth, A. 1988. "Ethical Universalism and Particularism." *Journal of Philosophy* 85:283–302.

Goodin, R. E. 1988. "What Is So Special about Our Fellow Countrymen?" *Ethics* 98:663–87.

Gordon, A. D. 1952. *The Nation and the Labour*. Jerusalem: The Zionist Library. (in Hebrew)

Graham, G. 1986. *Politics in Its Place: A Study of Six Ideologies*. Oxford: Clarendon Press.

Gray, J. 1986. *Liberalism*. Milton Keynes, England: Open University Press.

Greenfeld, L. 1994. "Review of Liberal Nationalism" in *American Political Science Review* 88:455

Gunsteren, H. R. van. "Admission to Citizenship." *Ethics* 98:731–42.

Gurr, T. R., et al. 1993. *Minorities at Risk: A Global View of Ethnopolitical Conflicts*. Washington, DC: United States Institute of Peace.

Gutmann, A. 1985. "Communitarian Critique of Liberalism." *Philosophy and Public Affairs* 14:308–322.

Gutmann, A., ed. 1994. *Multiculturalism: Examining the Politics of Recognition*. Princeton, N. J.: Princeton University Press.

Hampshire, S. 1983. *Morality and Conflict*. Oxford: Blackwell.

Hare, R. H. 1981. *Moral Thinking*. Oxford: Oxford University Press.

Hart, H. L. A. 1955. "Are There Any Natural Rights." In Waldron, ed., *Theories of Rights*.

Hegel, G. 1967. *Hegel's Philosophy of Right*. Oxford: Oxford University Press.

Henry, N. O. 1970. "Political Obligations and Collective Goods." *Political and Legal Obligations*. Nomos 12. New York: New York University Press, pp. 263–89.

Hertz, F. 1944. *Nationality in History and Politics*. London: Routledge & Kegan Paul.

Higgens, R. 1963. *The Development of International Law Through the Political Organs of the United Nations*. Oxford: Oxford University Press.

———. 1982. "Judge Dillard and the Right of Self-Determination." *Virginia Journal of International Law* 23:389–94.

Hirsch, H. M. 1986. "The Threnody of Liberalism." *Political Theory* 14:423–49.

Hobsbawm, E. 1990. *Nations and Nationalism since 1780*. Cambridge: Cambridge University Press.

Hobsbawm, E., and T. Ranger, eds. 1983. *The Invention of Traditions*. Cambridge: Cambridge University Press.

Hollis, M. 1977. *Models of Man: Philosophical Thought on Social Action*. Cambridge: Cambridge University Press.

———. 1985. "Of Masks and Men." In Carrithers, Collins, and Lukes, eds., *The Category of the Person*.

Horowitz, D. L. 1985. *Ethnic Groups in Conflict*. Berkeley, Calif.: University of California Press.

Houser, R. 1971. "International Protection of Minorities and the Right to National Self-Determination." *Israeli Yearbook of Human Rights* 1:92–95.

Ichilov, O. 1993. *The Development of Civic Education in Israel*. Sifriat Hapoalim (in Hebrew).

Jaeger, G., and P. Selznick. 1964. "A Normative Theory of Culture." *American Sociological Review* 29:653–69.

Kamenka, E., ed. 1979. *Nationalism, the Nature and Evolution of an Idea*. Canberra: Edward Arnold.

Kasher, A. 1985. "Justice and Affirmative Action: Naturalization and the Law of Return." *Israeli Yearbook of Human Rights*, pp. 101–12.

Kedourie, E. 1985. *Nationalism*. Rev. ed. London: Hutchinson.

Kingsbury, B. 1984. "Indigenous Peoples and International Community." Unpublished M.Phil. thesis, Oxford.

Klosko, G. 1987. "Presumptive Benefit, Fairness, and Political Obligations." *Philosophy and Public Affairs* 16: 241–59.

Kohn, H. 1966. *American Nationalism*. New York: Collier Books.

———. 1966. *The Idea of Nationalism*. New York: Collier McMillan.

———. 1974. "Nationalism." In *Encyclopedia Britannica*.

———. 1979. "Nationalism." In the *Dictionary of the History of Ideas*.

Krejci, K. "From Ideal Types of Multidimensional Concepts: The Concept of the 'Nation' in Changing Europe." *History of European Ideas* 6:287–95.

Kymlicka, W. 1988. "Liberalism and Communitarianism." *Canadian Journal of Philosophy* 18:181–203.

———. 1989. *Liberalism, Community and Culture*. Oxford: Clarendon Press.

———. 1990. *Contemporary Political Philosophy*. Oxford: Oxford University Press.

Larmore, C. E. 1987. *Patterns of Moral Complexity*. Cambridge: Cambridge University Press.

Lijphart, A. 1977. *Democracy in Plural Societies*. New Haven, Conn.: Yale University Press.

———. 1986. *The Politics of Accommodation*. Berkeley, Calif.: University of California Press.

Lloyd, C. 1983. *Social Theory and Political Practice*. Oxford: Clarendon Press.

Lucas C. J. 1972. *Our Western Educational Heritage*. New York: Macmillan.

Lukes, S. 1973. *Individualism*. Oxford: Blackwell.

———. 1985. "Conclusion." In Carrithers, Collins, and Lukes, eds., *The Category of the Person*.

———. 1988. "Making Sense of Moral Conflict." Unpublished paper.

MacCormick, N. 1981. *Legal Right and Social Democracy*. Oxford: Clarendon Press.

———. 1991. "Is Nationalism Philosophically Credible?" In W. Twining, *Issues of Self-Determination*. Aberdeen: Aberdeen University Press.

———. 1994. "What Place for Nationalism in the Modern World?' Unpublished paper given at the Stevenson Lectures in Citizenship, University of Glasgow.

MacDonald, M. 1949. "Natural Rights." In Waldron, ed., *Theories of Rights*.

MacIntyre, A. 1981. *After Virtue*. London: Duckworth.

———. 1983. "The Magic in the Pronoun 'My.'" *Ethics* 94:112–25.

———. 1984. *Is Patriotism a Virtue?* The Lindley Lecture, University of Kansas.

McLellan, D. 1986. *Ideology*. Milton Keynes, England: Open University Press.

McLennan, G., D. Held, and S. Hall, eds. 1984. *The Idea of the Modern State*. Milton Keynes, England: Open University Press.

Macpherson, C. B. 1973. "Rawls' Models of Man and Society." *Philosophy and Social Science* 3:341–47.

Margalit, A., and J. Raz. 1990. "National Self-Determination." *Journal of Philosophy* 87:439–61.

Mauss, M. 1938. "A Category of the Human Mind: The Notion of Person; the Notion of Self." In Carrithers, Collins, and Lukes, eds., *The Category of the Person*.

Mazzini, J. 1907. *The Duties of Man and Other Essays*. London: J. M. Dent & Sons.

Mendus, S. 1989. *Toleration and the Limits of Liberalism*. London: Macmillan.

Mendus-Flor, P. R., J. and Rienharz., eds. 1980. *The Jews in the Modern World*. Oxford: Oxford University Press.

Mill, J. S. 1975. *Three Essays: Consideration on Representative Government, On Liberty, The Subjection of Women*. Oxford: Oxford University Press.

Miller, D. 1987. "In What Sense Must Socialism Be Communitarian?" Paper presented at the conference on "Capitalism and Socialism," Social Philosophy and Policy Centre, Key Biscayne, Florida.

———. 1988. "The Ethics of Nationalism." *Ethics* 98:647–62.

Miller, D., and L. Siedentop, eds. 1983. *The Nature of Political Theory*. Oxford: Clarendon Press.

Mitchell, W. J. T. 1982. *The Politics of Interpretation*. Chicago, Ill.: University of Chicago Press.

Montefiore, A. 1973. *Philosophy and Personal Relations*. London: Routledge & Kegan Paul.

———, ed. 1975. *Neutrality and Impartiality, The University and Political Commitment*. Cambridge: Cambridge University Press.

Mulhall, S. 1987. "The Theoretical Foundations of Liberalism." Unpublished paper.

Nagel, T. 1975. "Rawls on Justice." In Daniels, ed., *Reading Rawls*.
———. 1987. "Moral Conflict and Political Legitimacy." *Philosophy and Public Affairs* 16:215–40.
Nandy, A. 1987. "Cultural Frames for Transformative Politics: A Credo." In B. Parekh and T. Pantham, eds., *Political Discourse: Explorations in Indian and Western Political Thought*. London: Sage.
Niran, T. 1977. *The Break-Up of Britain*. London: NLB.
Norman, R. 1983. *The Moral Philosophers*. Oxford: Oxford University Press.
Nowell-Smith, P. H. 1975. "A Theory of Justice?" *Philosophy and Social Science* 3:315–29.
Nozick, R. 1974. *Anarchy, State and Utopia*. New York: Basic Books.
O'Brien, C. C. 1988. "Nationalism and the French Revolution." In G. Best, ed., *The Permanent Revolution*. London: Fontana Press.
———. 1991. "Nationalists and Democrats." *TLS* (Aug. 15).
Okin, S. M. 1987. "Justice and Gender." *Philosophy and Public Affairs* 16:42–72.
———. 1989. "Humanistic Liberalism." In N. L. Rosenblum, ed., *Liberalism and the Moral life*. Cambridge: Harvard University Press.
Oppenheim, F. E. 1987. "National Interest, Rationality and Morality." *Political Theory* 15.
Osterud, O. 1987. "Nation Building." In the *Blackwell Encyclopedia of Political Institutions*.
O'Sullivan See, K. 1986. *The First World Nationalism*. Chicago, Ill.: University of Chicago Press.
Pateman, C. 1983. "Feminist Critics of the Public/Private Dichotomy." In Benn & Gaus, eds., *Public and Private in Social Life*.
———. 1985. *The Problem of Political Obligation*. Cambridge: Polity Press.
———. 1986. "Problem of Liberalism." *Ethics* 96:375–85.
Partidge, H. 1971. *Consensus and Consent*. London: Macmillan.
Pennock, J. R., and J. W. Chapman, eds. 1977. *Human Nature in Politics*. Nomos 17. New York: New York University Press.
———. 1979. *Political Obligations*. Nomos 10. New York: New York University Press.
———. 1983. *Liberal Democracy*. Nomos 26. New York: New York University Press.
Pitkin, H. 1972. "Obligations and Consent." In P. Laslett, W. G. Runciman, and Q. Skinner, eds. *Philosophy, Politics and Society*. Oxford: Blackwell.
Plamenatz, J. 1968. *Consent, Freedom and Political Obligation*. Oxford: Oxford University Press.

Pitkin, H. 1973. "Liberalism." In *The Dictionary of the History of Ideas.*

———. 1976. "Two Types of Nationalism." In Kamenka, ed., *Nationalism.*

Pogge, T. 1988. "Rawls and Global Justice." *Canadian Journal of Philosophy* 18:227–55.

Popper, K. R. 1962. *The Open Society and Its Enemies.* London: Routledge & Kegan Paul.

Pye, L. W., and S. Verba, 1966. *Political Culture and Political Development.* Princeton, N.J.: Princeton University Press.

Ranger, T. 1983. "The Invention of Tradition in Colonial Africa." In Hobsbawm and Ranger, eds., *The Invention of Traditions.*

Raphael, D. D. 1970. *Problems of Political Philosophy.* London: Macmillan.

Rawls, J. 1972. *A Theory of Justice.* Oxford: Oxford University Press.

———. 1980. "On Kantian Constructivism in Moral Theory." *Journal of Philosophy* 77:515–72.

———. 1982. "Social Unity and Primary Goods." In A. Sen and B. Williams, eds., *Utilitarianism and Beyond.* Cambridge: Cambridge University Press.

———. 1985. "Justice as Fairness: Political Not Metaphysical." *Philosophy and Public Affairs* 14:223–51.

———. 1988. "The Idea of an Overlapping Consensus." *Oxford Journal of Legal Studies* 7:1–25.

Raz, J. 1986. *The Morality of Freedom.* Oxford: Clarendon Press.

Roelofs, H. M. 1958. *The Tensions of Citizenship: Private Man and Public Duty.* New York: Rinehart.

Rousseau, J. J. 1965. *Emile.* New York: Basic Books.

Ryan, A. 1983. "Private Selves and Public Parts." In Benn & Gaus, eds., *Public and Private in Social Life.*

Said, E. 1987. "Miami Twice." *London Review of Books.* (December 10):3–6.

Sandel, M. 1982. *Liberalism and the Limits of Justice.* Cambridge: Cambridge University Press.

———. 1984. *Liberalism and Its Critics.* Oxford: Blackwell.

———. 1984. "The Procedural Republic and the Unencumbered Self." *Political Theory* 12:81–95.

———. 1991. "Religious Liberty: Freedom of Conscience or Freedom of Choice?" Unpublished paper.

Senor, T. D. 1987. "What If There Are No Political Obligations." *Philosophy and Public Affairs* 16:260–68.

Seton-Watson, H. 1977. *Nations and States.* London: Methuen.

187

Shapiro, M. J. 1986. "Charles Taylor's Moral Subject." *Political Theory* 14:311–22.

Shiloni, L. 1989. "How to Make Use of Life." *Ha'Aretz*, p. 106. (in Hebrew)

Simmons, A. J. 1979. *Moral Principles and Political Obligations*. Princeton, N.J.: Princeton University Press.

———. 1987. "The Anarchist Position: A Reply to Klosko and Senor." *Philosophy and Public Affairs* 16:271–79.

Singer, M. 1970. "The Concept of Culture." In *The Dictionary of the History of Ideas*.

Smith, A. 1983. *Theories of Nationalism*. London: Duckworth.

———. 1986. *The Ethnic Origins of Nations*. Oxford: Blackwell.

———. 1987. "Ethnic Nationalism" and "Nation-State." In the *Blackwell Encyclopedia of Political Institutions*.

Snyder, L. L. 1954. *The Meaning of Nationalism*. Westport, Conn.: Greenwood Press.

———. 1964. *The Dynamics of Nationalism*. Princeton, N.J.: D. Van Nostrand.

Steinberg, S. 1981. *The Ethnic Myth*. Boston, Mass.: Beacon Press.

Stevenson, L. 1974. *Seven Theories of Human Nature*. Oxford: Oxford University Press.

Sureda, R. 1973. *The Evolution of the Right of Self-Determination*. Leiden: A. W. Sijthoff.

Svennson, F., 1979. "Liberal Democracy and Group Rights: The Legacy of Individualism and Its Impact on American Indian Tribes." *Political Studies* 27, no. 3.

Symmons-Symonolewicz, K. 1968. *Modern Nationalism*. New York: Polish Institute of Arts and Sciences in America.

Taylor, C. 1985a. "The Person." In Carrithers, Collins, and Lukes, eds., *The Category of the Person*.

———. 1985b. *Philosophical Papers*. 2 vols. Cambridge: Cambridge University Press.

Taylor, C. 1989. *Sources of the Self: The Making of Modern Identity*. Cambridge: Cambridge University Press.

———. 1994. "The Politics of Recognition", in A. Gutmann, ed., *Multiculturalism*. Princeton, N. J.: Princeton University Press.

Taylor, G. 1936. *Environment and Nation*. Chicago, Ill.: University of Chicago Press.

Thornberry, P. 1989. "Self-Determination, Minorities, Human Rights: A Review of International Instruments." *International and Comparative Law Quarterly* 38:867–89.

Titly, C., ed. 1975. *The Formation of the National States in Western Europe.* Princeton, N.J.: Princeton University Press.

Treitschke, H. V. 1977. "Politics." in M. Zliger, ed., *A Reader in Political Philosophy.* Jerusalem: Hebrew University.

Trilling, L. 1972. *Sincerity and Authenticity.* Oxford: Oxford University Press.

Tussman, J. 1960. *Obligation and the Public Body.* Oxford: Oxford University Press.

Urwin, D. W. 1985. "The Price of a Kingdom: Territory, Identity, and Centre-Periphery Dimension in Western Europe." In Y. Meny, and V. Wright, eds., *Centre-Periphery Relations in Western Europe.* London: Allen & Unwin.

Verba, S. 1966. "Conclusions." In Pye & Verba, eds., *Political Culture and Political Development.*

Waldron, J. ed., 1984. *Theories of Rights.* Oxford: Oxford University Press.

————. 1987a. "Can Communal Goods be Human Rights," a paper delivered at a conference on Development, Environment, and Peace as Human Rights, Oxford.

————. 1987b. *Nonsense on Stiles.* London: Methuen.

————. 1990. "When Justice Replaces Affection: The Need for Rights." *Harvard Journal of Law and Public Policy* 11:625–47.

Walicki, A. 1982. *Philosophy and Romantic Nationalism: The Case of Poland.* Oxford: Oxford University Press.

Walzer, M. 1971. *Obligation: Essays on Disobedience, War and Citizenship.* New York: Simon & Schuster.

————. 1983. *Spheres of Justice.* Oxford: Oxford University Press.

————. 1984. "Liberalism and the Art of Separation." *Political Theory* 12:315–29.

————. 1986. "The Reform of the International System." In O. Osterude, ed., *Studies in War and Peace.* Oslo: Norwegian University Press.

————. 1987. *Interpretation and Social Criticism.* Cambridge, Mass.: Harvard University Press.

————. 1989a. *Two Kinds of Universalism.* Tanner Lectures, Oxford.

————. 1989b. *The National Question Revised.* Tanner Lectures, Oxford.

————. 1990. "The Communitarian Critique of Liberalism." *Political Theory* 18:6–23.

————. 1991. "The Civil Society Argument." Gunnar Myrdal Lecture, University of Stockholm.

Walzer, M. 1992. "Pluralism: A Political Perspective." In *What It Means to Be an American*. Marsilio.

Weil, S. 1952. *The Need for Roots*. London: Routledge & Kegan Paul.

Welch, S. 1987. "Review Article: Issues in the Study of Political Culture—The Example of Communist Party States." *Political Theory* 12:479–500.

Whelam, F. G. 1983. "Democratic Theory and the Boundary Problem." In Pennock and Chapman, eds., *Liberal Democracy*.

Wildavsky, A. 1987. "Choosing Preferences by Constructing Institutions: A Cultural Theory of Preferences Formation." *American Political Science Review* 81:5–21.

Williams, B. 1966. "Morality and Emotions." Inaugural lecture.

_____. 1973. *Problems of the Self*. Cambridge: Cambridge University Press.

_____. 1981. *Moral Luck*. Cambridge: Cambridge University Press.

_____. 1985. *Ethics and the Limits of Philosophy*. Cambridge, Mass.: Harvard University Press.

Williams, R. 1971. *The Long Revolution*. New York: Penguin Books.

_____. 1981. *Culture*. Glasgow: Fontana Press.

Wintrop, N. 1983. *Liberal Democracy, Theory and Critics*. London: Croom Helm.

Wolf, R. P. 1968. *The Poverty of Liberalism*. New York: Beacon Press.

Young, I. 1987. "Impartiality and the Civic Culture." In S. Benhabib, and D. Cornell, *Feminism as Critique*. Oxford: Polity Press.

_____. 1989. "Polity and Group Differences: A Critique of the Ideal of Universal Citizenship." *Ethics* 99.

INDEX

aboriginal peoples, 38, 40–41, 76
academic freedom, 114
Ackerman, B. A., 19, 127–28
Address to the German Nation (Fichte), 89, 91
affirmative action, 47, 48
agents, 23
Agnon, S. Y., 96
Algeria, 90
alienation, 11, 163
alternative communities, 49
American culture, 85. *See also* United States
American ethnic groups, 50
American Revolution, 60
Anderson, B., 8, 68, 172n.25
Arabs, 66
armies, 164. *See also* military service; wars
assimilation: cultural plurality and, 30; deportation and, 162; difficulty of, 27; of Jews, 92; language and, 152; nationalist view of, 26; political process and, 161; social mobility and, 28; UN charter and, 76
association, freedom of, 44, 104
associative obligations, 99–102, 110, 130, 131, 134–39
authenticity problem, 48–53
autonomy. *See* individual autonomy; political sovereignty; self-rule

Balkanisation, 143
Baltic republics, 160. *See also* Estonians; Latvia
Bangladesh, 143
Barry, B. M., 115, 121–22, 123, 157
belonging, feelings of, 137, 138
Ben-Yehuda, Eliezer, 88
benefit theory, 132–33
Berlin, Isaiah, 6, 13, 71–72, 98, 114–15
betrayal, 98
birthrights, 124–30
black people, 85
Bosanquant, 19
boundaries, state, 122–24, 140, 166, 174n.11. *See also* territorial disputes

Brodzinski, Kazimierz, 92
Brown, Roger, 35
Burke, Edmund, 62–63

Canadian Indians, 38, 49, 149–50
career choices, 29–30
"causal neutrality," 146
changes, 21
chauvinism, 94
choices: of communal affiliations, 21–22, 25–32, 37; cultural, 7, 35–56, 154; liberal nationalism and, 84; of moral identity, 22–25; of state membership, 125
chosen people concept, 81–82
church/state separation, 154
citizenship, 10, 124–30; of minorities, 163; national membership and, 144; political obligations and, 134–35; of Russian-Estonians, 158, 159; state abstractness and, 141; state sovereignty and, 61
civic competence, 129
civil duties. *See* obligations
civil obedience theory, 132
civil rights, 71, 72
civil rights movement, 25, 141
classes, social, 51, 155
Cobban, A., 65
Collini, S., 23, 25
communal affiliations: choice of, 7, 21–22, 25–32, 37; citizenship and, 127, 128–30; cleavages in, 157; moral identity and, 20–21; right to culture and, 35–56
communal egoism, 113, 114, 119
communal goods, 45–46
communal morality. *See* morality of community
communal obligations, 131
communal rights, 42–48, 75. *See also* national rights
communism, 94
communists, 90, 146, 149
communitarianism, 103–4
competition, 31
conceptions of the good, 146, 147
consent theory, 131–32, 135
consociational democracy, 156–58, 165

constitutive ties, 99–102
contextual individuals, 32–34, 36, 104–5, 107, 134
contractarian theory: citizenship and, 125, 129; demarcation and, 127; distributive justice and, 120–21; social egoism and, 119; voluntarism and, 122
Convention of Irish Patriots (1792), 91
Convention on the Elimination of all Forms of Racial Discrimination, 160
conversion to Judaism, 154
Covenant on Human Rights (1960), 62
cricket (game), 49
cross-national cooperation. *See* cooperation
Cubans, 86
cultural choices, 7, 35–56, 154
cultural dialogue, 90
cultural homogeneity, 162
cultural nationalism, 83–86, 163–67
cultural neutrality, 141, 145–47, 148, 149
cultural pluralism, 30–31, 32, 79
cultural rights, 8, 34, 35–56, 111
cultural self-determination. *See* individual identity; national self-determination
cultural vouchers, 54, 55, 56
culture: adoption of, 170n.31; citizenship and, 128, 129; history and, 64; human development and, 16; instrumental value of, 36–37; mutual recognition and, 67–68; ordinary actions and, 85; personal selection from, 171n.3; political, 147–50, 161, 163; universal, 166–67; Western, 49
Czechoslovakia, 143

Dagger, R., 112, 113
Dancing at Lughansa (Friel), 24
Darwinism, 93
Davis, Uri, 90
deception, 98
Declaration of Independence, 60
demarcation, 121, 123, 124, 127
democracy, 61, 71, 156–58, 165, 174–75n.11. *See also* liberal states; self-rule
demographic changes, 158–59
D'Entreves, A. P., 59
deportation, 162
determinism, 25
Deutsch, K., 58
Dewey, John, 19
dialogue, 90, 128
diaspora groups, 97, 138, 158
Dinstein, Y., 76
Diponegaro, Prince, 172n.25

discovered identity, 20
distributive justice, 10, 117–21, 146, 147
divine right, 60
dual loyalties, 112. *See also* moral dilemmas
Dunn, J., 95
duties. *See* obligations
Dworkin, Ronald, 19, 99–100, 101, 131
dynastic right, 60
Dyson, K., 59

Eastern Europe, 78, 83, 165
EC, 151–52, 153, 165
eccentric preferences, 40
economic cooperation, 150, 165
economic wellbeing, 161–62
egoism, 97, 113, 114, 119. *See also* selfishness
Elon, Amos, 78
emigration. *See* deportation; immigration
empires, 144
Estonians, 158, 159
ethical individualism, 83–84
ethical particularism, 113
ethics. *See* morality
Ethiopian Jews, 66, 100
ethnic minorities. *See* minorities
ethnocentric nationalism. *See* nationalism
Europe: Eastern, 78, 83, 165; liberal nationalism in, 92; nationalities of, 140, 142, 143, 144–45; unification of, 71, 151–52, 165, 172n.38; Western, 143, 153
European Community, 151–52, 153, 165
evaluators, 22–23, 36

fascism, 93
favouritism, 100, 111, 112–16, 160
feelings of belonging, 137, 138
feminism, 25
Fichte, Johann Gottlieb, 14, 84, 89, 91
First Propagandist Decree (1792), 91
Fourteen Points (Wilson), 142
freedom: academic, 114; of association, 44, 104; of movement, 158 (*see also* immigration); religious, 37, 38–39, 39–40, 154; of speech, 37
French Revolution, 60, 91
Friel, Brian, 24
fundamentalism, religious, 3

Gandhi, Mahatma, 95
Gaulle, Charles de, 90
Gaus, G. F., 18–19
Geertz, Clifford, 15–16, 148, 149

Gellner, E., 5, 164–65
generational obligations, 110–11
geography, 38, 57, 75, 142, 171n.9. See
also boundaries, state; territorial
disputes
Gewirth, A., 113
Ghandi, Sonia, 28
Girondins, 91
global contracts, 119
"going native," 24
Goldman, Simha, 39, 40, 53
good, conceptions of the, 146, 147
Gordon, Aaron David, 92
gratitude theory, 132–33
Great Knesset, 148
Green, T. H., 19

Hampshire, Stuart, 57, 66–67
handicapped persons, 169n.7
Hare, R. H., 107, 109
Hearst, Patricia, 25
Hebrew language, 88, 148
Hegel, Georg Wilhelm Friedrich, 62, 63,
106
Herder, Johann Gottfried von, 14, 79
Hertz, F., 58–59
historical continuity, 29, 64, 121, 124
Hitler, Adolf, 93
Hobhouse, L. T., 19
Hobsbawm, E., 64
Holland, 156, 157
homosexuals, 169n.7
"horizon of evaluation," 23
human nature, 7, 13–34, 57
Human Rights Committee, 71
Hume, David, 106

ideal communities, 102–3
"identity renewal," 26, 29. See also individual identity
illiberal cultures, 31
"imaginary communities," 8, 68, 85, 110
immigration: community borders and,
166; consociational democracy and,
158; liberal states and, 126–27; minority status and, 42; national self-determination and, 159–60, 161. See also deportation
imperialism, 93
independence struggles, 92
Indian culture, 46, 49, 149–50
indigenous peoples, 38, 40–41, 76
individual achievements, 85, 86, 96
individual autonomy, 31, 36, 37, 51, 70
individual identity, 19–22, 23, 35–36, 73,
137

individual preferences, 40, 171n.7
individual rights: communal aspects of,
44; liberal nationalism and, 9; national
self-determination as, 73, 75; right to
culture as, 43, 45, 46–47, 53–56
individual self-fulfillment, 84, 98
individual values, 23–25
individualism, 63, 115. See also ethical individualism
infidelity, 98
instrumental cultural value, 36–37
international cooperation. See cooperation
international organisations, 144, 152. See
also regional organisations
Inuits, 149–50
invented traditions, 64, 172n.25
isolated persons, 43, 44, 45, 73. See also
stateless persons
Israel: diaspora Jews and, 97; Ethiopian
Jews and, 66, 100; Knesset, 148; "Law
of Return," 160; national culture of, 52;
national pride of, 96; Palestinians and,
82, 102; political parties in, 158; post-
nationalism in, 78; religious rights in,
47; West Bank and, 114, 136

Jews: as chosen people, 81; of diaspora,
97; dietary laws of, 41; Ethiopian, 66,
100; "Law of Return" and, 160; marriage to, 154; national status of, 66; Orthodox, 24, 47; persecution of, 169n.7;
public prayers of, 56; self-identity of,
28, 29; Soviet, 88; Supreme Court and,
39–40; Zionism and, 92
Joyce, James, 86
just communities, 101, 104, 122, 133–34,
136
justice, 9–10, 97, 99, 104–12; community
and, 118; distributive, 10, 117–21, 146,
147; political obligations and, 134;
Rawls on, 74, 97, 105, 110–11, 119–20.
See also morality

Kant, Immanuel, 106, 115
Kasher, A., 160
Kenyan elite, 49
Knesset, 148
Kohn, H., 83–84
Kymlicka, W. on: choice, 21; civil rights
movement, 141; minorities, 149; right
to culture, 38, 39, 40, 48–49

languages, 128, 152, 159
"Law of Return" (Israel), 160
League of Nations, 144